From **Teacher** *to* **Manager**

Managing Language Teaching Organizations

Ron White   *Andy Hockley*   *Julie van der Horst Jansen*   *Melissa S. Laughner*

CAMBRIDGE
UNIVERSITY PRESS

CAMBRIDGE UNIVERSITY PRESS
Cambridge, New York, Melbourne, Madrid, Cape Town, Singapore, São Paulo, Delhi

Cambridge University Press
The Edinburgh Building, Cambridge CB2 8RU, UK

www.cambridge.org
Information on this title: www.cambridge.org/9780521709095

First published 2008

Printed in the United Kingdom at the University Press, Cambridge

A catalogue record for this publication is available from the British Library

Library of Congress Cataloguing in Publication data
Library of Congress Cataloguing data applied for.

ISBN 978-0-521-709095

Contents

Thanks and acknowledgements   v

Introduction   1

1 Managing in the LTO   5

2 Organizational behaviour and management   25

3 Human resource management   51

4 Marketing and sales   79

5 Customer service   113

6 Strategic financial management   151

7 Operational financial management   177

8 Academic management   201

9 Managing change   233

10 Project management   255

Appendix   271

References & further reading   277

Index   283

Thanks & acknowledgements

Thanks

A multi-authored work is already the product of many hands, yet behind us are many other hands and minds who have contributed to our experience and thinking and the writing of this book. First among these are individuals at the institutions with which we have been or are associated in our professional lives, including Donald Freeman and Stephen Fitch at The School for International Training in Brattleboro, Vermont, and friends and colleagues at the Centre for Applied Language Studies, University of Reading, the Bell Educational Trust, in the UK and worldwide, the Institute of Continuing & TESOL Education at the University of Queensland, and Cambridge ESOL in the UK. Next, there are past MA students and participants on the International Diploma in Language Teaching Management. They will recognize themselves in the vignettes. Finally, there are significant individuals who have given us support throughout: our partners and families, CUP's Associate Publishing Director, Nóirín Burke, and most importantly, Jenny Johnson, who took on the invaluable role of Critical Friend, and our editor, Helen Forrest, whose efficiency, good humour and skill brought the project to successful fruition. To them all, our gratitude. And to anyone we have overlooked, and for any errors and omissions, our apologies.

Acknowledgements

The authors and publishers acknowledge the following sources of copyright material and are grateful for the permissions granted. While every effort has been made, it has not always been possible to identify the sources of all the material used, or to trace all copyright holders. If any omissions are brought to our notice, we will be happy to include the appropriate acknowledgements on reprinting.

John Wiley & Sons, Inc for quote on p. 2 and fig 9.7 on p. 244: 'Comparison of departments' from *Leading in a Culture of Change* by M Fullan, published by Jossey-Bass (2001). Reproduced by permission of John Wiley & Sons, Inc. Harvard Business for quote on p. 2: How to Put Meaning Back into Leading, by Martha Lagace, published 10 January 2005 from http://hbswk.hbs.edu/item/4563.html, for the text and table on p. 38: Two dimensions, four cultures from 'What Holds a Modern Company Together?' *Harvard Business Review on Managing People* by Goffee and Jones, published by Harvard Business School Press, for the text and table on pp. 145–146: 'Designing Services that Deliver'. *Harvard Business Review 62/1*, pp.133–139, for the text on p. 243: *Leading Change* by J Kotter, published by Harvard Business School Press, 1996. Reproduced by permission of Harvard Business. Elsevier and HarperCollins Publishers (US) for quotes on p. 10 and p. 233: *Management: Tasks, Responsibilities and Practices* Copyright © 1973, 1974 Peter F Drucker. Reprinted by permission of HarperCollins Publishers (US) and Elsevier. Pearson Education Limited for fig 1.2 on p. 11: 'Five essential stages of management control, figure 21.2' from *Management and Organizational*

Behaviour, 6th edition, by L J Mullins. Copyright © 2002, Pearson Education, for fig 9.1 on p. 234: 'Environmental influences on an LTO', (adapted from Mullins, 1985, p13) from *Management and Organisational Behaviour*, by L J Mullins. Copyright © 1985, Pitman, London. Reproduced by permission of Pearson Education Limited. Open University Press for adapted fig 1.5 on p. 17: 'Teachers in public sector schools and in LTOs' and for adapted fig 1.7 on p. 19: 'Principals/head teachers in public sector schools and heads of LTOs' from *Educational Leadership and Learning* by Law and Glover. Published by Open University Press, Copyright © 2000. Reproduced by kind permission of the Open University Press Publishing Company. TESOL Publications for the KASA headings on pp. 20–22 and for fig 1.9 on p. 23: 'KASA framework summary' from 'Teacher Training, Development and Decision Making: A Model of Teaching and Related Strategies for Language Teacher Education' by Donald Freeman *TESOL Quarterly*, Vol 23, No 1, March 1989. Reproduced by permission of TESOL Publications. Palgrave Macmillan for the quotes on p. 25 and p. 40: *Analysing Organisations* by Sandra Dawson, Macmillan Education, 1986. Reproduced with permission of Palgrave Macmillan. Profile Books for fig 2.3 on p. 28: 'Inverted organigram' from *The Twelve Organisational Capabilities* by Bob Garratt. Reproduced by permission of Profile Books. Carter McNamara for fig 2.4 on p. 32: 'Overview of organisational life cycles' from http://www.managementhelp.org/org_thry/org_cycl.htm. Copyright Carter McNamara 1997–2007. Reproduced by permission of Carter McNamara, Authenticity Consulting, LLC. International House World Organisation for p. 40: 'Mission Statement' from http://www.ihworld.com/about_us/mission.asp Reproduced by permission of International House World Organisation. The Random House Group Limited for 2 quotes on p. 43: *The Fifth Discipline: The Art and Practice of the Learning Organisation* by Peter Senge, published by Century. Reprinted by permission of the Random House Group Ltd and Doubleday, a division of Random House, Inc. Instituto Brasil Estados Unidos for information on p. 45: 'Case Study: IBEU'. Reproduced by kind permission of Instituto Brasil Estados Unidos (IBEU). John Wiley & Sons Limited for fig 2.7 on p. 48: 'Basic model of learning by doing' from *An Intelligent Organisation* by P Sydänmaanlakka. Copyright © 2002 John Wiley & Sons Limited. Reproduced with permission. NTL Institute for the text on pp. 65–66: 'Giving effective feedback' from 'Giving and Receiving Feedback; It Will Never Be Easy, But It Can Be Better' by Larry Porter from *NTL Reading Book for Human Relations Training*. Copyright © 1982 NTL Institute. Reproduced by permission of the NTL Institute. Blackwell Publishing for the text on p. 81: 'Definition for market' by Cooper and Argyris from *The Concise Blackwell Encyclopaedia of Management*. Reproduced by permission of Blackwell Publishing. The American marketing Association for p. 81: 'Definition of Marketing' from http://www.marketingpower.com/content4620.php, for fig 5.8 on p. 129: 'The 'Gaps' model' from 'Figure 1: conceptual Model of Service Quality' from *Journal of Marketing*, April 1988. Reprinted with permission of The American Marketing Association. British Council for summarized ideas on pp. 84–85: *English Next* by David Graddol. Copyright © British Council, 2006. The Australian Government for fig 4.2 on p. 87: 'Overseas student enrolments in Australia by major sector, 2003–2006, for fig 4.3 on p. 87: 'Student enrolments in Australia from top 10 source countries, 2003–2006, for fig. 4.4 on p. 89: 'Regional market share by state/territory, 2006. Copyright Commonwealth of Australia, reproduced by permission. Business Resource Software, Inc for fig 4.12 on p. 99: 'Boston Matrix' and for fig. 4.13 on p. 100: 'Strategic Business Units' from http://www.brs-inc.com/models/model14.asp. Reproduced by permission of Business Resource Software, Inc. Australian College of English Pty Ltd for fig 4.14 on p. 102: 'ACE Mission Statement' from the ACE website http://www.ace.edu.au/aboutus.html. Copyright Australian College of English Pty Ltd. Bell International for fig 4.14 on p. 102: 'Bell Mission Statement' from the website http://www.bell-centres.com/aboutbell/default.asp. Copyright © Bell International. Cambridge University Press for fig 4.16 on p. 109: 'The ELT salesperson' from *Management in English Language Teaching* (1991), fig 8.2, written by White et al, for text on p. 208: 'Statement of principles' from *Curriculum Development in Language Teaching* (2001), written by Jack C Richards, for fig 8.3 on p. 209: 'Decision-making roles' from *The Second Language Curriculum* (1989), table 1, written by Robert Keith Johnson. Reproduced by permission of Cambridge University Press. Emerald Group Publishing Limited for the text on p. 113: 'Client views of TESOL', for fig 5.1 on p. 115: 'Comparison of client satisfaction predictors and recommendation predictors', for fig 5.10 on p. 130: 'Client satisfaction rating scale' from 'Client satisfaction with English language centre service: insights from a New Zealand national survey', written by J Walker *International Journal of Educational Management*. Copyright © 2003 Emerald Group Publishing Limited, all rights reserved. Elsevier Limited for the text on pp. 114–115 and for fig 5.2 on p. 116: 'Group preferences' from 'Learners' preferences regarding types of language school: An exploratory market research' by E Cristobal and E Llurda. *System* 34, for fig 5.17 on p. 143: 'Relationship ladder' from *Relationship Marketing for Competitive Advantage,* written by A Payne, M Clark and H Peck. Published by Butterworth Heinemann, 1997. Reproduced by permission of Elsevier Limited. McGraw-Hill Publishing Company for the text on p. 119: 'What is service?' from *Principles and Practices of Marketing*, 3rd edition, written by D Jobber. Published by McGraw-Hill, London 2001. Reproduced with kind permission of the McGraw-Hill Publishing Company. George Pickering for the text and fig 5.3 on p. 122: 'The revised quality model' from 'Roads to quality street: perspectives on quality in ELT'. *ELT Management,* December 1999. Reproduced by permission of George Pickering. Tribune Media Services for fig 5.7 on p. 128: 'Zone of tolerance' from 'Understanding Customer Expectations of Service' from *MIT Sloan Management Review*, Spring 1991, written by A Parasuraman, Leonard L Berry and Valarie A Zeithaml. Copyright 1991 by Massachusetts Institute of Technology. All rights reserved. Distributed by Tribune Media Services. Dr John Walker for the text on p. 128: 'Gaps in the EFL Service', fig 5.20 on p. 146: 'Service System Blueprint Matrix', fig 5.21 on p. 148: 'EFL Service System Blurprint', for the text on p. 149: 'Blueprint applications' from 'Blueprinting the EFL Service Provision', *ELT Management*, no 24, July 1997. Reproduced by permission of Dr John Walker. Satmetrix Systems, Inc and Bain & Company for text on pp. 133–134: 'Net Promoter Score' from http://www.netpromoter.com/calculate/nps.php. Reproduced with permission for Satmetrix Systems Inc. The University of Texas for the adapted text on p. 134: 'Focus Groups' from Division of Instructional Innovation and Assessment, The University of Texas at Austin 'Focus Groups.' *Instructional Assessment Resources*. 2007. http://www.utexas.edu/academic/diia/assessment/iar/tech/plan/method/focus.php. Used by permission of The University of Texas, Austin. EAQUALS for fig 5.15 on p. 137: 'Extract from EAQUALS Inspection Scheme – Version 5.3', for fig 8.4 on p. 211: 'Course requirements' (adapted from EAQUALS, 2007) for fig 8.5 on p. 212: 'Teaching Standards (adapted from EAQUALS, 2007. Copyright © EQUALS 2004, updated January 2007. www.eaquals.org; British Council for text on p. 138: *Accreditation UK Handbook* from the website http://www.britishcouncil.org/accreditation.htm. Reproduced by permission of the British Council. Affinity Consulting for text on pp. 143–144 and fig 5.18: 'Customer loyalty grid' by Brian Ward from http://www.excellence2.com/customer-service/creating_customer_loyalty_the_customer_loyalty_grid.shtml. The Customer Loyalty Grid is a trademark of Affinity Consulting. Reproduced by permission of Affinity Consulting. Lovemarks.com for fig 5.19 on p. 144: 'Love/Respect Axis' from www.lovemarks.com. Reproduced by permission of Lovemarks.com. Dorling Kindersley Ltd for the text on pp. 177–178: 'Aims of budgeting' from *Essential Managers: Managing Budgets* by Stephen Brookson. Text © 2000 Stephen Brookson. Copyright © 2000 Dorling Kindersley Ltd. Reproduced by permission of Dorling Kindersley Ltd. Tutor2U Limited for fig 8.6 on p: 215: 'New product development stages'. Adapted from http://www.tutor2u.net/ Reproduced by permission of Tutor2U Limited. E L Gazette and Terry Phillips for fig 8.7 on p. 221: 'Resource management timetable' by Terry Phillips from *E L Gazette*. Reproduced by permission of Terry Phillips and EL Gazette, Unit 3 Constantine Court, Fairclough Street, London E1 1PW. www.elgazette.com. Eurocentres for fig 8.9 on p. 229: 'Eurocentres Scale of Language Proficiency' from http://www.eurocentres.com/en/eurocentres/Scale_of_Language_Proficiency,43.html. Copyright © 2005–2007 Eurocentres. All Rights Reserved. Council of Europe for the text on p. 230: 'Can do statement' from *A Common European Framework of Reference for Languages: Learning, Teaching, Assessment*. Copyright © Council of Europe; Simon & Schuster Adult Publishing Group for fig 9.4 on p. 238: 'Adoption/Innovation curve', for adapted text on p. 241: 'Influences on adopting innovations'. Adapted and reprinted with the permission of The Free press, a Division of Simon & Schuster Adult Publishing Group from *Diffusion of Innovations*, 5th edition by Everett M Rogers. Copyright © 1995, 2003 by Everett M Rogers. Copyright © 1962, 1971, 1983 by The Free Press. All rights reserved. Alta Book Center Publishers for the text and fig 9.6 on p. 242: 'Zone of innovation' from *A Handbook for Language Program Administrators* edited by Christison & Stoller, 1997. Reproduced by permission of Alter Book Center Publishers, www.altaesl.com. Teachers College Press for adapted text on pp. 242–244: *The New Meaning of Educational Change*, 4th edition, by Michael Fullan. Reprinted by permission of Teachers College Press, © 2007 by Teachers College, Columbia University. All rights reserved. Office of Government Commerce for fig 10.5 on p. 264: 'Risk tolerance matrix'. Crown © 2008.

Introduction

In 1989, a group of people met at a conference in Rio, where they suggested to Cambridge University Press that there was a need for an introductory book on management, aimed at people who were either becoming managers or were now in a management role. The result was *Management in English Language Teaching*, published in 1991, which provided a useful introduction to management for many people who are now in middle and senior management positions in what we are terming language teaching organizations (LTOs).

Since 1991, the global English Language Teaching (ELT) industry has expanded and evolved, with an incredibly wide range of enterprises, from tiny small-scale start-up operations to international chains with global reach. Whatever their size and scope, all these LTOs have to be managed; that is, people within the organization have to be led towards shared goals, activities and resources planned and organized, staff motivated and developed, and resources monitored and controlled. Ultimately, and perhaps most importantly, customers have to be satisfied. For one of the most significant changes that have taken place since 1991 is the reconfiguring, in both private and public sectors, of the traditional teacher–student relationship into a service provider–consumer relationship. LTOs have taken on an additional role to their educational one: they are service providers.

Meeting the demands of this additional role has involved a growing awareness of the importance of management, so anyone moving from a classroom to a supervisory or managerial role needs to extend existing skills relevant to their new job, as well as acquire new competencies and a new managerial perspective. This book is intended to be a contribution to such development.

The contents and approach of the book are built on the combined experience of the authors in a variety of management roles and a wide range of LTOs, either by direct experience, or by proxy through our involvement in training aspirant or existing LTO managers and directors. We owe a considerable debt to the scores of participants following courses leading to the International Diploma in Language Teaching Management (IDLTM), the management qualification designed and administered by the Universities of Cambridge and Queensland and the School for International Training. In addition, we are indebted to colleagues in the various institutions with which we are associated. Through them, we have gained insights into a vast variety of LTOs, at virtually every stage of their life cycle, from infancy to maturity, and ranging in size and scope and diversity. We have also seen how the job of LTO managers has changed, with middle managers, such as directors of study, assuming responsibilities outside their traditional role as leading professional. And we have observed how even not-for-profit (NFP) organizations have had to become more commercial in their outlook with a growth in competition, both domestically and internationally. From these observations, we have concluded that some LTOs, regardless of size, are more effective than others.

What, then, are some of the characteristics of an effective LTO? There is, of course, no simple answer to this question. Nonetheless, we have been able to draw some conclusions about what appears to make an LTO effective as an educational institution, as a service provider, as a profitable enterprise, and as a good employer.

Firstly, an effective LTO is clear about what it is, what it is doing, and why it exists. In short, it has a clear vision of itself, and a clear set of goals. These will not necessarily be embodied in vision and mission statements, but they will be demonstrated in what members of the LTO say about what they are doing, how they do it, and how in tune they are with the values and ambitions of the organization and its clientele. In short, an effective LTO has a sense of moral purpose, which Fullan (2001b, p. 3) has defined as:

> ...acting with the intention of making a positive difference in the lives of employees, customers and society as a whole.

And it is alignment between people's values and those of the organization which give meaning to work. Or, as Podolny, Khurana & Hill-Popper (2005) put it:

> To the extent that we understand our work within an organization as contributing to a goal or ideal that we value, our work will have meaning.

Secondly, derived from its sense of vocation and clarity of vision, an effective LTO will have a strategy about where it is going over the next year or more, how it is going to get there and how it will know whether or not it actually got there. In other words, an effective LTO is not a rudderless ship, buffeted by forces which it makes no attempt to deal with in a purposeful and coherent manner. Effective LTOs are definitely not characterized by laissez-faire management.

Thirdly, effective LTOs – or the directors, managers and staff – listen and learn. They listen to what their clientele tell them, and they learn from what they hear. This enables them to perceive and satisfy changing client needs. It means treating consumers as boss, and making sure that the organization has the capability – including the staff capability – of responding to the consumers' requirements in a timely manner.

Fourthly, they recruit and retain motivated, committed and loyal staff who are clear about what their jobs involve and require, and where they and their work fit into the organization as a whole. If there is purposeful management, good internal communication, and a collegiate culture, staff commitment and loyalty form part of a virtuous circle.

Fifthly, they are committed to maintaining and raising quality standards overall, and are profitable because of this, rather than because they prioritize profits and student volume at any cost. They provide excellent service levels to underscore the benefits of opting for their services. On the basis of this, they carefully build a reputation through good word of mouth.

Sixthly, effective LTOs are characterized by continuous improvement, adjustment, diversification of their portfolio of products, development of teaching staff, implementation of modern teaching techniques and teaching to certified and demonstrable levels of attainment. Effective LTOs are not static; they are learning organizations.

Finally, they have the ability to adapt while maintaining credibility and reliability. By intelligently reading changes in the environment and the market and by anticipating future trends, they are able to introduce well-judged innovations, and to change without sacrificing the unique identity and character that distinguish them from their competitors.

An effective LTO will not necessarily be an easy place to work in because people are expected to perform well. It will, however, be a rewarding place to work in, and in our view it is through effective management that this happy state of affairs is achieved.

In preparing this book, we have faced a problem: managing is an integrated process, so that decisions that are made in one aspect of an LTO's activities will either draw upon or have an impact on others. Since a book has to be organized as a series of chapters, it is easy to lose sight of such integration, as a point relevant in one chapter may be covered in greater depth in another. We have attempted to avoid lack of integration, while at the same time steering clear of unnecessary repetition, by use of cross-referencing, both as a reminder to readers, as well as a way of directing them forward or back to related aspects of management. We have also tried to link the contents of each chapter to the real world of the reader's LTO. This has been done in two ways.

Firstly, we have provided examples – vignettes – based on a range of actual LTOs. These vignettes are used to illustrate aspects of management and the ways in which different LTOs find solutions to a range of management issues. Readers may discover in these vignettes parallels with their own LTO, or thought-provoking insights into the way other LTOs operate.

Secondly, throughout the book there are tasks which invite readers to relate concepts, principles and practices to their own LTO. In many cases, the reader is invited to reflect on the area concerned; in others, the reader may be asked to investigate an area in some detail by obtaining information on how their LTO manages a particular aspect of its work or services. In the reflective activities, there is no right or wrong answer, and in any case, the information will often be specific to the LTO concerned. The idea is to look at the familiar and taken-for-granted from a new, analytical perspective. Reflecting and researching are important ways of applying management principles and practices and giving life to the content of this book. Such work may also reveal aspects of LTO practices which could be improved, or it may indicate a need for specific training that is outside the scope of a book like this.

In addition to training, managers (aspirant or practising) can extend their knowledge and skills by participating in the various professional forums which are available to them. These are of two kinds: those involving institutional membership, and those open to individuals. Trade associations, such as English UK and English Australia, are restricted to institutional membership, and they are concerned with promoting the interests of these corporate members. As part of their remit, they will also offer conference and training opportunities for individuals, such as directors and directors of study.

Related to, but independent of, such trade associations are national or regional accreditation schemes, such as Accreditation UK, the NEAS scheme in Australia, or EAQUALS in Europe and the UK. Accreditation by such schemes is increasingly a regulatory requirement, which means that LTOs have to reach threshold levels of management effectiveness. Being concerned with achieving and maintaining such levels can provide valuable development for individual managers as well as the LTO as an enterprise.

The second kind of forum is that open to individual membership, foremost among which are such associations as IATEFL and TESOL, and their national or local affiliates. Both IATEFL and TESOL have special interest groups (SIGs) for LTO managers and administrators, providing useful forums for interchange and development. The IATEFL management SIG is also one the few bodies which publishes articles directly related to LTO management.

Finally, there is a third kind of forum open to virtually everyone: the World Wide Web accessible via the Internet. In 1991, when *Management in English Language Teaching* was published, the first publicly available websites appeared and the use of the Internet as a research tool was in its infancy. Since then, the World Wide Web has become a global resource, and at the time of writing this book we are in the era of Web 2.0. This means that no one, least of all an LTO and its managers, can work without accessing and using the web. This text includes a searchable Glossary which you will find on CUP's website www.cambridge.org/elt/teachertomanager. For managers, the web is an invaluable source of ideas, and there are numerous search engines which managers can refer to for information and guidance, such as Ask.com., Google, Yahoo! and free online resources such as encyclopaedias (e.g. Wikipedia), dictionaries (e.g. 12Manage, BusinessDictionary.com, Free Management Library), and official government sources such as the Department for Children, Schools and Families (UK), Business Link (UK), and business.gov.au (Australia). Social network sites such as Facebook, MySpace and Bebo offer opportunities for marketing, advertising, recruitment, staff induction and communication.

In 1991, it would have taken some prescience to have predicted both the impact of the World Wide Web and the ways in which LTOs and the work of their managers would evolve. Seventeen years later, the present authors hope that *From Teacher to Manager* will meet the needs of newcomers and practising managers, will extend their understanding of management, will contribute to developing their management skills, and will lay a foundation for whatever specialized training and development they may undertake in the future.

Managing in the LTO

- THE LTO: VARIETY
- DEFINING MANAGEMENT
- THE TRANSITION TO LTO MANAGER

INTRODUCTION

English Language Teaching (ELT), also referred to as English for Speakers of Other Languages (ESOL), given the status of English as a global language, is a global phenomenon, taking place in virtually every country in the world and being provided in a wide range of institutions, or Language Teaching Organizations (LTOs). Indeed, one of the most striking characteristics of ESOL is the huge diversity of contexts and organizations in which it is provided. Many LTOs are commercial businesses, some are not-for-profit (NFP) enterprises which, nonetheless, have to be run commercially, and yet others are publicly funded, ranging from regular state sector schools, through further education (FE) institutions to universities. There is also tremendous variation in the size of LTOs, from small, owner-run schools to global chains.

Despite this diversity, there is one unifying factor: all of these LTOs, regardless of size and context, have to be managed. The role of management and administration in LTOs has, like ESOL itself, greatly expanded in the past twenty years, influenced by the widespread acceptance of management principles and practice, not only in the commercial, but also in the public and NFP sectors as well. This development, accompanied by a focus on quality, efficiency, improved productivity, self-management, accountability to stakeholders and an emphasis on service, is a feature of managerialism or New Public Management (Fitzsimons, 1999), which may be contrasted with professionalism, in which codes of practice and the interests of the client are prioritized. ESOL is not isolated from the tensions between managerialist and professional priorities, and without an understanding of management principles and practices, the ESOL professional in a management role can be disadvantaged and marginalized. One of the purposes of this book is to help achieve an effective and productive balance between these two sets of demands.

The LTO: variety

The diversity of ESOL contexts referred to above is illustrated in the following examples. This is not an exhaustive set, and you may well work in an LTO which does not actually match any of these examples.

HONG KONG: THE PUBLIC SECTOR SCHOOL

Angela is the departmental head of English in a medium-size public sector secondary school with an enrolment of around 900 students, which serves children from adjacent public housing. The school is English–medium, although the first language (L1) is extensively used in the classroom. Angela's job includes a lot of administrative chores, such as writing reports and plans for the Education Department, and attending meetings. Although her involvement is required, she is subordinate to the principal in appointing new staff, but it is she who has responsibility for helping, advising and developing teachers in her department. In addition, she is responsible for quality assurance through observing teachers, and checking the grading of homework. She also deals with complaints from students and parents, and she works quite closely with the principal on such matters. She has no financial responsibilities, as the budget for the school is managed by the principal, who in turn is responsible to the Education Department, which also specifies the curriculum and defines the assessment and other educational targets which the school has to meet.

UNITED KINGDOM: THE NFP CHAIN SCHOOL

Bruce is a director of studies (DOS), or senior academic manager, in a branch of a privately owned, NFP chain located in a small town. The centre has a capacity of around 250 students, and it is open all year, offering a mixture of individual and group courses. Around half of the students follow intensive English courses, while adult closed groups make up the other half. There is a small amount of teacher training for both native English and non-native English speakers. Bruce is responsible for recruiting and managing teachers, in collaboration with the central Human Resources manager. A small core of teachers are permanent, while others are employed on short-term contracts to match seasonal fluctuations in volume. Bruce is responsible for quality assurance, part of which includes four-yearly inspections under the Accreditation Scheme, as well as teacher development, and he collaborates with other DOSs in the chain on curriculum development. Sales and marketing for the group are handled centrally in consultation with branches. Bruce works closely with a colleague who is responsible for student services, covering accommodation and social and excursion programmes, and each also manages annual budgets. Both report to the head of schools, who is based at headquarters.

AUSTRALIA: THE COLLEGE OF FURTHER EDUCATION

Lee is head of department (HOD) in a large FE college which serves two types of clientele: immigrants who are settling in the country, and language travel students who come for periods ranging from a few weeks to nine months to combine an English language course with part-time employment on a student visa. The adult migrant programme is federally funded, whereas the language travel programme operates on a commercial for-profit basis. Recently the college has developed a small IELTS programme to meet the rising demand among students aspiring to enter tertiary education, for which an IELTS score at a specified level is an entry requirement. The staff are either on casual, hourly paid terms or on annual contracts. As HOD, Lee has responsibility for managing the departmental budget, which is set through an annual budget round in competition with other heads of department. Much of her work involves attending various college meetings to represent the interests of her department, devising plans in line with college strategic planning, monitoring ongoing student and staff numbers and performance against targets, and reporting regularly to her head of division. The majority of the curriculum development, quality assurance and temporary staff recruitment and supervision is devolved to the two DOSs, who regularly report to her.

GREECE: THE OWNER-RUN FRONTISTERIA

Melina runs a very small language school, or *frontisteria*, in a provincial town where there is a lot of competition from similar LTOs. Aspiring to obtain one of the limited number of teaching posts in the state school system, Melina was persuaded to open her school as a temporary measure until such employment came her way. Backed by some family money, she rented some premises and used contacts to recruit students who are mostly youngsters and teenagers from the neighbourhood, following general English and exam preparation courses. Five years on, the school is established, and staffed by Melina and a small number of part-time teachers. Melina manages the entire operation, although she relies on a cousin to manage the accounts, and she is also responsible for meeting parents and recruiting students, dealing with staffing matters, devising courses, and ensuring that things run smoothly and profitably. She is still hoping for a state school appointment.

THE MIDDLE EAST: THE ENGLISH LANGUAGE SUPPORT UNIT

Bob is the head of the English Language Support Unit in a large English-medium university in the Middle East. The unit is charged with bringing the entering students up to the levels of English required to cope with the course they enter, as well as offering support to the undergraduate student body by way of language labs, academic writing support, and ongoing EAP (English for Academic Purposes) classes. The unit has ten expatriate (native English speaker) staff and four locally hired teachers. Bob's work involves ensuring that the courses are being delivered as planned and in line with the university's needs. Much of his role is actually devoted to attending meetings to try and gain funding for the unit, and dealing with some intense inter-faculty politics which often leave the unit sidelined as not being part of the academic programme.

JAPAN: THE FOR-PROFIT NATIONAL CHAIN

Hafwen works for a large LTO chain in Japan. Founded in the early 1980s, it is wholly owned by company shareholders as part of a corporation which includes health insurance for foreign employees, publishing, a travel agency, and a study-abroad placement agent. In 2006 there were about 800 branches nationwide, the chain commanding nearly two thirds of the total student numbers for the English conversation schools nationwide. In 2006 two thirds of the total work force were foreigners, having an average age of 25.

Comprehensive marketing and mass advertising have made the chain a recognizable brand throughout the country. It offers a range of products and a flexible booking system and times, with an emphasis on meeting the customers' requirements for convenience and flexibility. Product specifications and systems are closely defined and controlled to ensure brand unity.

The LTO is hierarchically structured, with centralized decision-making, including financial planning and staff recruitment. Operational management is devolved through an area and branch management network. Lesson Management Plans, which are devised by a centralized Education Division, must be used. There are also manuals for training sessions and some specific personal development sessions, for which branch managers are responsible. There is a Code of Conduct given to each new recruit at orientation and this is reinforced throughout employment.

TASK

Before reading any further, complete the table in Figure 1.1 opposite for the examples above, and for yourself and the LTO you work in. The idea in this activity is to start looking at your LTO from the viewpoint of a manager, starting with who is responsible for what. Activities in this and subsequent chapters will involve further analysis of specific aspects of managing an LTO.

What these examples illustrate is how diverse LTOs are in size, type, ownership and complexity. In all of them, in addition to the core or central activity – teaching – there is a range of other activities which go on in support of the teaching function and the various services provided by the LTO.

MANAGEMENT

Defining management

Management is something which is fundamental to the way any organization, including any LTO, operates, survives and develops. What, then, is management? In his book *The Twelve Organizational Capabilities*, Bob Garratt (2000, p. 51) explains that the English word 'manager' derives from the Latin for 'hand', and that it entered English in Tudor times via the Italian *manegiare*, as applied to the breaking of horses. Two centuries later, the word 'management' assumed an additional meaning from the French *ménager*, which concerns the domestic economy of the kitchen. Garratt contrasts these two views of management, the former prioritizing control, the other being more 'emotionally nurturing'.

It is precisely these contrasts which reflect the ways in which people approach and experience management. In some cases, management can be very hands-on – and even heavy-handed – prioritizing getting things done, that is, task achievement. In some cases, it can be very hands-off, or even laissez-faire, resulting in lack of direction and confusion. In yet other cases, it can be democratic, with effective delegation, a concern with harnessing and developing people's skills, and encouraging motivation and commitment

LTO	What type of LTO?	Who manages it?	Who recruits staff?	Who is responsible for staff development?	Who designs the curriculum?	Who manages budgets?	Who is responsible for quality assurance?
Angela's					Education Department		
Bruce's	NFP chain		DOS				
Lee's						Head of Department	
Melina's		The owner					
Bob's							
Hafwen's			Central recruitment			Branch managers reporting to headquarters	Branch managers and Education Division
Yours							

FIGURE 1.1: *LTO responsibilities*

to achieve shared goals. It is this last sense which informs our approach to management in this book.

Management functions

Management operates through various functions, often classified as planning, organizing, leading/motivating and controlling:

- planning: deciding what has to happen in the future (today, next week, next month, next year, over the next five years, etc.) and producing plans to achieve intended goals
- organizing: making optimum use of the resources required to enable the successful carrying out of plans
- leading/motivating: employing skills in these areas for getting others to play an effective part in achieving plans and developing people's skills
- controlling: checking progress against plans, which may need modification based on feedback.

Drucker (1973, p. 73), who sees both for-profit and NFP organizations as being essentially businesses, takes the view that 'managing a business must be a creative rather than an adaptive task' and he lists three tasks, 'equally important but essentially different, which management has to perform to enable the institution in its charge to function and to make its contribution' (p. 40):

- the specific purpose and mission of the institution, whether business enterprise, hospital, or university
- making work productive and the worker achieving
- managing social impacts and social responsibilities.

For Drucker (1973, p. 39), business enterprises, including public-service institutions, 'are organs of society', and 'management, in turn, is the organ of the institution'. In other words, management 'has no existence in itself', being defined in and through its tasks, such as those in the list of management functions above.

Management control

Two of the management functions outlined above, organizing and leading, are also stages in a management control system. Whatever the nature of control, there are five essential elements in such a system:

1   planning what is desired, which in an organization includes long-term strategic as well as day-to-day operational planning
2   establishing standards of performance, which are guidelines set up as a basis for measurement, including tolerance of deviation from performance standards
3   monitoring actual performance, using reported results and observation
4   comparing actual achievement against the planned target, taking into account acceptable variance from standards of performance
5   rectifying and taking corrective action by finding the cause of variation and taking timely action to correct or remove the cause.

Mullins (2002, p. 770) has incorporated these in a management control model:

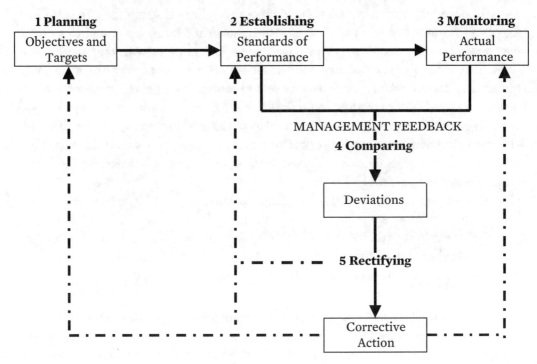

FIGURE 1.2: *The five essential stages of management control*

What will strike any teacher is the parallel between this model and teaching. Teachers, to a varying extent in consultation with students, define goals and establish standards of performance. Having taught something, teachers monitor subsequent student performance against a criterion and, depending on the closeness of the performance to this measure, will take corrective action, which can also include reviewing objectives. So, if language learning goals prove to be taxing for the learners, teachers can adjust the goals and performance criteria, as well as the content and amount of teaching and practice.

There are many items in an LTO which will need to be controlled following the scheme outlined by Mullins. While it is advisable to avoid falling into the managerialist trap of attempting to measure and to set targets for everything, there are many aspects of an LTO which need to be quantified in order to evaluate performance or to account for the use of resources. In some areas, such as financial management, managers will have no choice about complying with the accounting and legal requirements which underlie corporate governance, while there are bureaucratic and marketing pressures on managers to quantify performance, such as exam pass rates and customer satisfaction.

REFLECTION

As with any reflective activity, there is no right or wrong answer to this task. The idea is, as with all the reflective activities, to look at the familiar and taken-for-granted from a new, analytical perspective. This should lead to new insights, and to making links between the theory or principles concerned and your own experience and practice. In this activity, you are asked to apply the concept of control to aspects of activities and resources in the LTO. Control involves measurement against a standard or criterion (such as past performance, or an established plan, such as a budget), making a decision about the observed level of activity or performance, and then, if necessary, taking action to modify future activity to bring it in line with the criterion or goal. Here are some questions to get you started:

- How can you decide which items to control in your LTO?
- First, decide on what basis you will exclude something.
- Then make a list of things which, as an LTO manager, you will need to control so as to make the most efficient use of resources.
- Take one of these items and describe how it could be controlled.

Almost inevitably when deciding which items to control, managers nominate photocopying as a priority. Measuring photocopy usage is easy. Controlling it is less easy, however, as imposing restrictions can be counterproductive. Perhaps you have already found effective ways of controlling this particular resource. If so, what did you do, and why was it successful? If controlling photocopying is not an issue, choose a significant item and consider how to control it effectively and efficiently. Keep in mind that it is important to avoid squandering time and resources on controlling something, and in so doing cancelling out any benefits derived from your efforts.

Functions and departments

In most businesses, the main functions which have to be carried out are spread across different departments or units.

Function	Department
Human resource management	HR (Personnel)
Operations management	Student & Academic Services
Strategic management	Board & Senior Management
Marketing management	Marketing & Sales
Financial management	Bursar or Accounts
Information Technology and Systems	IT Services

FIGURE 1.3: *Functions and departments*

Most of these functions are also covered elsewhere in this book: Chapters 2 and 3 on organizational behaviour and human resource management, Chapters 4 and 5 on marketing and customer services, Chapters 6 and 7 on strategic and operational financial management, Chapters 8 and 9 on academic management and managing change, and the final chapter on project management.

Managerial levels/hierarchy

As will be described in more detail in Chapter 2, organizations tend to be hierarchical, and in a large corporation the management will typically have three levels:

1   senior management (or 'top management' or 'upper management')
2   middle management
3   lower management.

Senior management is generally a team of individuals at the highest level of organizational management who have the day-to-day responsibilities of managing the business. Senior management are managed by and are responsible to a board of directors (or in an NFP organization, a board of trustees) and those who own the company, the shareholders or the owners in a for-profit organization. It is the directors and senior management who define organizational strategy and policies and ensure that they are implemented. They need to be knowledgeable as far as management roles and skills are concerned, since they are responsible for the appointment and supervision of middle managers.

Middle management is a layer of management in an organization whose primary job is to translate the organization's strategy into action and results. They are responsible for getting things done, for which they require appropriate expertise, and they are the link between strategic plans and results. They are also the link between senior management, lower management and operations staff, that is, the majority of organizational members who do not occupy designated management positions.

Effective middle managers help the staff to stay focused on the most important work by communicating what is expected and why it is important, providing constant feedback on the work not only to the staff but to senior management as well. Effective middle managers also develop others by encouraging an organizational culture that fosters and supports continuous learning through the work itself. They also clarify performance expectations and establish a clear connection between work and the organization's strategic goals and mission. Finally, they ensure that there is an alignment between staff and the values and goals of the organization so as to foster enthusiasm, motivation and commitment.

Accountability: corporate governance

It is expected that the directors and managers of a corporation (whether for-profit or NFP) will act ethically, and in the best interests of the organization, its shareholders, its staff and its clientele. The process by which corporations are directed and controlled is known as corporate governance, which is a means of ensuring that formal procedures are in place to hold managers accountable to the board, shareholders and staff over the use of the assets of the business.

Corporate governance specifies the distribution of rights and responsibilities among the main groups of participants:

- the board of directors or trustees (sometimes called 'governors')
- the managers
- the staff
- the shareholders or owners
- regulatory authorities (such as Charity Commissioners)
- customers
- the community
- suppliers.

The system of corporate governance includes:

- national law concerning the setting up and running of corporate bodies such as an LTO
- the rules set up by the corporation itself (sometimes called 'bylaws', which cannot supersede national law)
- the organizational structure of the corporate body.

An organization's own bylaws are drafted by its founders or its directors under the authority of its Charter or Articles of Association. Bylaws typically specify how directors are elected, how meetings of directors (and in the case of a business, shareholders) are conducted, what officers the organization will have and a description of their duties.

Issues involving corporate governance principles include:

- oversight of the preparation of the corporation's financial statements
- internal controls and the independence of the corporation's auditors
- review of the compensation arrangements for the chief executive officer and other senior executives (but not for other staff, whose compensation may be subject to enterprise bargaining with a union)
- the way in which individuals are nominated for positions on the board
- the resources made available to directors in carrying out their duties (such as travel and other out-of-pocket expenses)
- oversight and management of risk
- dividend policy (in the case of a for-profit business with shareholders).

Accountability and fiduciary duty, integrity and ethical behaviour, disclosure and transparency, and the equitable treatment of stakeholders are key aspects of corporate governance. In all jurisdictions there will be legal and regulatory frameworks which establish the basis of corporate governance, but there may also be local and corporate ways in which such governance requirements are realized in practice. Expectations formed under one set of conventions may be challenged when confronted with such local variations, and given the global spread and mobility in the ELT world, these can be a source of conflict between staff, management and directors in LTOs with nationally diverse members.

> **REFLECTION**
>
> It is not unusual for staff to be quite ignorant of the corporate governance of the LTO they work for, yet it provides the basic framework for the proper running of the organization. This activity is designed to stimulate some thinking about the taken-for-granted corporate governance of your LTO.
> - What do you know about the corporate governance of your LTO?
> - How is information about the way the LTO is governed made available?
> - What does the availability (or not) of such information suggest about the transparency of governance in your LTO?
> - How does the transparency or opacity of governance affect staff attitudes towards the LTO?

The work of the LTO manager

What job responsibilities fall to the LTO manager in order to make things happen? There are various ways of classifying and grouping these responsibilities, and Figure 1.4 on p. 16 is one of them. The allocation of different responsibilities will differ from one individual to another, depending on the LTO, the status of the manager, and the areas that come under his or her responsibility. A lower-level manager might have few or no responsibilities in some areas, but a lot in others, whereas the picture might change for a middle or senior manager.

> **TASK**
>
> Complete the % column in Figure 1.4 for your own job. The idea is to allocate approximate percentages to each category so that altogether they total 100. For example, if you are a DOS with a major responsibility for academic management, 40% of more of your work might be devoted to this particular area, while a low percentage – 5% – might be given to resources management. Although there will be some seasonal variation in the amount of time given to different parts of the job, try to take an annual view of your job.
> - What does the allocation of percentages tell you about the 'shape' of your job?
> - How has this shape changed as you have moved up the management hierarchy?
> - Would you like to change your job shape (the allocation of responsibilities)? If so, in what ways, and why?

As is illustrated in the LTO examples on pp. 6–7, there are big differences in the duties of the managers, reflecting not only the context in which they work, but also their status

	Responsibilities	%
1	**Academic management** curriculum development, course planning, assessment, teaching, materials selection & development	
2	**Business management** monitoring volume & profitability, costing & budgeting, assessing risk, meeting targets	
3	**Resources management** procuring, allocating & maintaining teaching materials, IT, study centre, classroom furniture & equipment	
4	**Entrepreneurial & customer relations** identifying new products, promoting & selling the offer monitoring customer satisfaction building relationships with customers	
5	**Managing people** recruiting, inducting, assigning, training, mentoring, motivating, problem solving, grievance & conflict handling, dismissing	
6	**Administration** overseeing the running of day-to-day systems, e.g. registration, timetabling, student placement, teacher assignment , social and excursion programme	
7	**Professional leadership** demonstrating technical competence & teaching skills identifying and meeting training needs of staff maintaining quality standards advising pupils, parents, staff acting as spokesperson vis-a-vis educational & professional matters	
8	**Diplomatic and representational** liaising with clients participating in institutional policy development external professional organization involvement liaising with accrediting & funding agencies, sponsors, international agencies	
9	**Corporate leadership** articulating strategic focus & direction allocating & co-ordinating a range of organizational functions acting as organizational broker, referee	

FIGURE 1.4: *LTO management responsibilities*

within the organization. Angela's responsibilities exclude business, entrepreneurial, diplomatic, representational, and leadership areas. Bruce's areas of responsibility are similar, but as he is working in a commercial organization, he has some business responsibilities as well as responsibility for resources, and he has some input into identifying and developing new products. In comparison, Lee has limited academic and administration responsibilities (most of these are delegated to the DOSs), but she does have responsibilities in all other areas. This reflects both her institutional context and her status as head of department. Then there is Melina. As an owner-manager, she has responsibilities in all areas, her LTO being too small to support a staff to whom work could be delegated. Bob's responsibilities are mostly political, securing resources for a service unit within an organization in which academic departments are given priority. Finally, Hafwen works within an LTO which is run as a profit-making business. As a block trainer, her role is highly prescribed, with limited autonomy or room for initiative, being largely concerned with implementing decisions that have been made by others elsewhere in the organization.

Changing job perspectives

The shape and scope of people's jobs change as they move up the management hierarchy. Jobs themselves also change in response to external and internal circumstances, an aspect of change management to be discussed in Chapter 9. In particular, the scope of leadership, management and administration will change. While leadership focuses on the initiation of new directions, management is concerned with implementing such initiatives, while administration involves implementation at operational level.

What, then, is the distribution of leadership, management and administrative functions in schools and LTOs? What leadership and management responsibilities do teachers have? One answer is provided by Law & Glover (2000, p. 15) in the table below. In the first column, their list, contextualized in public sector schools, is set out, while to the right a list is suggested for teachers in LTOs.

	Public sector schools	**LTOs**
Focus	Curriculum delivery	Service provision
through	Schemes of work	Materials, methods, activities
Leadership	Classroom tone Subject mission Teaching and learning style	Service mission Teaching and learning style
Management	Materials development Resource use Curriculum tracking Student assessment	Service and curriculum development, provision, monitoring and tracking Assessment and evaluation
Administration	Student records Teaching and learning records	Student, teaching, learning and evaluation records

FIGURE 1.5: *Teachers in public sector schools and in LTOs* (adapted from Law & Glover, 2000, p. 15)

As professionals and as managers, teachers draw on technical, human and conceptual skills in their classrooms. They provide leadership in establishing and maintaining the tone of the classroom, by realizing the curriculum goals of their subject, and through the teaching and learning style they promote. Their managerial responsibilities involve managing resources and activities to achieve learning outcomes. But teachers also occupy several potentially conflicting roles: as facilitators of learning, as providers of a service to consumers, and as gatekeepers. In the classroom context, theirs is not a relationship of equality with their co-participants, being based on asymmetrical distribution of power derived from positional authority and expertise. So, while the answer to the question 'Do teachers manage?' is affirmative, their role as managers is largely confined to the setting of the classroom.

It is in the role of subject leader/DOS – a middle manager in the management hierarchy – that Law & Glover suggest a range of responsibilities which extends beyond the classroom to the department. While the class teacher (Figure 1.5) is responsible for leading and managing the work of students, who are not status equals, the subject leader (Figure 1.6) is responsible for leading and managing the work of colleagues, who are. The second column in Figure 1.6 illustrates how this applies to the responsibilities of the DOS.

	Public sector schools	LTOs
Focus	Subject department	ELT service and academic provision
through	Departmental development plan	ELT service and curriculum development plan
Leadership	Departmental aims Targets Resource bidding Team cohesion Subject policies	Service and curriculum aims Targets Resource bidding Team cohesion ESOL policies
Management	Resource allocation Subject staff development Curriculum organization Monitoring and evaluation Student progress	Budgeting Resource allocation Marketing Curriculum development Syllabus development Student placement Student progress and satisfaction checking Articulation among levels Test development and curriculum trialling Teacher recruitment, induction and evaluation Teacher training and development
Administration	Staff records Resource tracking Maintaining records	Staff records Resource tracking Budget monitoring

FIGURE 1.6: *Subject leaders in public sector schools and DOSs in LTOs* (adapted from Law & Glover, 2000, p. 15)

Extension in the scope of responsibilities of the subject leader/DOS inv
the work of others through allocation of resources, monitoring and evalu
development. This is a significant shift, involving a different perspective
frames the work of the teacher.

Similarly, with the role of principal/head teacher – a senior manager in the hie
Law & Glover outline a further change of perspective, involving responsibility for the
whole school and all its members. This is shown with its LTO application in Figure 1.7.
Although she is not a principal, Lee's role as head of department in a large college
incorporates many aspects of these responsibilities.

	Public sector schools	LTOs
Focus	Whole school/college	Whole of LTO
through	Institutional development plan	Institutional development and business plan
Leadership	Vision Aims and objectives Strategy Team formation Organizational policies	Vision Strategy Goals, aims and objectives Organizational policies Team formation
Management	Overall control of resource base Overall development of staff	Overall control of resource base (including finance) Overall development of staff
Administration	Responsible but not active	Responsible but not active

FIGURE 1.7: *Principals/head teachers in public sector schools and heads of LTOs* (adapted
from Law & Glover, 2000, p. 15)

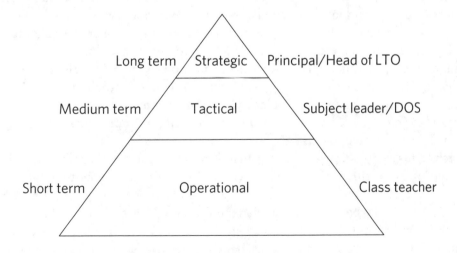

FIGURE 1.8: *Organizational hierarchy and management levels*

The differences in the scope of responsibilities of teachers, subject co-ordinators and principals matches the differences in range and scope of operational, tactical and strategic management, as defined in the traditional hierarchy of levels in an organization (Figure 1.8). Positional authority and increasing span of control are characteristic of such hierarchies – the higher up the hierarchy, the larger the number of people and activities for which a manager is responsible, and the more extensive in scope is the perspective.

Managing an LTO involves, to a varying extent, all the roles indicated above and the range of responsibilities and skills outlined earlier. What probably makes LTO management unique is the tension between meeting both educational and commercial interests, and professional and managerial concerns, particularly in private – and increasingly in state sector – institutions. There is also another pressure which the LTO manager has to meet: the emphasis on service, to be considered in detail in Chapter 5.

THE TRANSITION TO LTO MANAGER

As often happens in other fields, managers are typically recruited from among employees within the organization. We have already noted that there are significant changes in perspective in the transition from level to level within the organizational hierarchy. How easy is it for teachers to make the transition from classroom to manager's office? What competencies do they already have and which ones need to be developed, and how can teachers go about developing them? The KASA (Knowledge, Skills, Attitudes and Awareness) framework (Freeman, 1989) provides a useful basis for teachers to analyse and answer these questions.

Knowledge: knowing about

'What information do I need to manage this school successfully?'

LTO managers need a lot of information in order to do their job well. This knowledge includes market information (who the clients and customers are, what the untapped part of the market consists of, who the competition are); resource information (what the LTO has at its disposal: financial resources, technological resources, building resources, human resources); institutional history and organizational structure. It also involves knowledge of the product that is being sold, in our case language teaching (as well as exams, curricula, coursebooks, etc.). Finally it requires a knowledge of management theory and practices, just as teaching requires a knowledge of approaches to teaching and of methodologies and techniques.

Much of this information is already available to any teacher who has recently been promoted into the management position. Teachers know their students, they have an idea of the market and of the human and material resources they can draw upon. Depending on how long they have been working at the school, they will have a sense of the institution's history, its values, and its academic structure. What they may not be aware of are the detailed financial information, the market (in terms of external factors and potential rather than actual students), and of course the non-academic aspects of the school management, coupled with the very real challenge of looking at the organization from an entirely different perspective. In many instances, it may be that teachers lack a real sense of what management actually is, often a result of negative experiences from being badly managed themselves. In effect they have been the recipients of management, and as such have had a different sense of needs and expectations than as the providers of management.

There are a number of ways of coming by some of this information: books such as this could provide some of the management theory. The departing manager is obviously an invaluable source of knowledge, which in many cases can be easily drawn on, particularly if there is an overlap in the handover period. Shadowing the manager for a week or two before he or she leaves is an extremely useful exercise. Obviously, working with the administrative staff is another important part of the process. Training courses or workshops can also help with some of the aspects of management theory and an understanding of how organizations work.

Skills: knowing how

'What skills do I already have that I need to adapt, and which skills do I need to acquire?'

This may be the most important area for a new manager. Many management skills are fairly easy to transfer from the classroom, while others will need to be acquired. Some of the former might be:
- time management
- the general management cycle as summarized in Figure 1.2 on p. 11 (planning, establishing, monitoring, comparing, rectifying – all very familiar to teachers)
- communication – and in particular listening, an essential management skill.

This last skill might include teacher supervision and evaluation, marketing, financial management, and customer relations.

Based on our experience of training, the two areas of management that most strike fear into the former teacher are financial management and marketing and sales. This is not because those skills are considered to be harder to learn than any others, but because most people feel as if they are starting from scratch, having never before managed organizational budgets, done market research, or sold a programme.

As with any other field, skills are difficult to pick up from a book, and in this area of competency acquisition, training courses and mentoring are particularly valuable. If you know a manager at another institution (probably not a competitor) try to tap into their abilities. If there are other managers at your LTO (and particularly if you are lucky enough to have a marketing and financial department), use them. If there is a director above you at the LTO, then find out if he or she would be willing to act as a mentor.

Attitudes: knowing why

'Why do people behave the way they do? How can I become more aware of their attitudes?'

Finding out people's motivations or the reasons behind certain facts can be tricky. Teachers are forced to do this all the time – asking why their students are there, what motivates them to study the language, what learning style they each have, which ones among them respond to which activities and techniques, and so on. A new manager may know something about the attitudes of his or her clients and customers, and even some of his or her staff – particularly the teachers – but might need more information. Why do my colleagues choose to work here? What motivates my colleagues (and particularly the teachers)? What historical issues are at play in the interactions and structure of the organization? What makes us tick, organizationally and from a human resource perspective?

Many of the abilities needed to determine these attitudes, values and motivations can be transferred directly from the classroom, but others will need to be acquired from other sources. A course in organizational behaviour or human resource management would be a good start, as would consulting the relevant chapters of this book. Other ways include attending conference presentations, joining special interest groups (SIGs) in a professional organization such as TESOL or IATEFL, and sharing ideas with other managers.

More locally, and specifically to your LTO, there is clearly a good case for sitting down with all your staff in one-on-one interviews to ask them what it is they like about their jobs, what they would like to change, and how their work life could be made more satisfying – but without raising their expectations that you will be able to wave a magic wand to bring about instant improvements!

In this way, not only do you get a sense of who your staff are, what brings them to work, what frustrates them, and what motivates them, but you also get to learn a lot about the organization that you might not have already known. One way of doing this successfully is to start with a 'job model' activity; this is essentially a task in which both you and the staff member individually list what you feel their job involves and what its priorities are. This can provide an excellent set of information from which the conversation can evolve. You will almost certainly be surprised at the difference between your perception of someone's role and their own!

Awareness: knowing oneself

'Who am I as a manager? What am I bringing to this role?'

This is the easiest and simultaneously most challenging of the four areas. Here is an example from the past of one of the authors:

> When I began my career as a teacher one of my primary concerns in the classroom was to get my students to like me. It took quite a long time before I became aware that this was my teaching personality, and realized that this might even be overriding other considerations, such as helping them learn English. This kind of self-awareness is something that you have to reacquire when you move into a management position. Now, of course, it is about learning what your management personality is.

One of the biggest challenges for a new manager who has recently been promoted out of the classroom is to deal with the shift in his or her relationships with the other teachers. However difficult it is to accept and however much everybody may hope that it does not happen, there is a definite shift in the dynamic. It is not unusual for teachers who have been promoted to a managerial role to struggle with the fact that their friends in the staffroom are no longer – at least at work – their friends. There is not necessarily any solution to this problem except for an awareness that it will occur, whether you like it or not.

So, who are you as a manager? Think about your first months in the classroom as a teacher and remember how you became aware of who you were as a teacher. This is an excellent way of speeding up the process!

CONCLUSION

	Needs	Where from?
Knowledge: **knowing about**	Resource information Academic programmes Market	Books Shadowing outgoing manager
Getting information	Management theory, etc.	Management courses Talking to staff and other 'experts'
Skills: **knowing how** **Developing expertise**	All management skills: Budgeting and financial management Communication Marketing Academic management Human resource management Customer relations Conflict management Teacher supervision and observation, etc.	Management courses and programmes Books Mentoring
Attitudes: **knowing why** **Discovering explanations**	Staff motivations Staff needs Staff priorities Organizational structure Communication channels Institutional history	Face-to-face meetings with staff 'Job model' activity Management courses Organizational behaviour books
Awareness: **knowing oneself**	Who am I as a manager? What are my strengths and weaknesses? How am I perceived by staff/ customers? What do I think makes a good manager?	Reflection Feedback from others

FIGURE 1.9: *KASA framework summary* (Freeman, 1989)

In this chapter, we have looked at the range of institutional contexts in which ESOL takes place, and considered the functions of management: planning, organizing, leading/ motivating and controlling. Not everything needs to be controlled, however, and managers need to decide what does not need to be controlled, as well as what does, and devise efficient and effective control systems.

Hierarchically different levels of management have different areas of responsibility which are differently distributed across the work of different managers, resulting in different job shapes or profiles. Likewise, the scope of responsibilities under leadership, management and administration varies according to position on the management hierarchy.

What characterizes an effective LTO is an organization in which there is strong alignment between its vision and goals and its staff and clientele. Just as teachers develop their competencies through a combination of training, experience, discussion and reflection, so, too, do managers. Furthermore, just as training is regarded as a vital part of becoming a teacher, and continuing professional development (CPD) is a way of continuing to learn and grow, so, too, are training and CPD vital for teachers who are becoming managers. The KASA framework outlined on pp. 20–3 is a good starting model to ensure that one remembers to take into account all aspects of management rather than focusing only on the more obvious need for skill building.

Books, such as this one, can help put the aspiring or practising manager on the path to good management, but just as with teaching, books alone are not enough, and training, tied closely to mentoring, is the clearest path to success for the language teacher moving into the manager's office. The following chapters will focus on different areas of LTO management, and will extend and apply many of the management concepts introduced in the current chapter.

2 Organizational behaviour and management

- ORGANIZATIONAL STRUCTURE
- VISION, MISSION AND STRATEGIC PLANNING
- THE LEARNING ORGANIZATION

INTRODUCTION

Organizations have been defined by Dawson (1986, p. xviii) as:

> collections of people joining together in order to achieve group or individual objectives. At least one set of objectives of any organization will relate to the production and output of specific goods and services to individuals, groups and organizations.

As we saw in Chapter 1, there are many kinds of LTO, and as organizations they take on many forms, as shown in these examples:

- a small, fairly new private language school in a European town: focused on teaching English and other languages to that city's middle-class residents, staffed by its founder/owner/director/teacher, two other teachers, and an administrator
- an English Language Support Unit in a large English-medium university in the Middle East: providing academically focused English language classes for incoming students, the unit exists as a non-faculty department of the university
- a school which exists to provide support for refugee resettlement in the United States: funding comes from federal and state government, and the school provides English and vocational courses
- an English school in Japan: employing 40 teachers and 12 admin staff, it exists as part of a large nationwide chain
- an Intensive English Program in the US: based on a university campus and serving the non-native-English speaking population of the college, the IEP is run as an outsourced business, not affiliated with the university in any way
- a British Council teaching centre in a provincial city: the centre itself is semi-autonomous, but the DOS's manager operates out of the office in the capital city, and the global organization offers a number of benefits and imposes a number of restrictions on activities
- a language school in a major European capital: established 20 years ago as a small business, and since expanding to employ more than 50 teachers spread over five branches throughout the city.

Looking at the definition and the examples of different language teaching organizations that began this chapter, it can be seen that all clearly fit the definition of an organization despite the great dissimilarities among them. All these organizations have in common the fact that they offer language classes, but as organizations they are very different. It is, however, possible to generalize and link these apparently unconnected situations to one another, based on organizational behaviour theories.

The study of organizational behaviour has developed rapidly over the last 50 years, and is now considered one of the social sciences. The purpose of this chapter is to link the study and theory of organizational behaviour to the needs and realities of language teaching organizations.

ORGANIZATIONAL STRUCTURE

When looking at organizational structure, we are interested in determining what an organization looks like – both from outside and from within, how it came to be that way, and whether or not the current structure best suits the needs of the LTO.

Organigrams

Organigrams (also referred to as 'organograms' or 'organizational charts') are the traditional way of graphically illustrating the way in which an organization functions. Figure 2.1 shows an example of a simple LTO organigram, which may or may not have similarities to your LTO's structure.

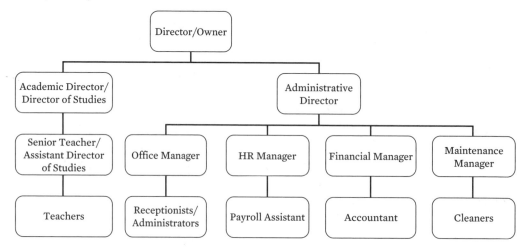

FIGURE 2.1: *Simple LTO organigram*

Chain of command/communication

Typically the organigram illustrates the chain of command. That is, it shows the reporting relationships within an organization and defines who is everyone's boss. It also gives an indication of span of control (see p. 30), that is to say, the number of people under each line manager.

Occasionally an organigram is modified to include the lines of communication. Rather than just being a set of formal reporting relationships, it also features lines (usually dotted) that illustrate the formal lines of communication.

In Figure 2.1 it is clear, for example, that while the payroll assistant has no reporting relationship with the Finance department, there must be a communication relationship between the two. This can be illustrated on the chart by a separate dotted line.

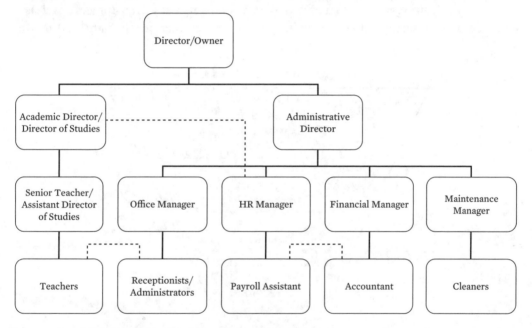

FIGURE 2.2: *LTO organigram with communication lines*

In an LTO, while there is typically no departmental relationship between teachers and receptionists, it is usually very valuable to formalize a communication relationship between these two 'departments' which are the main points of contact with the organization for its clients, the students and/or person or organization funding the course of study. By utilizing the organigram in this way, one can see where formal relationships need to be established. The next stage, of course, is to work out how exactly these relationships can be created and formalized.

In larger organizations the organigram can be an indication of one of the typical problems that often arise, that of lack of communication within organizations, and particularly between departments. Even quite small LTOs can often encounter this problem between the two major branches of the organization: the academic and the administrative sides. This lack of communication between departments is referred to as 'silo-ization'. The departments act as silos, in which everything is contained and the only entrance/exit for information is at the top. If there is little communication in your organization between the academic and administrative silos, ways of engendering communication need to be found. One such way is by staff members working together in teams on projects (see Chapter 10).

Inverted hierarchy/fronted organigram

It is important to note that the standard organigram tends to mirror the traditional hierarchical structure with the directors at the top of the chart (Figure 2.1, p. 26). This standard pyramidical hierarchy is how most of us perceive the organization from within.

Inverting this picture, though, can be quite helpful for us to see the organization from another angle. If an organization is defined by its relationship with its customers, as LTOs tend to be, we can end up with the following pictorial representation (Garratt, 2000, p. 48):

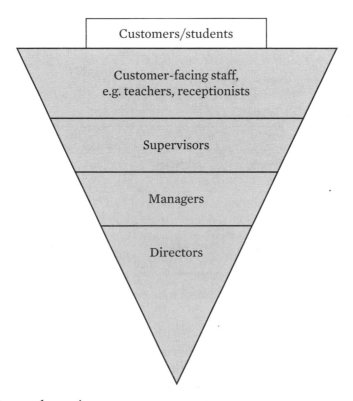

FIGURE 2.3: *Inverted organigram*

In this diagram, not only are the customers located at the top of the diagram, giving them the prominence they ought to be given, but also one can see that the most important members of an organization are the staff who have the contact with the customers (teachers, receptionists, etc.), and the supervisors, managers and directors are responsible for supporting their work. It may take a slight repositioning of our standard view of how things work, but it does help considerably with viewing the organization in a different light and in ensuring that the work is focused on the things that ought to drive it. In this representation the 'moments of truth' (those which determine the success or otherwise of the organization) happen at the top of the diagram, in the interactions between customers and staff.

Charles (1993) in 'The Fronted Organigram' prefers a sideways-on model, such that teachers will feel 'up front' in the organization and such that there is no clear 'up' and 'down'; a teacher moving into a management position would be moving backstage rather than up (a little like moving off-stage in the theatre), while those who remain in teaching are 'frontstage', as shown in the service systems blueprint matrix in Chapter 5 (page 146).

Academic and administrative sides of the LTO: differences and similarities

As we have seen, there can often be a lack of connection between the academic (or teaching) side and the administrative (or office) side of the LTO. There are a number of possible reasons for this.

Firstly, the organizational structure of both sides tends to be somewhat different: the academic side tends to have a very flat hierarchy with a number of teachers, all of equal status, reporting to a DOS or academic director. In larger LTOs there may be one level of hierarchy between these two in the form of an assistant DOS (ADOS) or co-ordinators or senior teachers, but rarely are there more than three levels of the chain of command on that side of the organization. The administrative side, on the other hand, is typically much more rigidly hierarchical and much less 'flat'.

Secondly, there is often a cultural difference, in that the academic side tends to see itself as creative and flexible, while the administrative side tends to work (of necessity) in a much less flexible, bureaucratic way (see *Organizations as culture* on p. 35).

Finally, there is a tendency for teachers in any school to view their work as being the crux of the business with everyone else merely supporting them, which can of course lead to mistrust of the academic side from the admin side.

All these factors, when coupled with the potential for silo-ization between separate departments, mean that it is very important for managers to keep the channels of communication between these two distinct areas of the LTO open and in use.

Other elements of organizational structure

In addition to chain of command, Robbins (2001, p. 414), identifies five other elements of organizational structure. These are outlined below.

Departmentalization

How many departments are there? Are jobs grouped together in separate departments or other clusters, or silos? In an LTO, for example, is the teaching done through one broad academic department, or are there mini-groupings corresponding to discrete teaching needs (such as a Young Learners department, a Business English department, exam courses, groupings by level, etc.)? On the administrative side, are there separate departments for marketing, finance, human resources, customer service, maintenance, etc.?

Formalization

How many rules and regulations are there governing how the organization functions? Do people have a certain amount of autonomy in their work or are they locked into a certain set of tasks governed by their job description?

Teachers, by the nature of their work, tend to have a fair amount of autonomy in their work. Once the classroom door has closed, they are more or less on their own and free to fulfil their job responsibilities as they see fit (within reason). However, outside of the class, how much leeway do they have? Are there certain forms to be filled in, records to be kept, and, crucially for our discussion here, things that need to be communicated in a very clearly defined way (to whom, how, when, etc.)?

Span of control

This area has been touched upon already: how many people are supervised by each line manager? This is the second of Robbins' six elements which can easily be seen by looking at the organigram. It is also another of the commonly found differences between the academic and administrative sides of the organization: often we find a large teaching staff, all of whom report to the same person (perhaps an ADOS, or a satellite branch manager), whereas the administrative side (with a more vertical structure) tends to have a greater number of layers, with more people in the supervisory levels. Six receptionists may report, for example, to two office managers, who in turn report to the customer service director, who falls below the administrative director.

Centralization

Who makes the decisions? Who has the authority to make decisions? In a very centralized organization, decisions are all made by the director. This can result in complex systems for requesting anything, involving someone at the lower level of the organigram discovering the need for something, asking his line manager, who asks her line manager, who in turn asks the director. The director makes the decision, and then this decision is passed back down the same chain.

By contrast, in a very decentralized organization, decisions can be made by many people within the organization. The director does not need to be consulted and things can be decided at a much lower level in the organizational chart. This obviously simplifies things and speeds things up considerably. Upper management ends up with less control over what is going on, which is usually the reason why organizations are not as decentralized as they could perhaps be.

Work specialization

How specialized are people's jobs? Do people do very small, discrete tasks which together make up the totality of the organization's work, or do people do more integrated jobs incorporating many of these tasks?

Typically in LTOs, teachers do a fairly wide range of things, from planning classes, to teaching different levels, Business English and Young Learners courses, to record keeping. Are there other tasks they could be reasonably performing, such as registration, marketing, testing, etc.?

In very small LTOs there is typically a very low level of specialization; everybody is expected to participate in everything, from answering the phones to recruiting new teachers to making the coffee to teaching the classes, whereas in much larger educational organizations there may be a much higher level of specialization.

> ### *REFLECTION*
> Consider your own LTO and its organization.
> - How departmentalized is it?
> - How centralized is it?
> - How does it compare in this regard with other LTOs (or other organizations) you may have previously worked in?

Organizational design

How did the organization come to look the way it does? What factors led to the structure that now exists? Many factors contribute to organizational design and structure, some of them planned, some of them not. One factor influencing design will be the stage in the organizational life cycle.

Organizational life cycles

LTOs typically start out as small organizations which, if they are successful, evolve and grow into large organizations, with multiple centres. In other words organizations, like people, go through different life cycles, from infancy to maturity (Schein, 1985). Carter McNamara (1997–2007), drawing on earlier work by Richard L. Daft, summarizes these stages and their typical features (see Figure 2.4, p. 32).

During its life cycle, an organization's structure may move from the kind of organic organization described below to one that is more mechanistic, with extensive division of labour and formalization of systems, characteristic of organizations in midlife and maturity. Within a large enterprise, there may be sub-units which retain an organic structure, further complicating organizational structure. Recognizing the life cycle stage through which an organization is passing is one of the skills possessed by a good leader, as is managing the transition from a simple, non-bureaucratic organization to one with formalized systems, specialization, and multiple managers, without sacrificing aspects of organizational culture which make the smaller organization special.

Impact of organizational history and context on structure

Many privately owned or not-for-profit LTOs tend to have grown organically from modest roots. Often begun as a family-style operation, with one or two teachers who double as secretaries, managers, and cleaners, they (if successful) will grow while retaining much of their original ethos. Everybody is expected to participate in all aspects of the business, there are many overlapping tasks among staff, and everybody feels part of the enterprise as a whole. This kind of organization has an *organic* structure.

	Birth	Youth	Midlife	Maturity
Size	small	medium	large	very large
Level of bureaucracy	non-bureaucratic	pre-bureaucratic	bureaucratic	very bureaucratic
Division of labour	overlapping tasks	some departments	many departments	extensive, with small jobs and many descriptions
Centralization	one-person rule	two leaders rule	two department heads	top-management heavy
Formalization	no written rules	few rules	policy and procedures manuals	extensive
Administrative intensity	secretary, no professional staff	increasing clerical and maintenance	increasing professional and staff support	large: multiple departments
Internal systems	non-existent	crude budget and information system	control systems in place; budget, performance, reports, etc.	extensive: planning, financial, and personnel added
Lateral teams, task forces for co-ordination	none	top leaders only	some use of integrators and task forces	frequent at lower levels to break down bureaucracy

FIGURE 2.4: *Overview of organizational life cycles (McNamara, 1997–2007)*

An organic structure has a number of defining characteristics:

- flat hierarchy, with very little departmentalization (staff tend to perform many more tasks than their primary role)
- decisions often made in a very participatory way with most people having an input
- comprehensive information network: everybody knows what is going on, partly because everybody is very involved with the running of the organization.

A number of other factors can influence organizational design or structure. These can be categorized as follows:

Strategy: why the organization exists, and what its purpose is. Some LTOs, for example, were built from the ground up by a committed individual (or individuals), while others were created to fulfil a specific need by a larger organization. This latter type might include such LTOs as IEPs attached to US universities, for example. The type of business that the LTO is focused on also makes a difference. LTOs that focus their energies on Business English courses provided offsite will look very different from LTOs that specialize in Young Learners courses onsite.

Size: how large the organization is and what influences size has on design. While an organic structure may suit a smaller organization, a larger organization may require a higher degree of formalization and centralization, as indicated in McNamara's table opposite. This is discussed in greater depth on p. 34.

Environment: where is the organization and what kind of space does it occupy? There are LTOs, for example, in which the administrative staff occupy one area of the building and teaching staff another, and therefore all contact between the two departments happens formally when needed. This tends to affect organizational structure. Likewise, there are also LTOs in large spacious custom-built premises which have been designed with organizational interactions in mind. Again, this will have a large impact on organizational structure.

Technology: increasingly, information technology is the medium by which much communication takes place, and as such it may have an impact on organizational structure and design. If a school occupies two buildings in different parts of the city, perhaps much of the interaction between those two buildings has become more computer-based than previously. Paradoxically, technology may also be the point at which human interactions happen; a large proportion of casual interactions in LTOs might take place in the queue for the photocopier.

National culture: one of the determinants of organizational structure is often the prevailing culture in which the LTO operates. Traditional and hierarchical cultures will tend towards one structure, while more egalitarian cultures may tend towards another.

Many LTOs are bicultural environments: while the administrative side of the organization will be staffed with locals and tend towards the local national culture, the academic side is often staffed with expatriates who will tend to a different cultural orientation. In countries where large numbers of expatriate staff work side by side with local staff from a very different culture, these cultural differences can have a noticeable impact on the organizational culture, and indeed can introduce a divide between the administrative and academic sides of the organization. If the academic manager's job can be seen as acting as a bridge between the teaching staff and the admin department, and the wider organization and upper management, in such a context the manager's job is made doubly challenging by being required to act as a bridge between cultures as well as between departments.

REFLECTION

Consider your own LTO.
- How did its organizational structure develop?
- What historical and other factors played into the design of the organization?

Impact of growth: transition from organic to mechanistic

As an organization progresses through its life cycle, an organic structure tends to be less and less easy to sustain when the organization grows in size. There is often a drive for more formalization and more centralization, and much more rigidity and clear job descriptions. This drive can come from within (staff concerns about lack of clear direction from management or lack of a clear reporting structure), or without (customers expressing a need for a clear and effective enquiries procedure).

An extremely formalized and centralized organization is regarded as having a *mechanistic* structure. Such a structure, in contrast to an organic structure, is characterized as being quite centralized, having a high degree of formalization, extensive departmentalization and usually a much more limited information network (staff know what they need to know for their work, but very little about other aspects of the organization).

One of the problems often encountered in LTOs is the fact that many of these organizations reach a critical point in their development, when the organic structure that has served them so well and seen them grow to this point becomes no longer workable, and a new, more mechanistic structure is needed, while not of course losing the advantages of the former organic structure.

Another occasional effect of growth on organizational structure is that new courses (or course types) are added to the LTO's portfolio, necessitating the creation of new positions and possibly even a new department. New working practices and technologies also create new roles within the organization. Twenty years ago, for example, very few enterprises had an IT department.

Organizational capacity and capability

The final factor influencing organizational structure and design is the capacity and capability of the organization (and of course the people within it). At first glance it may appear that it is the structure of the organization that determines its capacity and capability, rather than the other way around, and indeed to some extent this is the case.

However, it is also the case that the organization's capacity, for example, can influence the way it grows (or stops growing). If in an LTO we are presented with an opportunity to extend our offerings, then the capacity of the school and its systems, and capabilities of our staff, determine whether we can take up this opportunity or must turn it down (it may of course be that we end up turning it down even if we can do it).

For example, a large local corporation approaches an LTO to provide language courses for its staff. Obviously, doing so will be financially beneficial to the LTO, but it may be impossible to provide the teaching required because it does not have the capacity. The management of the LTO would then have to decide whether to restructure (and hire Business English experts), perhaps even adding a new department to take on the extra workload. Later on, of course, if the LTO loses such a lucrative contract, it may be left with a lopsided and overstaffed organization.

Organizational culture

While the study of organizational structure helps us understand how an organization looks and how it came to be that way, the following section presents two further tools of organizational analysis, all of which can help us to come to a greater understanding of exactly how LTOs function.

Organizations as culture

Some theorists look upon organizations as having many of the features of cultures (Brown, 1995). As with national and local cultures, organizational culture can be said to involve a pattern of beliefs, values and learned ways of coping with experience that have been developed during the course of an organization's history, and which tend to be manifested in its material arrangements and in the behaviour of its members. Put another way, the organizational culture is 'the way we do things around here'. Most of us who have worked in more than one organization will recognize the sense of 'culture' in the way things work and the way people interact.

Organizational culture fulfils a number of functions. It:
- creates distinctions between one organization and another
- conveys a sense of identity
- generates commitment to something larger than self-interest
- enhances social system stability
- holds organizations together by providing standards of what members should say and do
- guides and shapes attitudes and behaviour of employees
- provides, in a strong culture, shared meaning and direction
- influences organization–individual fit
- ensures that employees will act in a uniform, predictable manner.

In his seminal work *Understanding Organizations*, Charles Handy (1985) identified four separate organizational culture types.

POWER CULTURE

The power culture is typically pictured as a web; at its centre there is a very powerful and influential leader with rays of influence leading outwards. The closer people are to this central figure the more power they have. It is quite a political structure in that control comes directly from the centre and there can be much jostling for position in the outer rings in order to have a role in the balance of power. Power cultures are quite dynamic and able to adapt to change, but they can also struggle to sustain themselves as the organization grows larger. The competitive atmosphere can also be demotivating for some employees (and motivating for others).

ROLE CULTURE

The role culture could be renamed as the organigram culture; it is pictured by Handy as a temple, with pillars holding up a pediment. The pediment represents the senior management, overseeing the work done by the different departments (the pillars – or silos). It is the role here that is important, rather than the individuals in the position. Role cultures are less successful at coping with change than power cultures; they tend to be inflexible and slow to respond to the need for change. For the employees they can be seen as safe and predictable; the climb up the pillar is regulated and usually takes place at a foreseeable rate. It may be a frustrating place to work, though, for people who are ambitious or who want more control over their work. The organization as a whole is unlikely to take many risks.

TASK CULTURE

The task culture is job-oriented, that is to say, the emphasis is on getting the job done. A lot of emphasis is placed on teams being created to fulfil certain organizational needs. It is a very flexible culture with teams forming, working on certain projects and then disbanding. Teams are empowered to make decisions and as a result their members feel that they have significant control over their work and influence in the organization. This kind of culture thrives in a marketplace in which speed of reaction and creativity are valued above all else (such as, say, the dot.com market). However, if resources become limited, this kind of organization can start to struggle, with political power plays appearing as different team leaders compete for resources. As morale declines, individuals cease working entirely for the team and hence the organization itself, and begin revealing their personal, individual objectives. This may result in the culture/structure of the organization changing as managers begin to assert authority, leading us back to a power or a role culture.

PERSON CULTURE

The person culture is focused on the individual. Handy refers to it more as a 'cluster', with as little structure as possible. The organization exists to serve the people working for it, rather than the other way around. It mirrors, to an extent, the modern family with no power base, and some organizations have attempted to use this as a basis for work. Some places where it might be seen are in small consultancy firms or co-operatives. However, eventually, 'the organization achieves its own identity and begins to impose on its individuals' (Handy, 1985, p. 196). It is rare to find an organization which is predominantly person-cultured, but individuals within certain more traditional organizations may have a personal preference for this type of culture. A good example from many LTOs might be IT experts, who may not feel bound by the rules or structures of the company, and do not really fall within either the academic or administrative side of the LTO, but instead operate in a kind of separate world, free to pursue their own interests/career development, while the benefit to the organization of their presence is limited to whatever services they provide.

> ### *REFLECTION*
> Consider how Handy's cultural framework is reflected in your own LTO. Handy stresses that one or two of these cultures may be prevalent, or even dominant, but that an organization is unlikely to be entirely role-cultured, for example.
> - Which of the cultures most closely reflects your own organization?
> - What about organizations you have worked for in the past?
> - Which of these frameworks most appeals to you?
> - Does this change according to whether you are considering your role as a manager or an employee?

Bringing Handy's work to the specific case of LTOs, we can once again see the divide between academic and administrative sides of an LTO. In general, the administrative side of an LTO tends towards the role culture because much of its work calls for standardization. However, the academic side can exhibit a number of different cultural tendencies. In some cases, teachers are people-cultured and can act broadly autonomously within their classrooms. Obviously, they have an internal contract with their students such that they fulfil their role effectively, but they may not feel or act as part of the organization in any way. In other LTOs there exists something of a power culture within the academic side, with teachers jostling for position and influence and resources, perhaps with the DOS at the centre of the web as resource allocator. Some LTOs have more of a task focus. Whatever the culture of the different elements of the LTO, we can see that this is another aspect of possible conflict and misunderstanding between the two sides of the LTO.

Organizational culture, like organizational design, often tends to be built upon the philosophy of the organization's founders. As time goes by, the selection criteria by which new employees are chosen also have a profound effect on how the culture develops (the people hired will determine the direction of the organization). Culture is then built up around the top management's philosophies and approach, and the socialization inherent in the company.

The following are some of the factors influencing the development of organizational culture:
- history
- primary function and technology

- goals and objectives
- size
- location
- management and staffing
- the environment.

Sociability vs. solidarity

Goffee & Jones (1996), however, argue that there are merely two important factors in determining organizational culture; what they call 'sociability' and 'solidarity'. They propose a two-dimensional, four-culture model as can be seen in Figure 2.5.

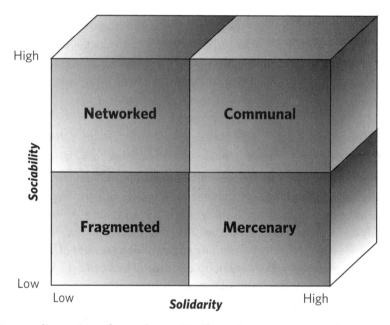

FIGURE 2.5: *Two dimensions, four cultures* (Goffee & Jones, 1996, p. 134)

With this model they argue that these two factors determine the way that the organization functions and operates as a culture or community. High sociability would characterize a workplace in which the employees get on very well with each other, perhaps socializing outside work too. High solidarity would be characteristic of one in which everybody within the workforce is committed to the organizational mission, vision and goals, and will work together for those aims, regardless of personal factors.

> *None of these cultures is 'the best'. In fact, each is appropriate for different business environments. In other words, managers need not begin the hue and cry for one cultural type over another. Instead they must know how to assess their own culture and whether it fits the competitive situation.* (Goffee & Jones, 1996, p. 13)

A networked organization (high sociability, low solidarity) is one in which there tends to be a great deal of informality. There may not be a lack of hierarchy, but there are always

ways of getting around it. It is typically politicized because employees build and use networks to get what they need and access resources. It tends to be a flexible and non-bureaucratic organization type. However, it also can be somewhat unfocused and difficult for the organization to agree on priorities. 'It is not uncommon to hear frequent calls for strong leadership to overcome the divisions of subcultures, cliques or warring factions in networked organizations.' (Goffee & Jones, 1996, p. 137)

At the opposite end of the spectrum is the mercenary organization, in which there is very little socialization and communication is focused on business matters. Such organizations are able to respond quickly to opportunities and threats: priorities are decided quickly by senior management and acted upon with little debate. Poor performance is not tolerated. However, the lack of strong personal ties also means there is little loyalty to the organization. Employees may like and respect their organization, but these feelings are not attached to individuals. Such organizations can be very productive, but can also lack inter-departmental co-operation.

The fragmented organization lacks both solidarity and sociability. Employees of such organizations show little consciousness of organizational membership; if asked what he does for a living, a teacher of a fragmented school will say 'I am a teacher' rather than 'I work for the Shakespeare School'. Employees will work with their doors closed, or at home, coming to the office only when necessary. They also will tend to disagree about organizational objectives or performance standards, for example. While this sounds like a recipe for an unsuccessful organization, they can work well, for example, in professional organizations such as university faculties, law firms, and also in LTOs (the management's focus needs to be on hiring the right people; their work requires little supervision).

Finally, the communal organization is one in which there is both a high degree of sociability and solidarity. People feel that they belong to something, and the mission statement evokes enthusiasm rather than cynicism. Members are friends both inside and outside the office. It sounds ideal, but Goffee & Jones are quick to caution that such organizations seem to be somewhat unstable, and that this state is difficult to sustain. During a period of change, for example, the possible conflict between sincere friendships and the dispassionate focus on achievement of goals characteristic of high solidarity, can create an unresolvable tension. Their research seems to suggest that only in such organizations as religious or political groups (in which people sign up to an ideal first and the job second) can such an organization be sustained for long periods.

So, what of the staffrooms in LTOs? There are some which exhibit features of the communal organization, especially in altruistic LTOs which provide low-cost or free language and vocational training to refugees or new immigrants, for example. There are some, as we have seen, which tend to the opposite, fragmented form. Sociability within LTOs is often quite high, especially in offshore LTOs in which the expatriate teachers all share a certain natural bond of the foreigner in a foreign town, burdened with the same challenges and perhaps similar interests. Solidarity is perhaps less so; teachers share a focus on their students' achievement, but possibly less interest in the organization as an entity, which for them may exist as a means to an end. This idea leads us into the next section of this chapter.

REFLECTION

Consider your own LTO.
- Which of the above cultures most closely reflects your own organization?
- What about organizations you have worked for in the past?
- Do you find that teachers or other employees in your LTO show high levels of solidarity, sociability or both?

VISION, MISSION AND STRATEGIC PLANNING

In the definition of an organization that began this chapter, there were two elements that defined what an organization is. The first of these, that an organization is a collection of people, we have looked at, and seen how these collections of people behave. The second is that the function of the organization is to 'achieve group or individual objectives' (Dawson, 1986, p. xviii). It is these objectives that we will look at in this section.

Mission statements

There are obviously many reasons why LTOs exist, beyond the broad–brush catch-all 'language teaching'. Defining what your raison d'être is can not only be of value to your potential customers (and therefore a valuable marketing strategy in and of itself), but can also help ensure that the organization as a whole is pulling together to achieve a common goal. The alternative is that everybody comes to work every day knowing exactly what their job is, but without having a sense of the wider context of why and how they are an integral part of the team. A famous and possibly apocryphal story is of a lavatory cleaner at NASA headquarters in Houston during the 1960s being asked what his job was. 'I'm helping to put a man on the moon' was his response.

An example mission statement is this one from International House World Organisation:

> IHWO is the leading language solutions provider worldwide and its goal is to promote excellence in language education. It supports a network of language schools to provide the highest quality of language learning and to promote innovation and standard setting in language teaching, learning and teacher training.

As a general rule a mission statement gains power and value if it is created by the staff as a whole. If everybody who works in an LTO comes together to forge a commonly agreed-upon statement of purpose, then it can be genuinely inclusive, and it can really focus the direction of the LTO. If it is imposed from on high, it tends to be ignored and/or misunderstood. An inclusive, cohesive, bonding mission statement can not only attract customers, but it can also be a motivator and driver of the LTO's staff. This is also the case with more internally oriented 'vision' statements.

Consider the mission statement of your own LTO, if it has one.
- Who wrote it? When?
- Has it ever been changed or has it always been the same?
- Do you think it could be improved upon?
- Is everyone in the LTO aware of it? Were you aware of it before this exercise?
- How often do you think about it?
- If your LTO does not have a mission statement, is there a reason why not?

Vision statements

Vision statements are similar to mission statements with one important difference. They are not directed at the public audience (though merely because they are designed by and for an internal market, not because they divulge hidden or secret information). They typically answer the question 'What kind of workplace or team do we want this to be?', and are written in such a way as to describe what the ultimate aim looks like. A vision statement of this type may be something like this:

> *We are a well-paid cutting edge team of professionals in a friendly and collegial environment, working for a financially stable and growing organization.*

While many organizations tend to have mission statements, it is much rarer that they have these internally driven outlines of vision. But, like mission statements, vision statements can be a very effective tool in planning as they provide an internal statement of intent and can be drawn upon when engaging in strategic thinking. Likewise, they can motivate staff as they attempt to develop themselves professionally. They are also especially useful in the context of LTOs as they can represent a more businesslike goal to complement the typically altruistic, socially valuable mission of the education service provider. While there is a need to have a mission statement setting out exactly what the LTO does as a service provider, it would be foolish to forget the need to be a *sustainable* service provider.

Strategic planning

In most of our cases, these broad-brush mission and vision statements are either already defined, or exist in some form. Having determined your organization's mission (and also possibly internal vision), it is essential to use these as a basis for setting out goals and strategy. Strategic planning in this context means the act of outlining the goals and aims for the long term future, perhaps the next three to five years.

The next step is to work out where you are in relation to that goal. Sometimes referred to as the 'current reality', this is conceived with reference to the mission/vision. From this the gap between the current state and the desired state can be worked out, and subsequently used as a tool for setting interim goals. One way of investigating the current reality is to use a SWOT analysis (see Chapter 9, p. 237).

Setting goals and objectives (planning)

The next stage in the strategic planning process is to look at the vision you have defined for the organization, and work to decide what concrete goals and objectives you have that, when taken together, will enable you to reach that vision. If the vision is the destination, and the current reality is the start point, then the interim goals are in some sense landmarks which help define the route you will take to get from A to B.

Having determined your organization's vision and mission and looked at where you currently stand in relation to that end point, the next step is to look at what goals and objectives you can set in order to get closer to attaining the vision. These objectives are much more concrete and are clear, achievable targets that can in themselves be broken down into steps and which can be assigned to specific people within the institution.

Objectives should have the following elements:
- when the objective will be accomplished
- who will be responsible for ensuring it is successfully completed
- where it will happen (if applicable)
- the scope of the work (how much and how many)
- what will be achieved.

Objective-setting is covered in greater detail in Chapter 10, p. 258.

Determining strategy

Once the goals and objectives have been established, the next step is to work out how they will be achieved. This is the strategy you will use.

First, translate your objectives into specific tasks. Tasks are:
- identifiable steps that can be sequenced on a timeline or calendar and assigned to particular people
- all the activities which must be carried out to accomplish the objective.

Then make a plan to complete them. Who will do what and by when? Which tasks need to be done before which other tasks? Can some tasks run concurrently?

Monitoring and evaluation

Finally it is necessary to determine how you will keep track of the plan, and how you will monitor and evaluate the success of your strategy. How will you check on progress? What indicators will you use? What steps will you take if one of your tasks runs longer than expected? What if the objectives or even the vision change at some point? There are many questions which you have to consider when thinking about how you will keep an eye on how your strategic plan is coming together in an operational sense.

For a more in-depth model of the planning process, see Chapter 10.

THE LEARNING ORGANIZATION

To wrap up this chapter, we come to the idea of the 'learning organization'.

The idea of the learning organization is concept mostly associated with the work of Peter Senge and outlined in his book *The Fifth Discipline*. He defined learning organizations as being '. . . organizations where people continually expand their capacity to create the results they truly desire, where new and expansive patterns of thinking are nurtured, where collective aspiration is set free, and where people are continually learning to see the whole together.' (Senge, 1990, p. 3)

In short, a learning organization is one which is flexible and dynamic and collectively learns from its actions. Just as individuals learn through a continuing cycle of action and reflection, so too, do organizations. Creating the conditions for this constant organizational action/reflection can lead to a more dynamic, creative, and ultimately successful organization.

Aspects of the learning organization

Senge outlines five 'disciplines' which, taken together, can help create the conditions for a learning 'organization' to thrive. Briefly, these disciplines may be outlined as:

Personal mastery

This is the idea that if organizations are to learn, then the individuals who make up the organization must also be constantly learning and developing their own personal goals. Crucially, this is a process not an end point, since learning itself is always a process.

Shared vision

If there is genuine vision (not lip-service to something imposed upon people) that the members of an organization collectively understand and 'own', people excel and continue to learn – not because they have to, but because they want to. As Senge puts it:

> The practice of shared vision involves the skills of unearthing shared 'pictures of the future' that foster genuine commitment and enrolment rather than compliance. In mastering this discipline, leaders learn the counter-productiveness of trying to dictate a vision, no matter how heartfelt. (Senge, 1990, p. 9)

Team learning

Broadly speaking, this involves dialogue and thinking together. When people are acting/reflecting together, the learning that can come out of this process can transcend anything that can be learned/gained by individuals. The process of brainstorming is often reported as achieving greater progress than individual thought, as thoughts expressed can spark off ideas in others.

Mental models

Our 'mental models' are the ways we think about the world. These are often assumptions which are so deeply ingrained in our consciousness that we are not aware of them. A good analogy is with cultural awareness: our perceptions of how the world is are shaped by our culture, and only when we experience another culture which sees the world slightly differently do we recognize this model of thinking for what it is. The key to this discipline then is to unearth those mental models, to reflect upon ourselves and our own thought processes. By working with others we can help expose the way we think and the processes we are using, and in so doing we can perhaps choose another mental model.

Systems thinking

This fifth discipline in many ways underpins all the others and is the cornerstone to Senge's work. On a very basic level it is understanding the fact that things work as complex systems, rather than as simple linear cause and effect chains. In so doing, systems thinking tends to a longer-term understanding of processes and of what would constitute effective action. It does not produce quick-fix solutions to individual problems, which ultimately can lead to long-term costs.

REFLECTION

Consider the disciplines above with reference to your own LTO.
- How can these concepts be brought to bear in an LTO?
- What concrete steps could you take in your institution to make it more of a learning organization?
- Have you ever worked for an LTO that is further along this road than others? In what ways?

Applying the idea of the learning organization to an LTO

There are six basic tenets of Senge's work that can be acted upon and used as tangible and concrete steps towards a learning organization. They could be characterized as follows:
- Shared vision
- Communication and feedback
- Transparency and participatory decision-making
- Team building
- Reflection
- Professional development.

The first of these, the idea of shared vision, has been described on p. 43. Some ideas for implementing the essence of the others follow.

Communication and feedback

Communication, both formal and informal, needs to be endemic and multi-directional at all levels of the organization. If there is a culture of communication in the organization, people will discuss their ideas with each other, think aloud about ideas, question decisions, explain and outline future steps. In this way, team learning can take place as well as giving people the space in which to challenge and deepen their mental models. Communication of this multi-directional type is upwards from teachers and admin staff to management, downward from management to staff (see p. 46), and sideways between teachers of different areas and between teachers and administrative staff.

A sense of openness to other ideas and each other's skills and knowledge is a vital step towards helping an organization learn and, therefore, work. A number of schools exist which have managed to encourage and facilitate conversation between teachers of

Case study: IBEU – a learning LTO?

IBEU (Instituto Brasil Estados Unidos) was founded in Rio de Janeiro in 1937 and over the years grew to embrace eleven branches all over the city, employing over 180 teachers, and serving, at its peak, an annual student body of over 15,000.

Its structure was characterized by an extremely centralized, very rigid hierarchy, with a high degree of formalization. Despite that, however, relationships were very important, and having strong links to the right people was a way of getting ahead. Through the lens of Handy's model it would be seen as a combination of a role and power culture.

Successful for many years in an uncrowded marketplace, it became clear in the late 1990s that the organization was unable to respond well to the fact that many new schools had moved into the Brazilian (and specifically Rio de Janeiro) market. Either the systems that had served it well for many years would need to be revamped or the organization, already suffering a drop off in student numbers, would continue to lose market share and possibly be forced to close branches.

A major change project was embarked upon, involving an internationally recognized in-service training course (the SIT TESOL Certificate) for all 180 teachers; the International Diploma in Language Teaching Management (IDLTM) for all eleven branch managers and the heads of the teacher training department; a new student assessment scheme; and a new professional development/performance management system.

This radical and visionary change not only re-invigorated the teaching and learning process at IBEU, but also created the conditions, through shared experience and language, for greatly increased internal communication and dialogue, an increased commitment to the organization, and a feeling of 'belonging'. Through the process, the staff as a whole devised a new vision statement, in addition to the creation of a new organizational mission statement which was proposed by one of the branch managers as part of her course work on the IDLTM and approved by the board.

For such a large and well-established (or entrenched) organization the changes were nothing short of revolutionary; IBEU is very much a human resource-oriented organization now, and one which is centred and focused on student learning. The changes have not only been felt on an organizational level but in the marketing sphere too. Obviously such a major change was not without its difficulties, nor without resistance from within, but in general the organization was revitalized (both in terms of staff energy, and in terms of market presence) by the changes.

different subject areas, who then went on to discover many interesting insights into the others' training and philosophy of teaching and were able to develop themselves by so doing. Likewise, opening channels of communication between academic and administrative sides of an LTO can have many unforeseen benefits as both groups have a different insight into the motivations of the students and other clients. A discussion of ways to improve communication, specifically feedback, can be found in Chapter 3, p. 65.

Transparency and participatory decision-making

Transparency is closely related to communication. Staff need to know why things are happening. This can be at the level of being informed as to why a particular class is in a particular room or can be at the level of what the strategic plans are for the LTO. If staff are left in the dark on any question which matters to them, they will probably assume the worst, or at least feel cut off from the workings of the organization as a whole. Of course, not everyone is interested in every last decision that is taken, and likewise there may be financial information that necessarily must remain confidential, but in general, transparent and open decisions are decisions which are more easily accepted. Likewise, as much as possible and as much as is practicable, decisions are best taken collectively. Full staff participation in decision making is highly recommended (even if the director has to make the final decision, or at least be the one who has to take responsibility for that decision), particularly for decisions of an important nature, such as strategic planning, coursebook selection, curriculum design, marketing campaigns, etc. Obviously if all decisions were devolved to all-staff meetings, very little would actually get done, and people would quickly tire of constantly having to make decisions, but it is the manager's role to make sure that relevant stakeholders in any decision are consulted and have some input in the decision-making process. Crucially, it is important to get staff buy-in to decisions. See the case study on p. 250, for an example of an innovation which involved relevant stakeholders.

Team building

Cross departmental teams increase communication. They can create a natural environment where dialogue can occur with a common goal in mind. As such they are an excellent way of creating space for team learning. An excellent way of building cross-departmental teams is through work on projects. Briefly, a project is often structured towards the production of some kind of tangible product, such as a new curriculum, a set of teaching materials in some area, or a new look for the school cafeteria. For a more in-depth look at projects and how they can increase team building, see Chapter 10.

Usually a project involves forming a team of people, making a plan of action, and then carrying out that plan while constantly monitoring and evaluating progress. In short, it is a fairly similar process to management writ large. By creating teams to work on projects, not only are links built between departments and members of staff, but more broadly, dialogue is enhanced, helping team learning and further enabling people to question their mental models.

Reflection

As educators we are familiar with the idea that reflection is an important part of the learning process. Allowing time and space for that reflection is an important part of the teaching and learning cycle. Yet, in our work as managers we often forget the importance of giving ourselves time to reflect, being constantly concerned with fighting fires or responding to crises. The 'experiential learning cycle' (Figure 2.6) illustrates how we can build this into our work routine (Kolb, 1984; Smith, 2001).

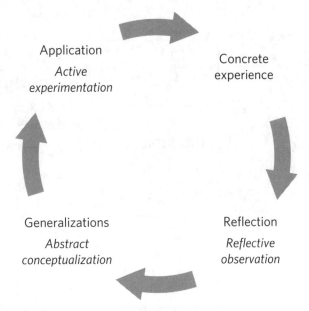

FIGURE 2.6: *Experiential learning cycle* (after Kolb, 1984)

Sydänmaanlakka (2002, p. 51) proposes a model of 'learning by doing' for organizations in order to embed the experiential learning cycle in the activities of the organization. See Figure 2.7 on p. 48.

Compare this model with Mullins' 'Five essential stages of management control' (Chapter 1, Figure 1.2, p. 11). Once again we begin with planning, leading into action, and subsequent reflection and correction. However, in this model, the organization itself is front and centre (as opposed to Mullins' model where the manager acts on the organization;) here, the organization, the teams and individuals act upon the organizational systems. Individuals (the central cycle) reflect upon and learn from their actions (gaining personal mastery). Likewise, teams within the organization are expected to reflect upon their work and their actions, and learn from that, transferring those 'learnings' into the wider organization (team learning, mental models). The organization as a whole translates these learnings into revised systems (systems thinking).

> **REFLECTION**
>
> How could this model apply to your LTO? Think of the activities that individuals and teams are engaged in and discuss what space and time could be given for the effective reflection upon and learning from the outcomes of those activities.

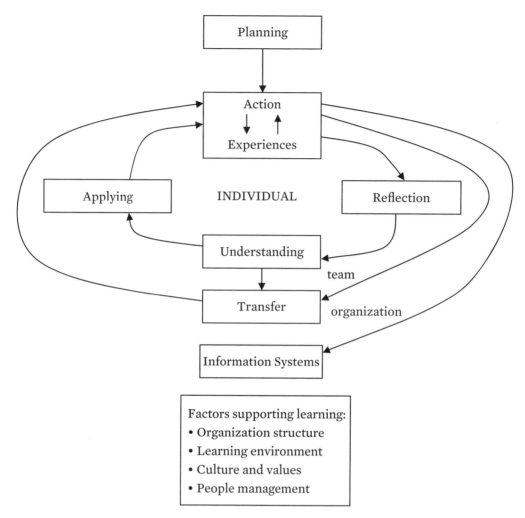

FIGURE 2.7: *Basic model of learning by doing* (Sydänmaanlakka, 2002, p. 51)

In support of the model above, we can incorporate Argyris & Schön's (1978, 1996) work on 'single-loop' and 'double-loop' learning. Broadly speaking this is another way to look at Senge's 'mental models' and 'systems thinking' ideas. Argyris & Schön posit that learning involves the detection and correction of error. Single-loop learning is finding another solution to the problem that has arisen, using the same parameters. Double-loop learning, on the other hand, is questioning the parameters themselves, and seeing if they can be changed, as exemplified in the punctuated equilibrium model of change discussed in Chapter 9 (p. 239).

Professional development
Encouraging staff to constantly develop their own professional goals and to enhance their skills and competencies as well as providing access to learning and development

opportunities is a very valuable way of increasing levels of personal mastery. This aspect will be looked at in more depth in Chapter 3.

CONCLUSION

The study of organizational behaviour can be an extremely interesting and informative undertaking. LTOs by their nature are somewhat different from many other organizations, but they have enough in common to benefit from many of the lessons of standard organizational behaviour theory, while also generating their own theories and set of problems and issues to be dealt with.

LTOs have a variety of historical contexts, from state institutions built as pre-fabricated structures and filled with staff who are treated as parts of an often dysfunctional machine, to small, organically formed LTOs built around an individual's drive and vision (and often starting out in that individual's home); from aggressive for-profit organizations which exist to make money, to not-for-profit or NGO foundation schools which exist to serve the community. Some are highly democratic organizations involving a great deal of discussion and collaboration, while others are highly centralized organizations in which a single individual makes all the decisions. Yet, all have some things in common. Typically LTOs have an academic side and an administrative side which may or may not communicate successfully with each other. Schools are mostly staffed by people who value the role of learning, and who are often motivated by the desire to positively impact society. This influences the organizational culture as well as the possibilities of moving towards a learning organization. All exist to serve their clients: students, parents, businesses.

By carrying out regular organizational analyses and rethinking or looking at the organization in different ways, managers can not only come closer to a better understanding of what they do and how things work, but can also make changes that will promote the successful functioning of schools, which in turn will improve the work lives of employees and better serve students.

TASK

The International Centre is a well-established language school in a large Eastern European capital city. It was set up in the early 1990s, and has grown steadily ever since, and it now, in a much more crowded market than the one in which it was born, has a reputation as one of the best-quality and most trusted schools in the city. While it was a small organization initially, the growing need for English and the good reputation of the school have meant that it has grown considerably and now employs 30 teachers and about half that number of administrative staff.

Its founding director was a fairly traditional educator and patrician boss. When he created the school, he made it clear what everyone's roles and responsibilities were, and formalized these roles in writing. Successive directors have either felt too in thrall to the founder, or have not wanted to disturb the status quo, and have therefore not seen fit to alter this formalized structure.

However, because of the school's growth over the years, positions and functions have been added to the departments which were not present at the outset. These positions tend to have much less written formalization and the members of staff occupying those positions have much more freedom to act as they see fit. There is one academic director in charge of all the teachers, while the current director herself is in charge of all fifteen administrative staff. The administrative staff nearly all have very strictly defined positions and rarely stray from their rigid job descriptions. There is almost no communication between admin staff and teaching staff. One exception is the IT 'department' (consisting of one person), which, since it is relatively new, does not yet have a clearly formalized role and is just broadly in charge of upkeep and purchasing of IT. This means that the IT specialist comes into contact with everyone (dealing with their IT problems) and is not specifically in the administrative half of the organization.

Recently an office manager was hired to deal with many of the administrative issues, since the director was finding that the task of dealing with the whole school along with direct micromanagement of all the administrative staff was too much. However it is not really clear what the office manager's responsibilities are and many of the longer standing admin staff still tend to come to the director with their problems and questions.

- Draw up a rough organigram for The International Centre based on the information above.
- Using the six categories as defined by Robbins, briefly carry out an organizational analysis of the school. What problems do you see in the way it is set up? What are the benefits and limitations of the current structure?
- Based on your organizational analysis, and putting yourself in the shoes of the director, what action would you take to improve the school's structure?

See Appendix, p. 271, for a suggested response to this Task.

3 Human resource management

- STAFFING
- MOTIVATION
- PERFORMANCE MANAGEMENT
- DELEGATING
- CONFLICT MANAGEMENT AND NEGOTIATION
- LEGISLATION

INTRODUCTION

An LTO in Saudi Arabia is experiencing problems with expatriate native-speaker teaching staff, who, unable to cope with both the wider national culture and the organizational culture, often leave a few months into their two-year contracts.

The academic director of an Intensive English Program based at a US university is having trouble keeping staff motivated as they feel marginalized and treated as 'second class citizens' within the academic culture of the university.

The recently appointed director of studies of an LTO in Spain is involved in a conflict with a teacher who has worked at the LTO for many years and who feels aggrieved at being passed over for promotion into the DOS position.

These situations all illustrate human resource management (HRM) issues. The subject of HRM includes discussion of what motivates your staff, how you can evaluate their performance, how your staff can develop themselves, and how to get the best out of your staff, as well as more detailed questions such as how to hire (and fire) staff, and dealing with local labour laws regarding staffing.

On a simple level, it has been said that what we call human resource management (or managing people) boils down to answering three fundamental questions:

1 Why do people work for you?
2 Why do people apply for jobs with you?
3 Why do people leave?

In this chapter we will look at all these questions, with the exception of specific details on local labour law, which is not within the scope of this book.

STAFFING

Organizational 'fit'

In Chapter 2 we saw how an organization can be seen more holistically than as merely a collection of roles, and that we should take into account the people who perform those functions, specifically their needs, values, talents, and personalities. It follows that when selecting staff for a new job, one of the most important questions to ask is whether the candidate will 'fit' the culture of the organization, and, conversely, how well the organization will fit that candidate. An LTO priding itself on the quality of its classes and its general levels of professionalism, for example, is unlikely to be a good mutual fit with an inexperienced teacher at the beginning of his/her career who regards teaching as an opportunity to travel. Other possible misalignments might include:

- an LTO of an organic 'family' type in which everybody is prepared to go beyond their job descriptions to help out the LTO, with a candidate who is not prepared to be flexible
- an LTO of a size that does not offer any advancement opportunities, with a candidate who is an ambitious career-focused teacher
- an LTO with a strongly hierarchical organizational culture which necessitates deference to authority, with a candidate who believes in the value of a collegiate culture.

Another question to consider is finding the right balance between hourly-paid teaching staff and those on a fixed contract to provide the organization with the flexibility to respond well to changes in demand, while still having organizational strength.

REFLECTION

What indicators would you look for as regards organizational fit in your LTO?

The recruitment process

The recruitment process runs from the identification of the need for a new hire all the way through to orientating the person recruited to their new job.

Figure 3.1 opposite illustrates the stages of the recruitment process.

Reference to vision and mission

In Chapter 2, we saw how an organizational mission and vision can be used as a basis for strategic planning. Staffing is another area where these two fundamentals of organizational planning can be used as a way of defining what the organization's needs actually are. If a teacher retires or moves on, the obvious step is to advertise for a new teacher. But before doing so, it is worth deciding whether this is what the organization actually needs. Would the LTO be better served by hiring a new teacher to replace the one who is retiring, or would the vision be better realized by restructuring departments, creating a teacher/administrator position, or some other organizational change?

In fact, if a teacher leaves, it is very rare that the obvious solution – that of replacing the teacher with another teacher – is not the best one. If the number of classes and students is the same, then clearly a new teacher is needed to fill the void left by the departing teacher.

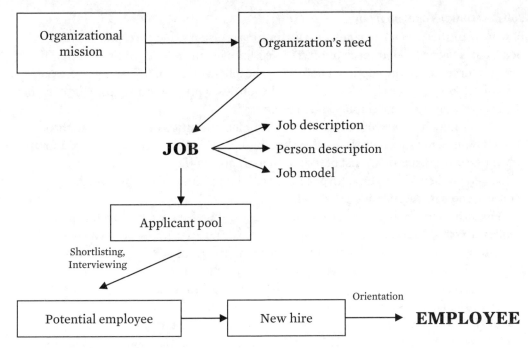

FIGURE 3.1: *The recruitment process*

In fact, staffing in such a cyclical business as that of the typical LTO is something that is looked at on an annual basis and organized from a point some time before the beginning of the academic year, although the exact number of teachers needed may be less easy to predict. Obviously, there will still be occasions when staff will need to be hired with slightly shorter notice: somebody leaves unexpectedly, a new group of students is formed, the LTO gets a new corporate client (since business contracts often do not follow the standard academic year/term/semester structure). But, in general, approximate staffing needs will often be known well in advance and can be addressed with foresight. Staffing in general is part of the strategic planning process, and should be treated as such.

The hiring committee

If the need for a new recruit has been identified, the process by which that post will be filled needs to be made clear. Many larger LTOs will have policies and procedures covering the recruiting process, and many of these are outlined below. One aspect that the LTO must consider is who will do the recruiting. In smaller LTOs it is common that one person is charged with defining the position, advertising the post, shortlisting, interviewing and hiring, whereas in larger organizations this is a task that is often carried out by a committee. The insights and differences that the hiring committee can give rise to are often invaluable and can help us overcome the constraints of our existing mental models (see Chapter 2, p. 43). If a committee is to be formed, it is worth doing so at this early stage in recruitment to ensure involving the committee members at all stages of the process.

Job descriptions and job models

Having identified a need for a new recruit, or for a redistribution of responsibilities, the next step is to create a job description. This is a list of all the responsibilities in a particular job, and serves to tell the applicant pool what the job involves, and the employer what kind of person might be right for the post. The job description will also form the basis for the contract that the new employee will be offered.

Increasingly, however, organizations are supplementing job descriptions with 'person descriptions' which are more helpful to the employer in determining who is right for the job. A person description is a list of requirements and qualifications, which gives a picture of the person they wish to hire. An example of a job description and a person description can be found in the Appendix, pp. 273–4.

A more in-depth approach is to use a job model; this is of great value to the potential employee as it includes real information that he or she needs to know as to what is expected in the position, as well as some contextual information regarding the kind of environment and situation in which he or she will be working. A job model has five categories:
- Results achievable (what the person will be expected to achieve)
- Priorities (what aspects of the job description are the priorities)
- Obstacles (what might make the achievement of the results difficult)
- Environment (what kind of situation the person will find themselves working in: colleagues, workspace, etc.)
- Management style (what kind of manager they will be working under).

Armed with this kind of information, the potential applicant will have a clearer idea as to whether they will fit into the organization successfully and find it a conducive place to work. Not inconsequentially, it also gives the employer and the LTO another opportunity to step back and take a look at themselves from an outside perspective, and ask themselves the question 'What is it like to work here?'

TASK

With reference to your organizational vision and mission, decide on a new position (this could be an amalgamation of old positions if necessary) that would help you to realize your vision. This job position will be worked on as you progress through the next few steps of the chapter. Alternatively, pick a position that already exists which you know you will soon have to refill.
- Create a job description.
- Create a person description for the job.
- Write a job model for the position you have identified.

Identifying and shortlisting applicants

Having concluded that there is a position in your organization, and decided what exactly that position will be, it is time to find someone to fill it. Obviously there are many ways of locating potential employees, from recruiting internally to putting an advertisement in a newspaper.

TASK

List as many ways as you can for finding the right person for your job. Which do you think would be the best source of potential applicants? Think about the advantages and disadvantages of the different places to publicize the job.

Some questions you might ask yourself as you decide where and how to advertise include:
- How many applicants do we want to get? (Advertising on popular ESL/EFL websites, where interested people can respond online, and have the opportunity to respond to large numbers of advertisements, is liable to glean large numbers of replies; advertising in the local paper is liable to glean far fewer.)
- What quality of applicants do we want? (An ADOS level position, for example, may suggest a certain recruitment strategy, which would not be appropriate for a less responsible position.)
- Do I want to recruit locally or from much further afield? (Urgent recruitment needs may suggest recruiting locally, which in turn will suggest a different place to advertise the job.)
- How do we ensure that we come across in the advertisement as a highly professional organization? (A job advertisement in the right place serves not only to attract candidates for the post, but can also raise the profile of the school in general.)

There are many legal requirements related to recruitment. There are laws regarding discrimination in most countries, and in many there are laws regarding whether or not new posts must be advertised publicly or whether they can be filled internally. It is your responsibility as a manager to ensure that your recruitment process is handled in a legal and ethical way.

Depending on a number of factors (e.g. where you advertise, what the current economic situation is in your region, the attractiveness of the job, number of potentially qualified people looking for work) you will hope to receive a rich selection of applicants from whom to choose. It should be noted, too, that you may receive unsolicited CVs and résumés throughout the year, even when you are not looking to recruit anyone. These, too, can be included in the applicant pool. The ideal situation is that you receive applications from a good number of suitable people from whom to choose, but not so many that you have to take up valuable time sifting through them all.

One of the advantages of the person description is that it allows you to sort through applications easily, eliminating the people who clearly do not match your needs. You have, in effect, already created a set of criteria by which to judge people's suitability for the job and their fit for the organization.

Some thought needs to be put into the question of responding to those applicants whom you will not be hiring. Will you respond to everyone who contacts you? A personal response to each application is unlikely to be practical, particularly in cases where a vacancy attracts hundreds of applications, but it is worth considering whether you wish to send a standard rejection letter to applicants whom you decide not to shortlist.

Having reduced the applications to those which fulfil your basic requirements, the next step is to come up with a shortlist of candidates who are well suited to the post. One way to accomplish this is to assign points to relevant areas of qualifications, experience, or background. Thus, for example, you may decide that for a teaching position in your LTO, 5+ years of relevant teaching experience would be worth 10 points on your scale and a DELTA or MA in TESOL would be worth 15 points. Or you might decide that for an offshore LTO teaching position, previous offshore experience would be worth some points on your ranking scale. Other factors such as experience with multilingual classes, Business English and Young Learners courses could also be considered, depending on your context.

> ### REFLECTION
> What factors do you look for when hiring a new teacher? What ranking points could you give each of them to weight them to your own satisfaction? Go back to the job you created earlier in this chapter and decide on what ranking system you would apply to it.

Once you (either alone or as a committee) have come up with these rankings, each candidate is scored according to the scale and those with the highest number are considered for interview. Once the scale is decided, the task of scoring the candidates is relatively simple, and indeed, if the LTO is large enough to permit it, is a task which could be carried out by an administrative person (in organizations which have an HR department, this is typically one of the functions of that department, such that the applicants only reach the recruitment committee once they have been shortlisted).

What this approach does remove is the element of intuition; occasionally reading a particularly well-written cover letter may give a sense that a person could be an excellent choice for the post, even though they may score slightly lower on the ranking system. Whether the removal of this intuitive element is a positive or a negative thing is the subject of much debate. It would be foolish, however, to imagine that there is no element of intuition in the hiring process. Indeed, the ranking system above might shift the intuitive element from the shortlisting process to the interview. If the recruitment committee or individual wishes to retain something of this intuitive element prior to the interview it is worth considering the option of sorting the applications into three piles:
- those which through the ranking system are clearly on the shortlist
- those which do not quite make the shortlist through the scoring system, but which the committee/individual responsible for hiring might want to skim-read just to see if there are any that stand out
- those which are definitely to be rejected.

Interviewing

By this stage in the process you have identified perhaps 6–10 people who may be right for the job, and it is now time to interview, to try to make sure you get the right person. It should, however, be noted that interviewing is notoriously unreliable – those who interview poorly, for example, are not necessarily going to be poor employees.

There are three questions you need answers to, both in shortlisting and in interviewing, but during interviewing it is essential you keep them very much in mind. They are:

1 Can they do the job? (capabilities)
2 Will they do the job? (motivation)
3 How well will they fit into the organization?

There are three main types of interview questions:
- those which ask about candidates' past experiences ('Tell us about your experience of teaching young learners in Turkey.')
- those which ask candidates to put themselves in a hypothetical situation ('What would you do if a student in a business class stopped attending the course?')
- those which test candidates' ability to solve a real problem but one not necessarily related to the job itself (for example, a logic puzzle to solve or some form of lateral thinking problem).

The last of these, the 'case interview' question, is often the most revealing and helpful in overcoming the unreliability of interviewing mentioned previously. Such questions can also be of value if they are presented as a task that all the candidates gathered together can be asked to solve as a group; the interviewers then have the chance to watch how people interact with each other, and what the various candidates would bring to the staffroom as a team member.

References and qualifications checking

References are of questionable value; candidates are only likely to supply references from those people who will give a glowing review. In addition, there is a sizeable (financial and time) cost in taking up references. Increasingly, therefore, references are used by employers as the final step in the recruitment process as a check to ensure that there are no obvious reasons why they should not employ that person, having already made the decision that they almost certainly will. In the UK, it is also now mandated by law that organizations do a criminal record check on any new recruit, which serves a similar purpose while also reducing the risk of employing someone who could be a threat to the well-being of students.

It is also important to do some kind of qualifications check on a new recruit. If they have been recruited locally, it is a simple matter to check their certificates, while those at a distance can be asked to fax a copy of their certificates, and bring along the originals when they take up the post.

Offering the job

Having chosen your ideal candidate, and checked their credentials to your satisfaction, you can go ahead and offer him/her the position. At this stage, in some countries and in some positions, this is the signal for negotiations to begin over salary and benefits. In most LTOs, though, this is unusual, and these items are fixed, or at least confined to limited bands (see *Compensation systems*, p. 63).

It is also quite possible that your preferred candidate will turn the position down for a different offer elsewhere. It is always worth, at the end of the shortlist/interview stage, having a backup choice or two for just this eventuality.

This highlights the time-sensitive nature of the recruitment process in many LTOs. If you start the process for the new academic year too soon, you run the risk that potential candidates have not yet decided on whether to move on from their current position. If you start too late, you run the risk that good teachers have already been snapped up and committed themselves to other offers. The danger is, of course, that if you do not get your top choice(s) of candidates the first time round, by the time the process has been repeated, you may be forced to select someone who you do not believe is the right fit for your LTO, just because you need someone qualified who is willing to accept the post.

Contracts

Once a candidate has been offered the job, and has accepted it, you will need to issue a contract. Much of what is included in this document will be mandated by local labour laws. Position-specific details like responsibilities can be drawn directly from the job description you drew up in the recruitment process. Some LTOs have two documents: the contract between the LTO and the individual, and a much weightier document known as the 'Terms and Conditions of Service' (sometimes shortened to TACOS) which sets out the legal details of the contract which applies to every member of staff. It is this longer document that comes up for renegotiation between management and staff representatives or unions on a regular basis. All that needs to be redrafted with a new hire, then, is the contract document itself.

Signing the contract signifies the agreement of both parties to the terms contained therein, and it is preferable from the point of view of both the LTO and the new hire that the contract is issued and signed as soon as possible after the candidate has accepted the post.

Orientation of new staff

Having made your new hire, the new person needs to be orientated to the workplace. There are two aspects to this, referred to as 'information' and 'socialization'.

Informational orientation involves giving your new employee all the information he or she needs to be able to do the job and successfully negotiate the first few weeks while they become accustomed to the work. This might involve forms to be filled in, information about payment, such as how and where salary will be paid, which office to go to in order to deal with which issue, email accounts, who to see for what, timetables, class information, etc. Clearly this is very important and it needs to be presented in such a way that it is memorable, but also easy to check (nobody can remember everything they learn in the first day on the job).

Socialization involves what we might call 'cultural' orientation (to the organization): helping the new employee deal with and understand the culture of the organization, how things work, who is who, etc. Some LTOs like to provide new teachers with mentors or 'buddies' (someone in the same position but who has been at the LTO for a while) who help guide the newcomer through the organization and what they need to know, and who can also help with acculturation to the national culture if necessary.

In the work of an offshore LTO, there is a third aspect that needs to be covered for the new foreign teacher, that of support, help and acculturation to the country and city in which they find themselves (which of course may also involve cultural pointers they will need to know in the classroom: subjects to be avoided, gestures open to misinterpretation, etc.).

Orientation occurs in three distinct phases:

- pre-arrival: the new hire, between signing a contract and actually starting work, begins the orientation process
- on arrival: this usually involves a specific programme taking place over the first few days of the contract (LTOs often have an intake of staff all at the same time, so this frequently happens as a group-based activity)
- ongoing: after the first week, when a great deal of information will have been taken in, and a great deal will have been forgotten, it is important to remember that new hires need ongoing support and will still have questions that need answering.

Case study: Staff orientation

Vicky, noticing the poor feedback on the orientation at the LTO in which she was a director of studies, decided to revisit the way new teachers were orientated. She worked in consultation with the staff who had recently been through the process and others at the LTO. One complaint from the teachers, for example, had been that finding somewhere to live was so stressful that they felt unable to take in much else until that basic need had been taken care of.

In response she devised an entirely new orientation procedure which included:
- signing all new teachers up to an online discussion board on which they could interact with each other, with current staff, and with the administration of the organization; this allowed them to meet some of their new colleagues virtually, ask important administrative questions that had not been clear from the documentation sent to them, and in some cases actually organize accommodation in advance
- dedicating an entire day early in the orientation week to finding accommodation (supported by local staff)
- instigating a mentoring system so that new teachers were paired with volunteers who had been at the school longer and who were on hand to help out and answer questions
- making sure that feedback on the orientation system was requested and acted upon.

Contracts

Depending on local labour laws, the employment market and other local factors, LTOs tend to have a mix of teaching staff contract types. Many teachers are likely to be contracted to a full-time teaching load (usually around 25 contact hours a week), others may be contracted on a part-time but fixed teaching load, while others may be working on a freelance or hourly-paid basis. This last group may also be working to a contract, but one which specifies they are only paid for the hours which they teach. Teachers on a temporary contract, for example to cover a particular course, are sometimes referred to as 'adjunct'.

Finding the right balance between hourly-paid teaching staff and those on a fixed contract to provide the organization with the flexibility to respond well to changes in demand, and to also have organizational strength, is a challenge for the LTO manager. The decision to hire mostly on fixed contracts, or to have a greater number of hourly-paid staff, is partly driven by law and by agreements between the LTO and unions, and partly by decisions that the management of the LTO takes based on a number of factors listed in Figure 3.2 below.

	Advantages	Disadvantages
Fixed contract	**More loyalty**: staff on fixed contracts will feel a greater degree of loyalty to the organization and will not be so easily enticed away by a competitor.	**Less flexible**: if there is a downturn in student numbers, teachers may not have a full timetable.
	More organizational involvement: staff who feel part of the team are more likely to get involved with other tasks when needs arise. Their contracts can also have written into them project work or other forms of cross-departmental interaction.	**More expensive**: health insurance, tax, cost of flights etc. (for offshore LTOs).
	Increased staff job security	
	Increased motivation: as staff who feel well treated by their organization, contracted staff are more likely to be motivated to do good work.	
Hourly-paid	**More flexible**: if there is demand for a new class, an hourly-paid teacher will usually be willing to take on that class. Likewise if demand slackens, money is not being spent on keeping an inactive teacher.	Can be **transient**: teachers may only remain with the LTO for a short time, creating a lack of continuity for the staffroom and also for students.
	Cheaper: hourly-paid staff typically are not awarded any benefits, such as health insurance and relocation expenses.	Danger of **less commitment**: if teachers are not on contract, they may not feel part of the team or contribute to the organizational culture.
	Can lead to a more **diverse and varied staffroom**, bringing freshness and new ideas to the classroom.	

FIGURE 3.2: *Contract types*

MOTIVATION

Satisfiers and dissatisfiers

It is a commonly held assumption that money is the prime motivator for most people in their work. This is, questionable, however. In his research on employee motivation, Frederick Herzberg (1987) identified two distinct types of factors governing motivation.

The first type were what he termed 'motivators' or 'satisfiers'. These are features of one's job that actually inspire and encourage. They include such elements as enjoyment of the work itself, responsibility, achievement, recognition, advancement and growth.

The second type he termed 'maintenance factors' or 'dissatisfiers': aspects of the job that in and of themselves do not actually motivate, but the absence of which can be demotivating. These include job security, salary, administration, supervision, interpersonal relationships, working conditions and status. According to Herzberg, then, an employee's salary in itself would not motivate him/her, but the lack of an adequate salary would serve to demotivate.

In further research based on Herzberg's findings, Hockley (2006) surveyed teachers and other staff in a number of LTOs, and concluded that teaching and other staff are motivated by similar factors to employees in other types of organizations, with the addition of a 'service' component: a desire to serve their students. The students themselves are a strong motivator for most people within an educational context.

Job enrichment

With a sense of what motivates our employees, we, as managers, can think about ways in which we can enrich and enhance the work of our teachers. Kohn (1995) proposes a model he refers to as 'job enrichment', with five steps to achieve this:

- Combine tasks, to increase skill variety and task identity.
- Create natural work units, to make work meaningful and provide 'ownership' of tasks.
- Establish client relationships, to increase skill variety and autonomy for employees.
- Expand jobs vertically, to give responsibility and increase employee autonomy.
- Open feedback channels, to improve employee awareness of performance level.

It is clear that teachers and other staff at an LTO are not, on the whole, lacking in client relationships (see Chapter 1, p. 16 on the features of services). Likewise, most teachers tend to have a natural work unit: they plan, design, teach classes, respond to student work, set, and mark tests. One possible way to increase these work units further, and also to combine tasks, is for them to be involved in registration (and re-registration) and placement testing. In many LTOs this is already the case.

This leaves the last two of Kohn's suggestions. In what ways can we expand our employees' jobs vertically, giving them more autonomy and more control? In many ways teachers already have a great deal of control over their jobs; once the classroom door has closed (in most LTOs), what goes on behind it is entirely within the remit of the teacher. But are there other ways? Could staff be given input into the strategic planning process of the organization? Is there a way in which they can be involved in making decisions on

TASK

What motivates you? Complete the survey below for yourself. Do you have similar motivators as the survey respondents? What motivates your staff? If it is possible do this as a group exercise with your colleagues, and see what the results are. Any surprises?

Below is a list of 25 possible motivating factors in the workplace. Please put a *X* or a ✓ next to the six items from the list which you believe are most important in motivating you to do your best work.

1 ☐ Steady employment
2 ☐ Respect for me as a person
3 ☐ Adequate rest periods or coffee breaks
4 ☐ Good pay
5 ☐ Good physical working conditions
6 ☐ Chance to turn out quality work
7 ☐ Getting along well with others on the job
8 ☐ Having a local employee newsletter
9 ☐ Chance for promotion
10 ☐ Opportunity to do interesting work
11 ☐ Pensions and other security benefits
12 ☐ Not having to work too hard
13 ☐ Knowing what is going on in my organization
14 ☐ Feeling my job is important
15 ☐ Having an employee council
16 ☐ Having a written job description
17 ☐ Being told by my boss when I do a good job
18 ☐ Getting a performance rating
19 ☐ Attending staff meetings
20 ☐ Agreement with organization's objectives
21 ☐ Opportunity for self-development and improvement
22 ☐ Fair vacation arrangements
23 ☐ Knowing that I will be disciplined if I do a bad job
24 ☐ Working under close supervision
25 ☐ Large amount of freedom on the job (chance to work not under direct or close supervision)

marketing campaigns? What about budgeting? Not only would many staff enjoy being involved in the planning process, but they might also have a lot to contribute. This also applies in marketing, as those with the closest link to the clients, such as teachers and receptionists, have a lot to offer and in most cases would appreciate being consulted. See the case study on p. 246, for an example of such job enrichment.

Three of the key motivators for LTO teachers and other staff identified by Hockley (2006) were 'Opportunity to do interesting work', 'Opportunity for self-development and improvement', and 'Feeling my job is important', which suggests that expanding jobs vertically would enhance motivation in general.

The budgetary process is also an area in which teachers could be involved, but this is an area which many might find quite intimidating, and they may be less interested in being involved. As with all such initiatives, it is important to offer the opportunity to participate in a consultation process, rather than demand involvement. Chapter 7 offers an introduction to creating and managing budgets.

Opening feedback channels is another important step to consider, particularly in the light of the features of the learning organization mentioned in Chapter 2. In the main, teachers are blessed with a job which by its nature includes regular feedback. They receive, from their students, constant informal feedback on their performance, both in terms of student success with the language being taught, and in terms of physical signs of student interest and involvement, and most will also include regular formal and informal feedback systems into their classes. But how much feedback do they receive from managers? Is it an annual performance evaluation, possibly tied to a lesson observation? How can constant, direct feedback be improved? Improving feedback is an area covered in depth later in this chapter (p. 65).

As managers of educational organizations it is important to be aware of what it is that motivates and demotivates our staff, and to get a sense of what alterations could be made to roles and responsibilities to heighten that motivation and keep staff interested and involved in their work. Although we may assume that teachers are motivated by the work of teaching itself, it is essential that we keep our ears and eyes open and constantly seek feedback from our staff on their work and how it is fulfilling them.

> ### *REFLECTION*
> How can you enrich the jobs of the staff in your LTO? Think of five concrete steps you could take to enrich the working conditions of your colleagues.

Compensation systems

Compensation can involve many elements. Obviously it involves salary, but it can also involve things like health insurance, bonuses, pension plans, and other fringe benefits. Salaries and other compensation can be determined by various methods. In some organizations, compensation is determined entirely on the basis of role, seniority and qualifications/experience, whereas in others it contains an element of performance-related pay. A typical example of the former type of pay scale is one in which there is a pre-determined salary band for teachers, with a fixed lowest and a fixed highest potential salary. Teachers are placed within the range depending on their qualifications and experience. An inexperienced teacher with a CELTA or equivalent might be at the low end of the scale while a teacher with twenty years of relevant experience and an MA might be at the upper end. These scales often operate under a simple points system (e.g. two years' experience = 1 point, DELTA = 1 point, MA = 1 point, up to a maximum of 10 points). These points are then linked to rates of pay.

A performance-related pay system has some advantages, but in the context of the LTO is difficult to implement and maintain. For performance-related pay to be successful, the performance must be objectively measurable, which is rarely the case in teaching. However, there are LTOs in which such a system can be operated as a supplement to the basic compensation system: in the case of an LTO which has a significant number of Business English classes for example, or one in which external project work makes up some of the work, those who write the project proposals and manage the projects can be given a bonus to allow them to benefit financially from their efforts which benefit the LTO as a whole.

Pitfalls that have to be avoided in any performance-related pay system include:
- subjectivity (or the suspicion of subjectivity)
- the creation of internal competition (any system that involves competing for limited bonuses is liable to create many more problems than it solves)
- confusion (it must be a clearly communicated system)
- too much focus on one area (if bonuses are tied to success in winning ESP contracts only, for example, then it is likely that teachers will gravitate towards that area and cease focusing on the regular language classes).

Ultimately, changing the way people are paid and how much they are paid is a move fraught with potential difficulties, and unless there are compelling reasons to do so, it is best avoided. If, however, the reasons are compelling, but internal expertise and experience are limited, drawing on external expertise will help avoid pitfalls.

Prioritization

Prioritization is not an area necessarily linked to motivation, but it can be affected by motivation and in turn have an impact itself. Some employees may choose to focus on the areas that motivate them, and leave the remaining tasks for another time, while others may prefer to prioritize the tasks they do not enjoy, and move on to the more interesting elements of their job later.

TASK

Work with a member of your staff.
- Ask him/her to write down the ten most important tasks in his/her job, and to rank them in order of importance.
- Do the same for that employee from your perspective: what are the most important elements of that person's job as you see it?
- Then sit down together and compare the answers. What has this exercise shown you? How can you use this information?
- Now do the same thing for yourself: have two or three employees list what they think are the most important elements of your job, and compare your responses with theirs.

PERFORMANCE MANAGEMENT

Arguably the question most central to HRM, and indeed management in general, is the one of managing the performance of your employees. How can you manage, monitor and evaluate their performance in a non-intrusive way that does not demotivate?

Feedback

Clear and timely feedback (internal feedback between employee and manager) is hugely important in what is an ongoing dialogue between employee and manager. Feedback:
- helps the receiver to form their self-concept
- reduces uncertainty about whether their behaviour is on track
- serves to signal which organizational goals are most important
- helps employees to master their environment and feel competent.

'Feedback' means both positive and negative feedback. Positive feedback is crucial in motivating staff, and while some managers are reluctant to give positive feedback as if it somehow overindulges the receiver, almost nobody, when asked, responds that they receive too much positive feedback. When praise is due, it should be given sincerely.

Giving negative feedback, on the other hand, can be as challenging as receiving it. If feedback can be delivered in such a way as to limit defensiveness and promote growth, it is useful and can be of great value to both employee and manager. If it is seen as an attack, it will not lead to any changes, and in fact is more likely to lead to a worsened situation.

Giving effective feedback

Feedback may be considered effective when the receiver clearly understands what is being said and does not become defensive. It keeps the channels of communication open and the relationship between the giver and receiver strong (not necessarily without conflict), and ensures that feedback is not avoided in the future.

Porter (1982) identifies thirteen criteria for effective feedback. Effective feedback:
- describes the behaviour that led to the feedback and does not use judgmental sentences, e.g. 'you haven't handed in your marks yet' rather than 'you've forgotten to hand in your marks'.
- comes as soon as possible after the behaviour. Providing immediate feedback gives the employee an opportunity to improve (telling someone six months later that their performance in one particular instance was poor is not helpful to that employee); it ensures that the incident is fresh in the mind of both parties; and, importantly, it keeps the employee–manager channel of communication open.
- is directly addressed from giver to receiver, not through a third party, or by trying to enlist the support of a third party, such as using statements such as 'I think the other teachers would be upset to learn that you haven't handed in your marks, when they have all done theirs.'

- is 'owned' by the giver, i.e. given using 'I' statements, and it is clear that the giver takes responsibility for them (and does not use statements like 'we feel . . .' or 'upper management would like . . .').
- includes the giver's real feelings about the behaviour, refers only to the behaviour, and does not include any speculation about the receiver's motives for the behaviour.
- is checked for clarity to ensure that the receiver has fully understood what has been said.
- asks relevant questions which seek information from the receiver of the feedback, and for which the receiver understands the reasons. This means avoiding questions which are really statements or which are leading questions rather than information-seeking, e.g. 'Were you late for class this morning?' in the knowledge that this was the case.
- specifies consequences of the behaviour either present or future, and does not use vague generalizations or 'should' statements.
- is solicited or somehow desired by the receiver and not imposed upon them.
- refers to behaviours about which the receiver can do something, not things over which he or she has little or no control.
- recognizes that feedback is a process and an interaction. Both giver and receiver have needs that they will strive to meet.
- affirms the receiver's worth, acknowledges their right to have the reactions he or she has to the feedback, and does not discount those feelings.
- acknowledges that it is a process, and if necessary addresses the need to improve that process while it is going on. It should not focus simply on content (the behaviour).

This is a very long list of criteria, but worth incorporating into the feedback process. With practice, many of these elements can easily become second nature.

It may not be possible, given human nature, to have a situation in which everybody is always happy to get feedback on their performance (particularly negative feedback), or indeed is actively seeking it out, but there are ways of making it more likely. One way of working towards this is to instil a culture of feedback. An organization where feedback is the norm and is offered whenever necessary is one in which people are likely to feel more open to feedback in general (see *The learning organization* in Chapter 2, p. 42).

> **TASK**
>
> Choose a situation at your LTO in which you have given poorly received feedback, or avoided giving feedback for fear of causing offence. Work through these thirteen points and work out exactly how you could go about giving that feedback in a helpful and constructive way. What would you say if that same problem arose again?

360° feedback

A 360° feedback system is one in which feedback does not merely go from the top down, as is traditional (i.e. managers give feedback to those beneath them in the hierarchy), but goes in all directions (staff give feedback to their line manager and to their peers and to anyone who reports to them, and likewise receive it from above, below and from peers). This kind of system has a number of advantages (as well as some potential drawbacks), chief of which is that it can really help to form a culture of feedback and take some of the fear out of feedback. If the manager is seen to be genuinely open to feedback, it is more likely to lead to others being similarly open. Other advantages of 360° feedback include:

- employee involvement
- positive reinforcement of the leader (if merited!)
- increased interest in feedback
- improved communication between leaders and others
- steps towards organizational culture change
- additional sources of input into the performance appraisal process (see below).

Some potential drawbacks include:

- retribution (people respond to negative feedback by giving negative feedback in return)
- defensiveness and denial (a potential problem with all feedback, as described opposite)
- conflicting ratings (how to respond if both positive and negative feedback is received from different people regarding the same action)
- lowered self-esteem (if negative feedback is received)
- cost (if the system is formalized, it will be expensive and time-consuming to implement effectively)
- increased expectations coupled with lack of change (if a good feedback system is introduced, and ideas surface as a result, a lack of action towards those ideas can be demotivating).

Another way that the manager can move towards instilling a culture of feedback is to check in with teachers regularly and informally, inquiring how certain classes are going, whether they feel they need anything, what would help them, and generally validating their work and the value you have in them as employees. This approach is sometimes referred to as 'MBWA' – management by walking around.

Performance appraisal

Performance management, including timely feedback and professional development, is an ongoing continuous process. Many organizations also include, as part of this process, something often referred to as a performance appraisal system. This is essentially an annual institutionalized feedback and professional development system. The term 'performance appraisal' is increasingly avoided as it implies some kind of judgement, but in order to distinguish this annual formal event from the wider whole of 'performance management' into which it feeds, for the sake of clarity we will use the term 'performance appraisal system' here to refer to this aspect of performance management. It is important to bear in mind that a 'performance appraisal system' is not a replacement for regular and timely feedback, but rather is a formalized addition to it.

A performance appraisal system typically involves the following steps. Every year, the employee and his/her manager schedule a meeting. Prior to the meeting both participants are required to fill in a form or questionnaire regarding the employee's goals for the previous year, the performance of the employee, and various questions regarding the employee's effectiveness as a worker and colleague. At the meeting the two discuss their responses to the questions and reach agreement on a mutually-worded set of responses to the questionnaire, as well as agreeing upon a new set of employee goals for the upcoming year. This agreed-upon document is signed by both and then placed in the employee's personal file. In addition, this meeting can be used to set professional development targets and to discuss possibilities for the employees' professional development (see p. 70).

In addition, the annual performance appraisal process is a good time to revisit and update the employee's job description; as the LTO changes, so the individual's role within it also changes. A person's job description often bears little resemblance to the job they are actually doing two or three years down the line.

Obviously there are slight variations on the above outline, but usually performance appraisal systems follow these guidelines fairly closely.

REFLECTION

Does your organization have a performance appraisal system? Does it follow the outline above? What differences are there, and why do you think there are differences?

If you do not have an appraisal system, is there a reason for not having one? Do you think it would be worth developing one? Design a performance appraisal system for your organization.

Teacher observations

In most LTOs, and specifically for the teaching staff, there is one addition to the above outline, and that is teacher observation. In many areas of business, managers have a good sense of how staff are performing in the most important areas of their jobs as they see them or interact with them on a daily basis through their work. The same is often not true of teachers, the bulk of whose work takes place behind closed doors and which managers do not experience (save through student feedback) in the same way. Many LTOs choose, therefore, to incorporate regular teacher observation into the performance appraisal cycle.

Teacher observations, while they are often used as part of the performance appraisal system of an LTO, are often fraught with problems. In theory, teacher observations ought, first and foremost, to be developmental. In practice, they are often perceived as being judgmental. When they are part of performance appraisal they are particularly so, since the word 'appraisal' implies judgment and rating. It is also difficult to base the annual feedback for a teacher on, say, one hour of observed teaching out of an annual load of something close to 1,000 hours, particularly when that hour, by its very nature, has a significant difference from all of the others – that of the presence of the observer.

If a culture of transparency and openness and a genuine interest in feedback exist, then this can be overcome, but this is rarely the case. Consequently, there is a good case to be made for removing teacher observations from the performance appraisal system altogether, including them as a clearly developmental tool, and making them part of the professional development side of performance management rather than the performance appraisal system. A comprehensive system of peer observations, whereby each teacher is contractually obliged to observe a number of his/her peers, and to be observed by them following a pre-presented model for offering feedback, is one possible way of dealing with this.

REFLECTION

Consider the role of lesson observations.
- How could you make teacher observations part of the 360° feedback system?
- On what basis should observed lessons be evaluated?
- What about a situation where an LTO manager does not have a teaching background? Should that manager still conduct teacher observations? If not, then how could the lesson observations be replaced with something else?

Discipline

Occasionally, and regrettably, despite excellent feedback and performance management systems, a staff member may need to be disciplined for some infraction. The important thing to remember here is that it must be completely clear why this staff member is being disciplined, and that a clear line of procedure has been followed. It should not be a surprise to the employee being disciplined, and there should be no suspicion of partiality.

It is, therefore, very important to have clear regulations governing what will trigger disciplinary proceedings, what the process is for such proceedings, and what the punishment will be. The manager should never be in a position of wondering whether someone should be disciplined or what action he or she should take.

There are also three important ways in which local context will play a role in the disciplinary process:
- disciplinary guidelines in accordance with local labour laws
- the legislated or negotiated role of unions in the process
- cultural considerations that need to be borne in mind: the role of discipline, the need for face-saving, the relationship between subordinates and managers, etc.

The section on grievances (p. 76) includes for an example format under which disciplinary procedures can be instituted.

Professional development

The topic of professional development (PD) is covered in more detail in Chapter 8. However, PD does fall under the umbrella of HRM, and as such needs to be touched upon here as well.

If we aspire to create a 'learning organization' (see Chapter 2, p. 42), it is clear that creating and offering professional development opportunities for our staff is an integral part of that overall process. One of Senge's five disciplines is personal mastery, which involves individuals in an organization constantly learning and developing their own personal goals. It is clear then that it is very important both for the employees and the organization to take the time to map out the learning and development goals of the individuals that make up the LTO, as much as it is to develop strategic organizational goals.

Sydänmaanlakka (2002) in defining an 'intelligent organization' links the ideas of the learning organization with the need for a well-constructed performance management system, with at its heart an understanding of professional development needs. Referring back to his model of such an organization (Chapter 2, Figure 2.7, p. 48), one can see that the core of the model is individual learning. This individual development is transferred through teamwork into the organization as a whole.

Many organizations these days use the traditional regular performance review process as a forward-looking performance preview. That is to say, the annual interview is used as a way of mapping out the individual's goals for the year ahead, both in professional development and in their relationship with the LTO.

DELEGATING

An effective manager is one who can delegate tasks successfully. We know this intuitively, and yet it often seems to be one of the most difficult elements a manager's job, often to the point where the manager actively avoids delegating and does things personally. Typical reasons that managers might give for this are:

- 'It's easier to do it myself.'
- 'By the time I've explained what I want to be done, I could have done it myself.'
- 'I still have to keep track of what people are doing, and that takes up time too.'
- 'It's not fair to ask my staff to do some of these tasks.'
- 'I can do it better.'

Managers may genuinely feel that they can 'do it better' and this may indeed be true; managers generally become managers by being promoted for performing effectively in their previous role. There are, however, many advantages of delegation. These include higher efficiency, which can be achieved by not carrying out tasks which could easily be performed by someone else (see also Chapter 8, p. 223). Motivation can be increased by giving staff different tasks to perform and entrusting them with responsibility (see p. 61). The skills of your team can be developed by giving them tasks that extend their repertoire. Finally, delegating creates better distribution of work through the group. The next section proposes a structure for effective delegation without losing managerial authority.

Case study: Performance management

A large LTO in Latin America decided to implement a new performance management system for the teachers. The system that was introduced was actually devised by a working group made up of the teachers themselves, elected representatives from each branch of the LTO.

This new system involved all teachers building up a portfolio of their teaching and professional development work, much in the way that students are increasingly being required to self-assess through the use of similar portfolios. Teachers compiled a portfolio of their own choosing to illustrate the work they had done that year: things they had learned, lessons they had taught, materials they had used; whatever summarized and encapsulated their year as they saw it. Keeping a portfolio is an ongoing project rather than something which involves answering some questions once a year (as was the case with the former performance review system), and hence teachers felt that the process was ongoing and based on what they perceived their role and professional achievements to be. In addition, they were encouraged to develop themselves and embrace opportunities for professional growth, as well as identifying areas of their own work which they felt that they would like to improve.

The annual performance management interview became a chance for the teacher to present his or her portfolio to the director of the branch, and to demonstrate what it was that they had been doing over the previous year and what it was they were especially proud of. In turn, the branch directors were given the opportunity to hear stories from the classrooms or from other aspects of their teachers' professional lives that they might not otherwise have heard about. The whole process served to raise teachers' sense of professionalism and professional self-worth, to improve communication between teachers and managers, and to support teachers in their professional development.

Delegating tasks effectively

Firstly, you will need to decide which tasks to delegate. One way to do this is to list all the tasks that you do, and then next to them write K (keep), S (share) or D (delegate), to decide who should take care of these elements of your work (you or someone else).

Once you have decided which tasks you will delegate, you need to decide who you will delegate them to. Think about who among your staff has the relevant skills; who has an interest in the task being delegated; who needs to develop their skills in a particular area; and who has the time to perform the task.

1   Consider the strengths and weaknesses of your staff and distribute tasks that allow them to use their strengths and work on their weaknesses. The easiest way to delegate is to give the majority of work to experienced employees, but it is also important to allow less experienced staff the opportunity to develop.

2   Having selected the person to whom you will delegate, you will need to explain the task and your expectations clearly and thoroughly. Include deadlines, and ensure that the person being given the task is given the appropriate authority to carry it out. Check that the task is understood.

3   Monitor and offer support, but without interfering, and allow the person to whom you have delegated the task to carry it out as they see fit. This may not be the way you would have done it.

4   Finally, seek feedback from the person who you assigned to the task. Keep in mind that ultimately, even though you have delegated the task to someone else, you are still responsible for making sure it is done on time and correctly.

An example of a task which the academic manager of an LTO often carries out is timetabling. It may be that this is quite an onerous and challenging and time-consuming task, particularly in a larger LTO which has many classes, many teachers, all of whom have preferences, and a limited number of classrooms. It could, however, be delegated. If we look at the question 'Who has an interest in this area?', it is unlikely that you will find someone who has listed timetabling as one of their main interests, but the task itself is one which requires a certain degree of logic and problem solving, like a puzzle. There may well be someone on the admin staff who would actually relish such a puzzle.

> **TASK**
>
> Take a task that you perform regularly that you would like to delegate. Draw up a plan to delegate it.
> - Who will you ask to perform the task?
> - How will you explain it?
> - What will you do to get feedback on the process and task from the employee to whom you delegate?

CONFLICT MANAGEMENT AND NEGOTIATION

Conflict happens. Much as we may like to avoid it, there will, from time to time, be conflict in any organization and any group. Indeed there are situations in which conflict can be advantageous (Figure 3.3).

> **REFLECTION**
>
> Think about a (work) conflict which you have been involved in, either as a participant or as a mediator.
> - What was the problem?
> - How did it arise?
> - How did you deal with it?
> - Did you feel it was resolved successfully?

Possible advantages of conflict	Possible disadvantages of conflict
Identification of issues of importance to others	Decreased performance
	Dissatisfaction
Resolution of underlying problems	Aggression
Enhancement of group development	Anxiety
Conflict between groups (inter-group conflict) can increase the internal cohesion of groups (intra-group)	Wasted time
	Wasted energy
	Reduced efficiency
Facilitation of organizational change	
Learning about self and others	
Avoidance of 'groupthink'	

FIGURE 3.3: *Advantages and disadvantages of conflict*

Motivations, needs and conflict styles

People involved in conflicts typically have different motivations, needs and consequent 'conflict management styles'. These styles vary according to their need to preserve relationships and their need to get the task done. Figure 3.4 on p. 74 illustrates this.

While this matrix refers to levels of assertion and co-operation, it is just as easy to think of it as task versus process; someone who is very concerned at getting the task done is likely to be more assertive, whereas someone who is concerned more with preserving relationships, and less with the task itself, is likely to be more co-operative.

There are advantages and disadvantages in every position. If the issue at hand is of very little importance to you, but the relationships are extremely important, then you will find yourself in the 'accommodation' quadrant. Alternatively, if this is an issue that you feel very strongly about, you may find yourself in the 'competition' quadrant. The value of referring to this model is that you can ascertain your own place in the grid and that of the person you are working with.

Compromising is appropriate when:
- goals are important but not worth the effort or potential disruption of more assertive modes
- opponents with equal power are committed to mutually exclusive goals
- it is desirable to achieve temporary settlements to complex issues
- time pressures necessitate expedient solutions
- collaboration or competition is unsuccessful.

An example of this in operation in an LTO might be two teachers who wish to teach the same class but have mutually incompatible timetables.

Competing is appropriate when:
- quick, decisive action is vital (e.g. emergencies)
- unpopular actions on important issues must be implemented (e.g. cost-cutting, implementing unpopular rules, enforcing discipline)

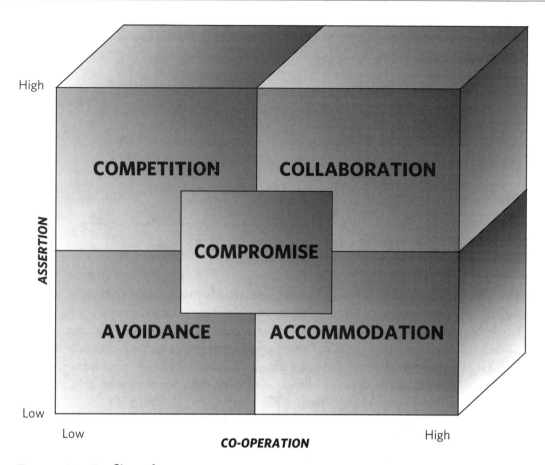

High

ASSERTION

COMPETITION   COLLABORATION

COMPROMISE

AVOIDANCE   ACCOMMODATION

Low

Low   High

CO-OPERATION

FIGURE 3.4: *Conflict styles*

- you know you are right regarding issues vital to the LTO's welfare, and timing is critical
- people will take advantage of non-competitive behaviour.

An example of this might be an LTO which has lost a major client and needs to trim staff and budgets in response.

Collaborating is appropriate when:
- an integrative solution must be found because both sets of concerns are too important to be compromised
- your objective is to learn
- insights from people with different perspectives should be considered jointly
- commitment can be gained by incorporating concerns into a consensus
- it is desirable to work through feelings that have interfered with a relationship.

An example of this might be a situation in which an LTO and one of its corporate clients are in conflict. The LTO needs to take the client's needs and wishes fully into account, while not compromising its principles.

Avoiding is appropriate when:
- an issue is trivial or more important issues are pressing
- you perceive no chance of satisfying your concerns
- potential disruption outweighs the benefits of resolution
- people must cool down to regain perspective
- gathering information supersedes immediate decision-making
- others can resolve the conflict more effectively
- issues seem tangential or symptomatic of other issues.

An example of this might be two teachers who are in conflict at the very end of an academic year, and one of them is finishing his contract and moving on. The disruption caused by dealing with the conflict might best be avoided until the conflict disappears naturally.

Accommodating is appropriate when:
- you find you are wrong
- you wish to allow a better position to be heard
- you wish to learn
- you wish to show your reasonableness
- issues are more important to others than to you
- you wish to satisfy others
- you need to maintain co-operation
- it is desirable to build social credits for later issues
- you are outmatched and losing (minimizes loss)
- it is desirable to allow others to develop by learning from mistakes.

An example of accommodating in an LTO might be when a teacher comes to you and asks if she can reorganize the materials for a certain level. From experience you suspect that this will not make much difference, but you wish to thank the teacher for taking this initiative.

The manager as arbitrator in conflict

As a manager you may well be called upon to arbitrate in a dispute. This dispute may be between two staff members, a teacher and a student, a staff member and a customer, or even, in the worst case scenario, between two factions of staff.

The most important action you can take is to listen to the two sides of the argument and hear them both. A staff member or a customer who feels that you have not listened to their perspective is not going to leave the conflict feeling that it has been resolved to their satisfaction. Indeed their anger or resentment may be transferred to you. In many cases a participant in a conflict who feels that their point of view has been really heard will often feel satisfied with that outcome, even if you do not offer to do what they asked initially.

One technique that is very useful for this approach is known as 'active listening'. This involves a way of responding to someone which (a) ensures that you really hear everything they say; and (b) makes it clear to them that you have, through paraphrasing, clarifying, and repeating back important points.

Beyond active listening, it is clear that as an arbitrator and as a manager you must act fairly and without prejudice. If the conflict is between a staff member with whom you have a good relationship and one with whom you have a poor relationship, the tendency is, of course, to side with one over the other (or, in some cases, to overcompensate and attempt to overcome your natural bias by going in the opposite direction). You must hear both sides of the argument, and then act in the best interests of the LTO. Having done so, you must then communicate clearly why you acted as you did and why you took the decision you did. In short, you need to remove the personal from the conflict, and make the outcome about the organization alone.

The manager as participant

There will, of course, come a time when you will be involved in a conflict not as a mediator, but as a participant. In general, in such situations, it is important to follow the same procedure as outlined above. Make sure you listen and make it clear you have listened. When conveying your feelings about the issue, do so bearing in mind the principles of effective feedback described on pp. 65–66. When trying to resolve the conflict, do so with the best interests of the organization at the forefront.

If the conflict proves to be too intractable for all of the above to work effectively, then it may need to be mediated by an outsider uninvolved in the conflict. This will almost certainly not be another member of staff under you, since to put such a person in such a position would be unreasonable, however open and approachable you feel yourself to be as a manager. It could be someone outside the organization, someone from a different department, or someone above you. The person needs to be accepted by both participants in the conflict, and it needs to be clear that both participants will accept their judgment, whatever that judgment proves to be.

Dealing with grievances

Many countries have national laws ensuring that all companies have an official grievance procedure, by which employees can register their complaints through an official process. Indeed, in this context a grievance is defined as a formal statement of complaint. Obviously, the hope of every manager is that there will be no such complaints, or that if there are they can be dealt with by unofficial means; we like to think that employees with a problem could approach us to discuss it rather than instituting official proceedings. However, it may happen that a staff member feels that an injustice has been done and that it needs to be addressed in an official manner.

If your LTO is in a country which does not have a legal requirement for a grievance procedure, it is still worth creating one. The usual model for such a procedure is as follows:

1   The employee should attempt to resolve the matter informally, either by addressing the problem directly, approaching his or her line manager, or if necessary, approaching the line manager's superior.
2   If this does not resolve matters satisfactorily, the employee should write a letter to their employer outlining in detail the grievance.

3   The employer should arrange a meeting in which to discuss the grievance. The employee has the right to be accompanied to the meeting by either a colleague or a union representative. At the end of the meeting the employer should make a decision as to the resolution of the problem.

4   If the employee is still not satisfied, he or she has the right of appeal. The appeals process roughly follows steps 2 and 3 above.

In dealing with conflict procedure it is essential to keep records of all the steps in the process and to follow the procedure to the letter.

LEGISLATION

Along with financial management, human resource management is the most legislated area of management. It is not within the remit of this book to outline national legislation in all the countries where LTOs exist. It is, however, extremely important for a manager, especially one who is dealing with the hiring and firing of staff, to become familiar with important aspects of national legislation.

In general, the best way to avoid falling foul of legislation is also the best way to work as a manager, that is, to act ethically at all times. Make sure you are not making decisions subjectively, maintain a dialogue with all your staff, solicit feedback, and generally be open to the continued development of your staff and your organization.

CONCLUSION

Arguably there is no area of managing an LTO more crucial than HRM. As we have seen, it ranges from administrative tasks such as the recruitment process and satisfying legal requirements, to higher issues of leadership and management involved in motivating staff and performance management.

Effective managers must be able to delegate tasks successfully, must be adept at both giving and receiving feedback, should understand the motivations and needs of staff and be able to speak to those motivations, must be able to deal with conflict, and has to find ways of supporting and developing staff professionally.

On the plus side, the 'soft skills' required by an effective HR manager are not dissimilar to many of those needed by a teacher (see Chapter 1, pp. 20–23). However, on the minus side, because of its nature as 'people management', a badly handled conflict or poorly delivered feedback can cause long term problems. Effective HRM is critically important to the success, effectiveness and harmony of the LTO.

TASK

You are the academic manager for a mid-sized language LTO in a European city. Within your teaching staff there is a certain amount of diversity. The language classes (primarily English, but also with a few other languages taught) are covered by three distinct types of teachers:

- native-speaker expatriate teachers, who have to be recruited externally and provided with various fringe benefits on top of the regular salary (flight at the beginning and end of contract, housing allowance, support with dealing with local bureaucracy, work permit, etc.); because local salaries are low in international terms, these teachers tend to be young people who have attended a one-month training course, and who want to experience life in another country
- local career teachers who are on full-time contracts and who have graduated from the pedagogic faculties of local universities
- local and expatriate part-time teachers who are teaching EFL on top of their regular jobs or as a way of supplementing their income.

The first of these categories has always proved a problem for the LTO; having native-speaker teachers is a market necessity (clients and customers expect the LTO to have them), but the teachers themselves rarely stay on beyond the two years of their contract (and frequently break their contracts to leave earlier). In addition to this lack of continuity, some of these teachers are quite often disruptive, complaining about the low salaries (which are on a par with competitors' salaries), and the difficulties of living in the city. By contrast, the second group of teachers typically get on with their teaching, work hard, and rarely complain. The one area where they do feel unhappy is that the native speakers receive more benefits and compensation, are (on an academic level) less qualified, and still complain about their situation.

- How could you devise a plan to help deal with these issues?
- What methods of motivation might be effective with both of these groups?
- What other strategies could you use to solve this problem?

See Appendix, p. 275, for a suggested response to this Task.

4 Marketing and sales

- STRATEGIC MARKETING
- FINDING OUT WHAT THE CUSTOMERS WANT
- MARKETING MIX
- MARKETING PLAN

INTRODUCTION

Although an LTO may have dedicated marketing and sales staff, everyone has a part to play in marketing and selling an LTO's services. Furthermore, in order to manage an LTO successfully, it is important to have an understanding of what marketing involves, and how essential effective marketing is to achieving the goals of the LTO. Some people have a virtually intuitive entrepreneurial flair, which they deploy with great success. Others, however, are less blessed, and less successful, as is demonstrated in Vignettes 4.1 and 4.2 below and on p. 80. This chapter aims to provide a basis in marketing and sales so as to help avoid the ineptness illustrated in these vignettes, and to build on the successful marketing practice exemplified in Vignette 4.3 on p. 80.

Vignette 4.1: Peter's LTO

This LTO specialized in corporate language training, and there was a sales team whose job it was to achieve centrally determined targets for the month, the quarter and the year. One member of the sales force negotiated a course package for an important new customer and returned to the LTO very pleased with his achievement. He handed over the list of requirements to Peter, the academic director, who noted, to his surprise, that a German course was on the list. 'But we don't teach German!' he protested. 'I know,' replied the salesman, 'but that's what the customer wants.' A German teacher was recruited, and the course was run for one participant. It was never repeated.

Discussion of vignettes

In Vignette 4.1, marketing is driven by the need to meet sales targets. The salesman promised to meet the client's needs without having first checked that the LTO had the capability of fulfilling the promise. This is symptomatic of an organization in which sales and marketing exist in isolation from academic staff, who are left trying to meet the short-term goals of the sales staff. In this case, fulfilling the salesman's promise did not involve any longer-term benefit for the LTO.

Vignette 4.2: Kim's LTO

The LTO owner, noting that competitors in Sydney were offering English for Business, decided that this must be a good market to enter. He refurbished a classroom with stylish and costly furniture and facilities and instructed Kim, the DOS, and the sales team to develop and promote Business English courses. Several months elapsed, during which only a handful of students enrolled. Meanwhile, teachers were tied up preparing and teaching, while the Business English classroom was out of bounds for overflow use when the LTO was running at maximum capacity, even though it was scarcely used. In the end, Business English courses were quietly dropped, with only the deluxe classroom serving as a reminder of this unsuccessful initiative.

Vignette 4.3: Sarah's LTO

Sarah's LTO is a branch of an international chain, located in a tropical city, where the market is highly seasonal. Centrally defined targets take limited account of this seasonal variation, however. Sarah and her colleagues had noticed that there were some students who liked to continue beyond the weeks that they had booked, so they surveyed them to find out what it was that encouraged them to stay on. This information was then used to develop a proposal for a package for continuing students. Targets were set for the first month, and the scheme was introduced. At the end of the month, Sarah and her team had met their targets, and the package was integrated into the portfolio of her branch, so helping to mitigate seasonal variation and meet the targets set by headquarters.

In Vignette 4.2, the LTO owner had noticed that competitors were offering a new product, so he decided to do likewise, but without having done a competitor analysis or a survey of the size and requirements of the market. His approach was to devise an offer, and hope that customers would buy it. This is a product-driven approach to marketing, and one which is quite widely followed. It is, however, not without risk, since it is based on an incomplete understanding of the market.

In Vignette 4.3, front-line staff – teachers and administrative staff – noted a small but potentially growing trend. They did some customer research, and estimated the potential size of the continuing market and the benefit to the branch of developing this segment for achieving the LTO's sales targets. Their proposal, approved by senior management, was successfully implemented. This is an example of effective, small-scale, local marketing practice making use of the initiative of customer-facing staff, who backed up their observations with survey data.

Marketing, as these vignettes illustrate, consists of more than selling, or trying to sell, something that customers may or may not want. It also involves more than attempting to meet customers' requirements at all costs. What, then, is marketing?

Defining marketing

Invariably when trying to define key terms like 'market' and 'marketing', we find that there is not always a set of commonly agreed definitions. So, without entering into a debate, we will define 'the market' as 'the existing or target group of customers for a particular product or service' (Cooper & Argyris, 1998, p. 387). The market can be subdivided (or segmented) into particular sets of buyers who are similar in terms of demographic (age, sex, nationality) and psychographic (social class, lifestyle, behaviour) and other characteristics. For LTOs a significant distinction concerns the geographical location of the market: onshore or offshore, to be discussed further below.

According to the American Marketing Association Board of Directors, marketing is:

> … the activity, set of institutions, and processes for creating, communicating, delivering, and exchanging offerings that have value for customers, clients, partners, and society at large.

In services marketing, a distinction is made between two approaches, summarized in Figure 4.1 below.

Transaction marketing	Relationship marketing
Orientation towards single purchase	Orientation towards repeat sales
Limited direct customer/supplier contact	Close, frequent customer/supplier contact
Focus on product benefits	Focus on value to customer
Emphasis on short-term performance	Emphasis on long-term performance
Limited level of customer service	High level of customer service
Goal of customer satisfaction	Goal of 'delighting' the customer
Quality is a manufacturing responsibility	Quality is the whole organization's responsibility

FIGURE 4.1: *Approaches to marketing*

The importance of relationship marketing will be developed further in Chapter 5, in which we deal with the management of customer services and satisfaction. It also underpins the approach to marketing described in this chapter.

Defining the customer

An LTO is involved in an act of exchange with its customers, the assumption being that both the customer and the organization value what the other has to offer. The party who buys the services of the LTO is not necessarily the party who uses them, however, which leads to this distinction:

Customer The party who purchases what the LTO provides, but may not actually use it, e.g. a parent.

Consumer The party who actually uses the LTO's services, but does not necessarily purchase them, e.g. a child or a corporate employee who actually follows a language course.

Client   The party in whose interests the services are provided. The term originally denoted a person under the protection and patronage of another; LTOs have a duty of care to their clients.

Sponsor   The party who is responsible for commissioning, and usually paying for, a service which is consumed by a third party. Sometimes the term 'client' is used to refer to this party. The training managers in the case study on p. 95 are both clients and sponsors.

One party may, and often does, occupy all of these roles. However, the roles may be distributed among a number of different individuals. Likewise, the role of supplier may be spread across a wide range of parties, some of whom, such as agents, occupy both a customer and supplier role. In this and the following chapter, 'customer' will be used as an all-purpose term embracing all four roles, the other terms being used when it is important to differentiate among these roles.

The distribution of these roles is also dependent on the kind of market that the LTO is engaged in: wholesale or retail. A wholesale market is one in which the LTO provides services to a client or sponsor who then recruits and supplies the students or consumers as a group. Corporate language training is an example of a wholesale market, where the customer/sponsor is the corporation, and the consumers are employees who actually take the course provided by the LTO. The retail market, by contrast, involves selling services to individuals who may occupy three roles: client, customer and consumer. The majority of LTOs operate in a retail market.

The parties involved in these roles and relationships will, of course, vary from one situation to another. If your LTO is involved in teaching young learners (ages 7–18, for instance), the customers are likely to be the parents of the learners, since it is they who actually pay their children's fees. Parents, as customers, will have certain expectations as to value for money (that they are not being overcharged, the course represents good value) and prestige (that the LTO is highly regarded within the community), while as clients, they will have expectations as to the LTO's duty of care (their children will be physically and morally safe), effectiveness of teaching (their children will actually learn something), examination success (high pass rates), and so on. The consumer will be the child, whose expectations may not entirely match those of their parents. Children may put more emphasis on the social aspects of the experience, for instance, although in some settings, as clients they may have high expectations as to the effectiveness of the teaching in achieving good examination results. Evidence for the success or otherwise of fulfilling the diverse expectations of these parties will be derived from various forms of feedback, some anecdotal, and some, based on surveys, quantifiable. Successful LTOs are good at collecting and attending to such feedback from the various parties who purchase and use their services, an area to be explored further in Chapter 5.

TASK

Analysing the various roles of the 'customer' can help us understand significant aspects of the relationship between an LTO and the users of its services. Here is a framework to start you thinking about this relationship and the parties involved.

Role	What do they expect?	How successfully do you meet their expectations?	What evidence do you have for meeting (or not meeting) their expectations?
Customer			
Consumer			
Client			
Sponsor			

Take a service purchased by one of your LTO's customers.

- Who actually uses (or consumes) the service purchased by this customer? Remember that customer and consumer (or user of the service) are not always the same party.
- What do customers look for in the service? In other words, what are their expectations?
- What does the consumer look for? Customers and consumers, you will remember, may have different concerns.
- Who is the client, and what concerns of the client are being met by the service concerned? The client, you will recall, is the party whose interests are to be prioritized in the provision of service. It is a teacher's duty, for instance, to place the concerns and well-being of students above their own.
- What issues can arise as a result of differences between what the customer or sponsor wants and what the consumer wants? And are there any conflicts of interest between the LTO as service provider and their duty to their client? If you can, give specific examples from your LTO.

STRATEGIC MARKETING

Strategic marketing is concerned with determining how an LTO competes against its competitors in the market. It also aims to develop a competitive advantage relative to the competition. As a process, strategic marketing involves a sequence of steps, which can be summarized as follows:

1   Develop a vision, a mission and a set of objectives.
2   Gather information about the business of the LTO itself, the local market environment, and the macro environment. Achieving this will involve analysing internal

performance over a period of years, as well as processing market and macro-environment data through the use of such tools as SWOT and STEP analysis respectively.

3   Make decisions and devise a marketing strategy. This will involve decisions about which parts of the business will be developed or allowed to decline, identifying the competitive advantages possessed by the LTO, identifying key segments and developing positioning strategies for each segment. Such positioning strategies involve defining the marketing mix, and planning how to communicate to the target markets.

4   Implement: (a) devise a marketing plan, and (b) prepare an action plan.

Step 1 is discussed in Chapter 2, p. 40.

Step 2 is the focus of the present chapter, while STEP and SWOT analyses are covered in Chapter 9.

Step 3, including the marketing mix and promotion, are covered below.

Step 4 is also dealt with below, while action plans are discussed in Chapter 10, p. 261.

External information

One of the things which the LTO manager needs to know is the potential size of the market. As noted in the previous section, demographic data, both national and local, can be used to estimate the potential market, as well as information on competitors, although this last will usually be more difficult to obtain. In language teaching services, there are two key distinctions: the first among what Graddol (2006, p. 82) terms 'models' of ELT, and the second between offshore and onshore markets.

Graddol's 'models' are defined on the basis of the following:

- target variety, e.g. native-speaker, such as British or American English, host country, local variety, etc.
- skills: the traditional four skills, and the priority given to each
- teacher skills: linguistic proficiency and pedagogical skill
- learner motives: instrumental, integrative (or neither)
- starting age: from birth to senior years
- primary purposes: a very wide range from communicating with native speakers to getting a job in one's own country
- citizenship: as a component of national, regional or global citizenship
- values: liberal, local, social and global issues, etc.
- learning environment: classroom, immersion, informal, online, etc.
- content materials: from international textbook to authentic materials
- assessment: variable, from informal to international test
- failure pattern: variable, depending on required proficiency level for purposes concerned.

Using these, Graddol distinguishes the following models, which reflect changes of focus as the demand for and availability of ELT have evolved:

- EFL (English as a Foreign Language): usually classroom-based, in students' home country, generally for business of leisure purposes with occasional visits to native-speaker countries

- ESL (English as a Second Language) (a): in a country where students now live (their host country), and they learn by immersion, possibly with some part-time ELT provision
- ESL (b): in students' home country where English is widely used, with local standard and non-standard varieties
- EYL (English for Young Learners): often provided in kindergarten and informal pre-school contexts
- Global English: with a focus on an internationally intelligible variety, taught in class, with instrumental goals.

Markets: onshore and offshore

The second distinction is between an offshore (overseas) and an onshore (domestic) market. EFL is provided in both contexts. When the EFL market is offshore, the LTO will have to recruit its customers (and consumers) in an overseas country, and bring them to the country in which the courses will actually be provided. Where the EFL market is onshore, the LTO and its customers live in the same community, and the LTO will usually deal directly with its customers.

For countries where English is spoken as a first language, the EFL market is predominantly offshore and customers have to be recruited from overseas and brought onshore. (A parallel situation exists for the teaching of European languages such as German, French, Spanish or Italian to students recruited from offshore markets elsewhere in Europe or the world at large.) The majority of EFL learners are taught in their own country, however, by locally based LTOs, for whom the market is a domestic one. Thus, in Latin America, Continental Europe and Asia, LTOs teaching EFL recruit their students locally. In parts of Asia where English is a national language (e.g. India, Singapore), EFL students are increasingly being recruited overseas to follow courses in the Anglophone country concerned.

In metropolitan countries like the US, the UK and Australia, there is also a significant domestic ESL market for immigrants. Unlike EFL students, such customers are mostly recruited onshore (since they are already living in the host country) and their ESOL course may be subsidized from the public purse as a means of encouraging social inclusion among resident newcomers. The recruitment process frequently involves social service agencies responsible for funding, and such ELT provision is often subject to changes in public policy.

There are some significant differences between offshore and onshore markets in terms of the kinds of services required by customers. These differences cover a wide range of parameters, including those listed by Graddol above, and the different models based on them.

One of the most significant features of offshore recruitment is that it involves recruiting in a diversity of different national catchment areas, and typically includes using agents based there, who act as the link between the LTO as supplier of language

TASK

Adapting Graddol's parameters, together with any others that you feel need to be added, compare and contrast two different types of provision in a market known to you. Consider the following:

- What is the variety of English that is taken as a model or goal?
- What is the balance among the four skills? This may differ considerably according to the type of course.
- What is the English language level of teachers? This could vary considerably in an LTO with a wide range of English-speaking teachers.
- How well qualified and experienced are they as language teachers? Are some bilingual and able to operate in the learners' own as well as the target language?
- How do the two examples differ and why? Do they differ because of the age, life stage, level and the motivations of the learners? Are there differences based on the content materials and forms of assessment?

Then compare the features of the provision with that in another, entirely different market. If yours is onshore, contrast it with an offshore market, and vice versa. This may involve doing some web searching to see what LTOs elsewhere offer, and how their offer compares with the examples you have already analysed.

teaching, and the student as customer/consumer. This means that agents need to be very aware of trends in the market, and to be well informed about the influence of economic and political factors on that market. Recent salutary examples of the impact of such factors include the Asian economic downturn of the late 1990s, and the events of 9/11 in New York in 2001. The impact of the former on offshore recruitment of students for LTOs in countries like Australia and of the latter for the US was considerable.

The LTO whose market is entirely onshore – domestic – has the benefit of being intimate with the market, and of being capable, for the most part, of dealing directly with the client and customer without the need for an intermediary. Furthermore, the onshore market, though varied along demographic and economic lines, will be more homogeneous than the culturally, linguistically and nationally diverse offshore market. Such an onshore market is, however, very vulnerable, because a serious downturn will leave LTOs highly exposed, as they will not be able to refocus their recruitment activities elsewhere, as can be done when serving a variety of offshore markets where a downturn in one market can be balanced by increasing recruitment efforts in another.

Offshore market comparison

The differences among different offshore markets is well illustrated by data from the Australian Government: Australian Education International website. Figure 4.2 shows student enrolments in each sector for 2006 compared with earlier years.

Sector	2003	2004	2005	2006	% Change 2005 to 2006
Higher Education	135,402	151,503	163,779	172,297	5.2%
Vocational Education	57,524	59,065	66,556	83,685	25.7%
School Education	27,044	27,341	25,156	24,717	−1.7%
ELICOS	62,262	61,873	64,998	77,468	19.2%
Other[1]	25,728	25,574	25,590	25,651	0.2%
Total	307,960	325,356	346,079	383,818	10.9%

FIGURE 4.2: *Overseas student enrolments in Australia by major sector, 2003–2006*
[1] *Other includes enabling, foundation and non-award courses*

Country	2003	2004	2005	2006	% Change 2005 to 2006
China	60,076	70,556	81,730	90,287	10.5%
India	14,374	20,752	27,605	39,166	41.9%
Korea, Republic of (South)	22,195	23,816	26,319	31,257	18.8%
Hong Kong	23,970	22,968	21,343	20,523	−3.8%
Malaysia	19,825	20,003	19,362	19,166	−1.0%
Thailand	17,093	16,316	16,514	17,889	8.3%
Japan	19,497	20,037	19,053	17,804	−6.6%
Indonesia	20,422	18,138	16,121	15,038	−6.7%
United States of America	12,584	12,793	12,585	12,045	−4.3%
Brazil	3,822	4,731	7,081	10,190	43.9%
Sub total	213,858	230,110	247,713	273,365	10.4%
Other nationalities	94,102	95,246	98,366	110,453	12.3%
Total	307,960	325,356	346,079	383,818	10.9%

FIGURE 4.3: *Student enrolments in Australia from top 10 source countries, 2003–2006*

Figure 4.3 summarizes student enrolments in the top 10 source countries over the same period, from which we see that there is some fluctuation over the period, with some 'gainers' and some 'losers'.

TASK

Study Figures 4.2 and 4.3 on p. 87.
- What conclusions can be drawn about the different sectors in Figure 4.2 in attracting offshore students? For example, what could explain the high volume of students in the higher education sector?
- What conclusions can be drawn about the offshore markets (Figure 4.3) concerned? (Keep in mind some of the STEP factors – see Chapter 9.)
- What are the implications for the LTO manager of fluctuations in these markets? In other words, what continuing adjustments will managers have to make as the source and nationality mixture of students vary?

Figure 4.4 shows market share by region for each state/territory in Australia for 2006. The states with the largest cities – New South Wales, Victoria, Queensland and South Australia – attract the highest percentage of offshore customers. There are some striking differences across different markets. For some reason, for instance, Western Australia attracts an unusually high percentage of customers from Sub-Saharan Africa.

TASK

Study Figure 4.4 opposite.
- What do these figures suggest about the relative attractiveness of different states?
- What do these differences tell us as far as domestic competition is concerned?
- What will be the implications of LTO location for selling in the various markets?
- How is the nationality mix of classes likely to differ between LTOs in, for example, New South Wales and Queensland?
- What are the marketing implications of the trends revealed in these figures? For instance, if you were running an LTO in Queensland, which regional markets might you target in order to increase your volume of students?

The kind of information which a sector organization like English Australia collects and makes available to its members is of considerable value to LTO management, particularly for strategic planning. Membership of such a trade organization is vital if LTO management is to be kept informed about developments in the market environment, which in turn informs situational analysis.

Internal information

The onshore market

To illustrate some features of internal information, we will use a simulated example in a domestic market. CLS operates in a city with a population of around 1 million, and it is estimated that there is a total ELT market of around 20,000. Figure 4.5 on p. 90

Region	New South Wales	Victoria	Queensland	Western Australia	South Australia	Australian Capital Territory	Tasmania	Northern Territory
Southern & Central Asia	39%	46%	6%	3%	4%	1%	0%	0%
South-East Asia	34%	33%	10%	14%	5%	2%	2%	0%
North-East Asia	41%	25%	17%	7%	7%	2%	1%	0%
North Africa & Middle East	38%	24%	22%	9%	4%	1%	1%	0%
Sub-Saharan Africa	17%	30%	13%	34%	4%	1%	1%	0%
Americas	44%	14%	30%	8%	2%	1%	1%	0%
Southern & Eastern Europe	66%	11%	13%	7%	2%	1%	0%	0%
North-West Europe	36%	16%	28%	13%	4%	2%	1%	0%
Oceania & Antarctica	34%	14%	44%	2%	2%	3%	0%	0%
Unknown	31%	21%	22%	11%	11%	1%	2%	0%
% of total market	39%	28%	16%	9%	5%	2%	1%	0%

FIGURE 4.4: *Regional market share by state/territory, 2006*

summarizes some features of this market which is subdivided according to age group (juniors 7–11, teenagers 12–18, adults 18+), examinations (such as Cambridge First Certificate, TOEIC) and in-company, in which employees are taught on company premises.

Market sector	Potential market size	% of total	Current provision	% of total	Headroom for growth
Juniors	3,000	15	1,800	14	1,200
Teenagers	4,000	20	3,200	25	800
Adults: general	6,000	30	4,200	33	1,800
Examinations	2,000	10	1,200	9	800
In-company	5,000	25	2,400	19	2,600
TOTAL	20,000	100	12,800	100	7,200

FIGURE 4.5: *CLS market potential*

The total potential size of this simulated market, based on demographic and economic figures, is taken as 20,000, and there are assumed to be 50 LTOs of various sizes which constitute suppliers in this particular marketplace. Of the 20,000 potential students, each segment is estimated to occupy a given percentage (e.g. juniors 15%, in-company 25%). Current provision refers to the estimated coverage of each segment by LTOs operating in this market, and the percentage occupied by each segment (e.g. juniors 14%, in-company 19%). The headroom for growth is the potential market size minus the current actual provision. Thus, for juniors this is 1,200, for in-company 2,600.

Why is this information important and useful? For LTO managers, such material provides a basis for comparison of the place occupied by their own LTO in the market as well as data for target-setting in planning expansion, including the kinds of language teaching services to be developed and provided. It is just this kind of data which was overlooked by the LTO owner in Vignette 4.2.

Figure 4.6 provides information on the percentage of each customer and course type for CLS from which such comparisons may be drawn with the estimated size of the market. From these comparisons, we see that CLS is well positioned in several sectors, suggesting that it is offering what the market wants, but may be failing to meet the requirements of the adult sector, in which there appears to be further room for expansion.

	Numbers	% of total
Juniors	213	17%
Teenagers	316	26%
Adults: general	160	13%
Examinations	187	15%
In-company	350	29%
TOTAL	1226	100%

FIGURE 4.6: *CLS student numbers and percentage*

The same information can also be presented in a pie chart (Figure 4.7), which is a useful graphic device to present data which shows percentages.

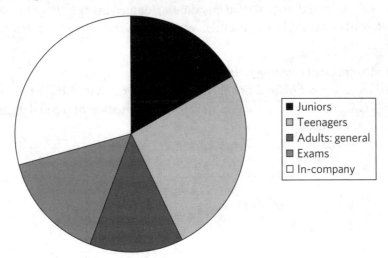

FIGURE 4.7: *CLS student enrolments*

In addition to comparison with the market, it is also vital to maintain records of LTO performance from year to year so as to depict market trends. Figure 4.8 illustrates a trend over a five-year period, indicating a decline in four out of five segments, the only one showing growth being corporate courses.

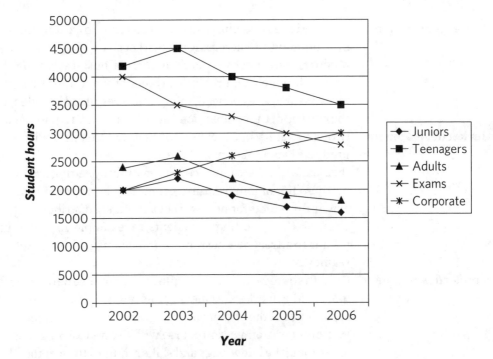

FIGURE 4.8: *CLS five-year trend*

Finally, analysis of volume and profitability of the LTO's portfolio of products will reveal which are the most profitable. The so-called 80/20 rule or Pareto Principle often applies: 80% of sales come from 20% of customers. Identifying the 20% of customers who contribute 80% of the profit is very useful in making decisions on where to focus time, effort and resources.

Trend data and marketing strategy: the Ansoff matrix

Trend data is used to prompt further analysis and to inform marketing strategy. The Ansoff matrix (Figure 4.9) provides a framework for evaluation of trend data and marketing decision-making.

	Existing products	New products
Existing markets	MARKET PENETRATION	PRODUCT DEVELOPMENT
New markets	MARKET DEVELOPMENT	DIVERSIFICATION

FIGURE 4.9: *Ansoff matrix*

Market penetration	Strategy based on selling existing products into existing markets by maintaining or increasing the market share of existing products and services. Essentially, this is a 'business as usual' approach, which requires little in the way of new resources and investment. It does depend, though, on a very good knowledge of the market, of the competition and of customers' requirements.
Market development	Growth strategy in which the LTO sets out to sell its existing products in new markets. There are various ways of achieving this: 'exporting' to a new market (possibly by setting up partnerships or joint ventures), repackaging and renaming existing products for new markets, changing distribution channels (by recruiting new agents, for example), or differential pricing to attract new customers or to open up new market segments.
Product development	Growth strategy in which the aim is to introduce new products into existing markets. Achieving this may involve developing the capabilities of the organization (e.g. a decision to offer an entirely new examination course will involve teaching staff developing the knowledge and skills required to meet the

requirements of the examination syllabus). It will also involve investment and development by the LTO.

Diversification   Growth strategy in which the LTO markets new products in new markets. At its most straightforward, this can simply mean recruiting a more diverse range of students – by nationality, by level, by goals. Accommodating such diversity within existing course provision can be problematic, and will require planning and preparation. Of the four marketing strategies, diversification is much the most risky, and any LTO contemplating this strategy needs to be very clear about what it expects to gain as well as doing a transparent and honest risk assessment. There is a very chequered history of attempts by LTOs to follow a diversification strategy.

Finally, products and services follow a sequence of stages from introduction, to growth, maturity and decline. It is important to recognize at which stage in the cycle the LTO's various products are situated, so as to align pricing policies and marketing strategies accordingly. For example, pricing may be reduced during the introduction, maturity and decline stages, but maintained during the growth stage. New features may be added during the maturity stage to differentiate the service from what competitors are offering. Once a product has reached the decline stage, a decision has to be made to discontinue.

TASK

Assemble trend data for your LTOs products, preferably over a five-year period. This data will include student volume for every course (product) for each year. This volume will usually be measured as student hours, days or weeks, depending on how the products are sold.
- What trends are revealed as far as these different products are concerned?
- At what stages in the product cycle are these located?
- What growth strategies is the LTO following for these various products?
- Are there any products which are in decline and should be discontinued?
- If so, what will replace them?

Assembling this information may involve some research, but if no one has ever done it before, you and your colleagues may learn something useful about the various courses (or products) that the LTO offers. Do you see a slow but steady growth – or, more worrying, decline – in some products? How long have you been offering these products? Do the trends suggest that some products have 'peaked' and are now mature, or that some are past their peak and are in decline? Are the trends revealed likely to continue? With reference to the Ansoff matrix, what are the strategies that the LTO is pursuing for each product? Are these strategies supported by the trends revealed in the data analysis?

Income streams and profitability

In addition to figures on sales volume and trends, the LTO director will also need information on the profitability of each income stream. There are various ways of measuring profitability. A very simple measure, also discussed in Chapter 7, is that of gross margin – sometimes called contribution – in which the direct cost of teachers is deducted from the hourly tuition income for any activity. An example will illustrate the principle. In Figure 4.10, the tuition rate per student is €6 per hour, and there are 10 students per class.

Class hourly income	Full-time hourly teacher's cost	Gross margin/contribution
€60.00	€20.00	€40.00

FIGURE 4.10: *Gross margin example*

The gross margin of €40.00 is equivalent to 67% of the tuition income per class hour. This margin can contribute to the meeting of indirect or fixed costs, such as administration, rent and utilities.

Selling more higher-margin courses will be more profitable than the reverse. Although it will be difficult for any LTO to focus solely on high-margin products, knowing what the margins are is an important piece of information for planning marketing strategy. Typically, there will be a mixture of high- and lower-margin products in the portfolio. Importantly, the manager should guard against low-margin products cannibalizing higher-margin ones, jeopardizing the viability of the LTO. Ultimately, it is important to combine volume, trend and profitability data, as none of these should be used in isolation as a basis for making marketing decisions.

FINDING OUT WHAT THE CUSTOMERS WANT

The obvious way to find out what the customers want is to ask them. However, as we noted on p. 81, defining the customer is not always easy. This is illustrated in the case study opposite. Steve, an experienced corporate language trainer, was planning to set up his own training service in Paris. Part of his planning included interviewing a key stakeholder group: the training managers who commission courses. He asked them to rate their own experience and that of their employees, who were the actual consumers of the services provided by the LTO.

Steve's approach to finding out what customers wanted was to use interviews. There are other ways using the same techniques which are used to evaluate customer satisfaction, as discussed in Chapter 5. In particular, Performance/Importance surveys (Chapter 5, p. 131) indicate what prospective or current customers are looking for.

There are other sources of information which make use of the contact which front-line staff have with customers. As noted in Chapter 2, p. 28, and as illustrated in Vignette 4.3 on p. 80, it is in their interactions with customers that customer-facing staff gain insights into what customers value. To make effective use of this source, customer-facing staff need to

Case study: Corporate training

The training managers

They were generally concerned with cost, administrative efficiency, and gathering feedback from the trainees. Their expectations included:

1　the satisfactory fulfilment of the specific needs and interests of the trainees, in order to meet their job requirements and/or personal wishes
2　a training centre located near their company (within five miles)
3　a brochure about the LTO to distribute to their employees
4　value for money with competitive pricing
5　administrative efficiency on behalf of the LTO (one of the most frequent complaints was that it was not made clear by the LTO who was responsible for the planning of the courses, which often led to trainees showing up with no instructor and vice versa)
6　a flexible cancellation policy as attendance is often precluded by other professional commitments of trainees
7　courses before 9.00 and after 18.00 preferred (i.e. out of working hours).

The trainees

Steve also obtained some information from the managers on the trainees' concerns based on feedback after their last cycle of training. From this, it emerged that trainees were, for the most part, concerned with the quality of the training itself, independent of any of the administrative issues which preoccupy training officers. Their concerns included:

8　late or absent teachers
9　an approach to teaching that they regarded as too scholarly or, at the other extreme, the instructor simply held informal 'chat' sessions
10　a lack of a planned pedagogical programme with objectives
11　a mismatch between the level of individual trainees and the rest of the group (i.e. the effect of mixed abilities on the effectiveness of the class)
12　lack of materials: students often finished the course with a flotsam of photocopies
13　homework either not assigned or assigned but not checked
14　a feeling among trainees that they had not made any progress
15　course content either unsuitable or irrelevant.

From this information, Steve could see that there were three sets of priorities:

• non-pedagogical: location (2), scheduling (6,7), value for money (4)
• pedagogical: alignment of needs and learning outcomes (1), (9), (10), (11), (14), (15)
• service efficiency: clarity of administration (3), (5), effectiveness of service provision (8), (12), (13)

Having clarified customers' preferences, Steve was then in a position to start planning his offer.

be encouraged to report their findings to the marketing team so that it can inform both new product development (Chapter 8, p. 213) and ways of promoting the offer (p. 103).

Segmentation

Typically, LTOs provide a range of services/courses aimed at specific customer groups, defined by age (Young Learners, Teenagers, Young Adults), level (Basic, Intermediate, Advanced), content (Business English), credentials (Examinations) or pathway (University Foundation). The assumption is that customer groups opting for these various offers will be relatively homogeneous, with similar needs and attitudes. While this is a sound organizing principle for the LTO's offers, it is a good idea continually to review the basis for segmentation, as identifying a new niche can provide an opportunity for developing new products.

There are several requirements for successful segmentation:
- members of the segment are the same or very similar (there is homogeneity within the segment)
- there are differences between segments (there is heterogeneity across segments)
- segment size and purchasing power are measurable
- the segment is large enough to be profitable
- the segment can be reached efficiently
- it is possible to develop a product or service for the segment.

A review of existing segments may reveal new segments. An example is the so-called General English course, a category which obscures significant differences among diverse customers. For example, in an LTO offering year-round continuous enrolment, there may prove to be two subsets within 'General English': those students who come for a short time (e.g. two to three weeks), and those who stay on for six months or more. Although they may be regarded as a homogeneous group as far as demographic characteristics (age, gender, nationality, life stage) and course type (General English) are concerned, they may actually differ in psychographic (personality, lifestyle, values, attitudes) and behavioural (benefits sought, rate of use/consumption, product end use) variables. In other words, within a customer segment classed as 'General English', there may be psychographic differences which identify new, internally homogeneous segments for whom new or different products and services could be developed and offered. The next task asks you to look closely at the portfolio of courses offered by your LTO from the viewpoint of market segmentation. By doing so, you may identify a new segment for which it would be profitable to develop a new product.

Defining segments on the basis of age or goal (e.g. an examination preparation course) is common. Less common is the use of psychographic variables as a basis for segmentation, yet in the contemporary world, lifestyle variables are increasingly used as a way of defining customer segments. It is useful to consider what such lifestyle variables will be in the market occupied by the LTO, and how they could define a new niche in line with the Ansoff matrix (Figure 4.9). Having done this, you can then consider what the demographic features of this new lifestyle niche might be: size, age, life stage, and so on.

Following this, you can consider the feasibility of developing a new product to sell into this particular niche market. Not all niche markets will prove feasible, or profitable.

> **TASK**
>
> Review the courses offered by your LTO.
> - What are the segments that these courses are intended for?
> - How are these segments defined? (See Figure 4.11 for variables used in segmentation.) Some of these, such as geographic variables, may be taken for granted, but they can have a significant impact on what an LTO can offer. For example, the widespread efficiency of IT infrastructure in South Korea opens up opportunities not available in a less 'wired' country like Indonesia.
> - Is there any customer segment excluded by your current offers?
> - If so, what is this segment and what are its characteristics?
> - In particular what product/course/service could you develop to meet the requirements of this segment?

Geographic variables	Psychographic variables
Region of the world or country: east, west, south, north, central, coastal, hilly, etc. Country size: metropolitan cities, small cities, towns Density of area: urban, semi-urban, rural Infrastructure: transport, communications Climate: hot, cold, humid, rainy, seasonal variation	Personality Lifestyle Values Attitude
Demographic variables	**Behavioural variables**
Age Gender Sexual orientation Family size Family life cycle Education: primary, secondary, college, university Income Occupation Education Socioeconomic status Religion Nationality/ethnicity Language Prior experience of learning English	Benefits sought (e.g. entry to next educational or career stage) Rate at which the service is consumed How the consumer intends to use or apply the service Readiness-to-buy stage Decision-making unit (e.g. the HR department, the family)

FIGURE 4.11: *Variables commonly used in segmentation*

MARKETING MIX

As we saw in the previous section, courses and services are usually developed to meet the requirements of specific customer segments or, in the case of one-to-one teaching, of an individual customer. There is a combination of components – the four Ps – which traditionally make up the marketing mix:

Product Specifications of the actual service, and how it relates to the customers' needs and wants.

Pricing What is exchanged for the product or service, which is usually money.

Promotion All those areas of publicity, such as press advertising and selling, as in direct sales, which are sometimes erroneously called 'marketing'.

Place Where the service is provided. In the LTO world, this is usually the actual LTO premises, but it can also include a virtual location (such as a website) or off-site premises (as is common in corporate language training).

There is also an additional set of Ps which are especially important for the kinds of services provided by LTOs:

People Range of people with whom the customer comes into contact, and who, as far as the customer is concerned, are an inseparable part of the total service. In language learning, as well as the teacher, these include fellow consumers/learners, who are typically co-present in the actual provision of the service/lesson. These people can have a significant influence on consumer satisfaction.

Process Process(es) involved in providing a service and the behaviour of people, which can be crucial to customer satisfaction. As is clear from the case study on p. 95, this is an important consideration for potential customers, and the surveys reported in Chapter 5, pp. 113–4 also confirm this.

Physical evidence Language teaching services cannot be experienced before they are actually provided, which adds to the risk of making a choice. To get round this, potential customers can be given an opportunity to see what a service is like through case studies, testimonials and video clips. Some examples of LTOs offering this may be found on the websites of the following organizations:
- AOI College of Languages
- EF International Language Schools
- Intrax International Institute
- University of Connecticut.

Packaging The way a service is packaged, through initial contact via a website or a brochure, is often the first contact that the prospect (prospective customer) has with the service.

Product

The way your services are specified needs to make sense to the prospect. There is a tendency for language teaching services to be specified in ways which make sense to teachers rather than the customer, who will not be familiar with the terminology used by members of the profession. The use of 'can do' statements in the Common European Framework (see Chapter 8, p. 228) is a move towards specifications which make sense to the non-professional and, increasingly, language courses are being described in terms of what the consumer/learner will be able to do as a result of following the course.

The rise in demand for customization of services also means that specifications need to consider individual needs. This has to be negotiated with care, as offering a plethora of choices – one route to customization – can result in a confusing range of options. Furthermore, it can be difficult for even a well-resourced LTO actually to cover a wide range of choices, leaving customers disappointed. So, product specification needs to achieve a judicious balance between restricted and excessive (or even confusing) choice.

Product portfolio

Even a small LTO will have a portfolio, or range, of products. Probably there will be differences in the way these perform as far as volume and income are concerned, both internally, as far as the LTO is concerned, and externally, in comparison with the competition. It is important for management to be able to plan its range of products in ways which match the LTO's strengths and which will enable it to exploit the most attractive opportunities as they arise.

A well-known method for such planning is the Boston Consulting Group Matrix (Figure 4.12). The method refers to Strategic Business Units (SBUs); for most LTOs this will mean courses, but in larger LTOs this may also cover departments or sections concerned with other services. The method depends on knowledge of market share of both competitors and your own business, information which, unfortunately, is rarely available in detail in our sector.

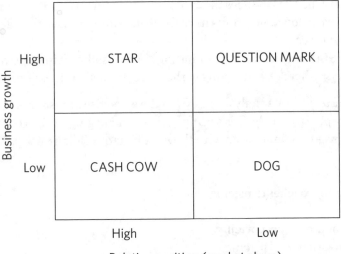

FIGURE 4.12: *Boston matrix* (Boston Consulting Group)

The characteristics of the four categories of SBUs revealed as a result of analysis are summarized in Figure 4.13 below.

Stars	Cash cows	Question marks	Dogs
High growth High share	Low growth High share	High growth Low share	Low growth Low share
SBU is likely to generate enough cash to be self-sustaining. Recommended tactics: • Promote aggressively • Expand your product or service • Invest in R & D	SBU can be used to support other business units. • Defend & maintain	SBU requires a lot of cash to maintain market share. • Invest more cash • Or, divest	SBU is a cash trap. • Focus on short term • Avoid risky project • Limited future

FIGURE 4.13: *Strategic Business Units* (Boston Consulting Group)

Once the SBUs (or courses in the case of an LTO) have been classified, management must decide what to do with them. Conventional strategic thinking suggests there are four possible strategies for each SBU:

1   Build share: here the LTO can invest to increase market share (for example turning a 'question mark' into a 'star').
2   Hold: here the LTO invests just enough to keep the SBU in its present position.
3   Harvest: here the LTO reduces the amount of investment in order to maximize the short-term cash flows and profits from the SBU. This may have the effect of turning 'stars' into 'cash cows'.
4   Divest: the SBU can be divested by phasing it out or selling it in order to use the resources elsewhere (e.g. investing in the more promising 'question marks').

Conducting a full-scale analysis is beyond the expertise or resources of most LTOs, but the basic concept of the analysis is a useful guide to managing the LTO's product portfolio, particularly if used in conjunction with the Ansoff matrix (Figure 4.9, p. 92).

Pricing

There are four approaches to pricing:
  • full-cost pricing
  • marginal (or direct) cost pricing
  • competitor-orientated pricing
  • market-orientated pricing.

Full-cost pricing is based on the total cost involved in providing the service and adding a margin. The problem with this approach is that it focuses on internal costs rather than the customers' willingness to pay. However, it does provide a basis for a break-even analysis – a critical indicator if an LTO is to continue in business.

Marginal cost pricing is based on calculating only direct costs, omitting overheads. This means that it does not represent the full costs of providing a service. Such pricing may be applied to reduce the 'perishability' of a service (see Chapter 5, p. 120) by attracting price-sensitive customers, but is best regarded as a short-term measure to reduce the impact of excess capacity, a common problem in the seasonal world of the LTO.

Competitor-orientated pricing includes going-rate pricing and competitive bidding. The former involves comparison with other LTOs' prices for the same service, and then either undercutting or else establishing a differential advantage (which could be any aspect of the marketing mix) and charging more. Competitive bidding is the norm when a contract is put out to tender. The provider has to meet the specifications drawn up by the customer, and set a price which will match the likely bid prices of competitors. This is common with corporate contracts of the type reported in the case study on p. 95.

Market-orientated pricing involves setting a price in line with the LTO 's own marketing strategy. This is both an art and a science, as it involves calculating the trade-off between price and quality, negotiating profit margins, and taking account of the state of the market and the willingness of customers to pay for the perceived value of the services you offer. If you are working with agents, they will also be concerned with how your market-orientated pricing compares with competitors', since they will, if the price is higher, have to justify this to their customers.

Price is the only element of the marketing mix which directly generates revenue and it is also the only component which can be changed quickly. However, competitors can also act quickly, and a price advantage can be speedily eroded. Market-orientated pricing, despite its more demanding requirements for the LTO manager, offers greater potential as far as increasing revenue and profitability are concerned.

USP

Variously called Unique Sales Proposition, Unique Selling Proposition or Unique Selling Point, your USP is what will attract potential customers and enable you to charge more. To ensure this, your USP really must be unique, providing something that other providers do not, cannot, or will not offer. You also have to be careful to ensure that the USP is not so subtle or trivial that customers will not actually notice it. For ELT providers, identifying and providing a USP is problematic, as illustrated in Figure 4.14 from the websites of two quality LTOs on different sides of the world. Some LTOs have clearly devoted a great deal of expertise and resources to defining and promoting their USP, and you can decide for yourself what this is and how effectively it is presented by visiting the websites of such schools as:

- EF International Language Schools
- Language Systems International
- Accurate English
- Langports.

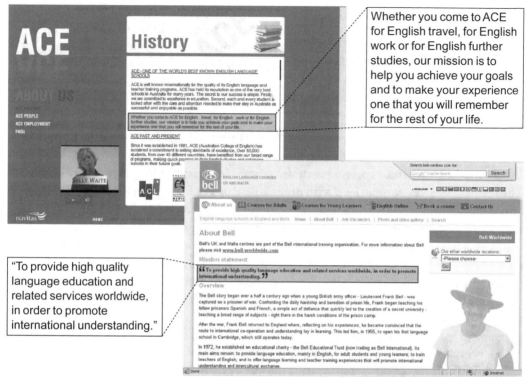

> Whether you come to ACE for English travel, for English work or for English further studies, our mission is to help you achieve your goals and to make your experience one that you will remember for the rest of your life.

> "To provide high quality language education and related services worldwide, in order to promote international understanding."

FIGURE 4.14: *LTO USPs*

TASK

Pricing is important, as it can make the difference between success and failure in selling a product, and making a profit.

- What is the basis for pricing in your LTO? In fact, pricing policy may have been decided by a manager who is no longer on the staff. How significant is pricing in relation to profitability?
- What is the going rate for similar services among your competitors? Virtually all LTOs have published prices (sometimes called the 'rack rate'), so it is relatively easy to establish the going rate for comparable courses. Discount rates and special deals are, of course, not made public, but by using a combination of taking note of local gossip and doing some 'mystery shopping' (see Vignette 4.4, p. 108), it is possible to gain an idea of what discounts competitors are offering.
- What benefits are your customers prepared to pay for? How is this reflected in (a) your offer, and (b) market-orientated pricing policy? Benefits could include airport pick-up, job placement, educational counselling and so on.
- What is your USP? How is this reflected in your pricing policy?
- What evidence do you have that your customers (a) are attracted by your USP, and (b) are happy to pay for it?

Promotion

Once you have products to sell, you have to promote them through two means: personal and non-personal. These are summarized in Figure 4.15 and discussed below.

Personal selling	personal (face-to-face, telephone, or Internet chat) presentation for the purpose of making sales and building relationships
Advertising	any form of non-personal presentation and promotion of your services through mass media such as newspapers, magazines, television or radio
Sales promotion	activity intended to boost sales, such as price promotions, loyalty incentives
Publicity and public relations	communicating with various publics in order to influence their perceptions and understanding of your sector or LTO
Trade and educational shows	putting your LTO in front of potential customers or prospects
Direct selling	establishing a direct relationship between your LTO and the final customer via mail, telemarketing, or e-commerce

FIGURE 4.15: *Promotional mix*

Personal selling

The choice of the means of promoting your services will depend on the context in which you operate, the market (on- or offshore) and the size and resources of the LTO. Given the nature of the services offered by an LTO, personal selling is very important. It has the advantage of facilitating lots of communication between the buyer and seller and explaining in detail the services on offer. It also helps build a relationship, which is important if closing the sale is going to take some time. It is, of course, costly, as it requires having a large enough sales force to handle the volume of encounters. The way front-line staff handle enquiries will influence a prospect's perceptions of quality, and this is exemplified in the experience of the mystery shopper in Vignette 4.4 (p. 107).

Cross-selling, which involves selling additional products or services other than those which have already been purchased, is best done through personal selling. In an LTO, teachers as well as designated sales staff can be involved in cross-selling, particularly as teachers have so much direct contact with consumers. Vignette 4.3 (p. 80) illustrates a form of cross-selling in which existing customers were offered the opportunity of continuing their course.

Advertising

Advertising objectives fall into three main categories:
- to inform, e.g. tell customers about a new product or service
- to persuade, e.g. encourage customers to switch to your LTO
- to remind, e.g. remind buyers where to find your services.

When planning any form of advertising, it is important to keep these three objectives in mind, as you need to be clear about why you are advertising as well as about what you are advertising. To be effective, advertising must be:

- meaningful. Customers should find the message relevant, which means that different messages may be needed for different customer segments, and if you are recruiting in offshore markets, this will usually mean advertising in the local language, and communicating both content and style in culturally appropriate ways.
- distinctive. It must capture the customer's attention. Highlighting your LTO's USP is important.
- believable. This is a difficult task, but one which is helped if claims are not exaggerated, and tangible evidence, such as credible testimonials, examination pass rates, etc., is provided. Again, cultural appropriacy is important. This is where a local agent and local knowledge can be critical.

The credibility of your advertising is also of concern to accreditation agencies. For example, Accreditation UK lists, among its criteria for both electronic and printed publicity, that it must be clear and accessible to non-native speakers, and it must be accurate with regard to premises, courses, costs, level of care, accommodation, leisure programme and teacher qualifications. Failure to meet these criteria is treated seriously.

The choice of medium will depend on resources and your target market. Increasingly, the Internet is the medium of choice, but, given the variation in Internet usage globally, it cannot be regarded as a universal form of advertising. For example, the Middle East has only 10% Internet penetration, while in Asia, such countries as South Korea, Singapore and Japan have very high rates of penetration (Internet World Stats, 2007).

Virtually all material produced and used by an LTO can be regarded as having a promotional or advertising function, so to project a professional image of the LTO will involve ensuring that there is a consistent style and standard for everything, including hand-outs. In the case study on p. 95, the students often finished the course with 'a flotsam of photocopies', which considerably detracts from any claims to professionalism and quality which the LTO may make. So, there needs to be internal quality control of such material to ensure that it fully represents the quality of the organization when it is seen by potential customers.

Like virtually all other activities in an LTO , advertising operates in cycles, with lead times and deadlines. The advertising year needs to be mapped onto the LTO year so that advertising is distributed in a timely manner so as to maximize its impact. A Gantt chart is a useful tool for plotting the advertising year together with other activities so that managers have an overview of all sequenced and timed activities (see Chapter 10, p. 261).

Sales promotion

Sales promotions through discounts and special offers have a useful place in the LTO's marketing strategy to help iron out seasonal fluctuations, to build volume if there is a recruitment shortfall or to establish a presence in a new market. Such seasonal discounts are widely used in the travel and hospitality industries for the same purpose, but they need to be used carefully in our sector because our customers spend a lot of time together and are in a good position to compare the cost of their course.

Encouraging repeat business is important and can be achieved through reward, discount and loyalty schemes. Again, these need to be carefully managed, as such schemes represent a cost to the organization. It is also important to avoid having discounted students supplanting full-fee students, thus reducing profitability.

Publicity, PR, trade and educational shows

Although LTOs differ widely in their size and status, even a small LTO may occupy a significant place in the local community by employing local people and using local suppliers. In Chapter 8, p. 204, we consider the roles of the head of an LTO, which include being accountable to the governing body, educational authorities, accreditation agency, government (the executive officer role), articulating the mission of the school (diplomat) and undertaking public relations with stakeholder communities and external bodies (publicist). All of these involve managing publicity and public relations.

Although few LTOs will have the resources to devote to maintaining extensive public relations and profile, it is important to perform the diplomat and publicist roles through:

- membership in local and national associations and lobby groups
- involvement in local civic initiatives (including local sponsorship)
- participation in trade and professional events and conferences
- ensuring that good news about your LTO is made available to the local media
- being well prepared to address the media and provide reassurance in the event of a crisis.

There are various channels available to promote public relations, and these can be used according to context, resources and purpose:

Media relations	Developing interesting story angles directed at the media. Using press kits and audio or video news releases.
Media tours	An LTO representative travelling to key locations to introduce a new product by being present on TV and radio talk shows and conducting interviews with print and Internet reporters and bloggers.
Newsletters	Contacting existing, past and potential customers, by either regular mail or electronic means. Newsletters provide content of interest to customers as well as information on products and promotions.
Special events	A wide range of events. Those that are linked with achievement, or an anniversary such as 50 years in business, can be used to target key participants.
Speaking engagements	Speaking at industry or professional conventions, trade association meetings, and other groups provides an opportunity for LTO members to demonstrate their expertise to potential clients/customers. These occasions are not explicitly for LTO or

product promotion, but are an opportunity to talk on a topic of interest to potential customers and to highlight the speaker's expertise.

Sponsorships   Building goodwill and LTO recognition by associating with an event or group.

Employee communications   Using Intranet, email, online and print newsletters, often in collaboration with HRM, to update employees with developments and opportunities.

Community relations and philanthropy   Building strong relationships with the local community through supporting local organizations and institutions, conducting workshops (e.g. for teachers, parents), donating products or services for community events and charitable fundraisers and demonstrating public benefit of the LTO.

It is particularly important to be able to represent your sector's interests in public forums and to promote a responsible, professional image. Given the propensity of authorities to regulate, being able to have a voice is vital, and this is usually best achieved through active membership of an organization which can represent your interests, such as English UK or English Australia. Maintaining an active and respected professional profile is also important, which is why staff development and conference participation have such a significant role. An LTO with an active, dynamic staff who are demonstrating their competence and expertise through their conference participation will have valuable public relations effects among fellow professionals who are, potentially, sources of recommendation for future customers, as well as potential recruits as employees.

Case study: ELS

From 1999 to 2003, New Zealand's previously small international education sector, in terms of enrolments of foreign fee-paying students, experienced rapid growth. Enrolment numbers rose by 318% over the five-year period to nearly 119,000, with an estimated economic value of NZ$2.2 billion to the New Zealand economy. English language schools (ELS) accounted for around half of this growth, peaking at nearly NZ$2.5 million in 2002 and 2003, but declining to NZ$0.9 million in 2006. The 'boom and bust' character of the ELS sector meant that from time to time there were some high profile failures, and in 2004, a non-accredited ELS went out of business, with a consequent loss of fees and income for students and staff.

A representative of ELS teachers appeared on the national TV news to comment on this closure, which had been widely reported in the national press. Dressed in a T-shirt, he looked as if he had strayed from the beach into the TV studio. To some viewers, his sartorial style tended to confirm the opinion that, whatever its aspirations to professional standing, the ELS sector was not to be regarded too seriously and such closures were only to be expected.

The importance of good public relations is nowhere demonstrated more significantly than when things go wrong, as illustrated in the case study opposite. Although there is an argument for avoiding slick presentation and aping a glossy corporate image, the semiotics of clothing can overpower the communicative content and intent.

Place

The case study on p. 95 demonstrated that convenient location was an important consideration for potential clients, confirming findings of surveys carried out in New Zealand (Walker, 2001) and in Spain (Cristobal & Llurda, 2006); see Chapter 5, pp. 113–4. The latter identify a factor which they call 'accessibility', which includes not only location, the appearance and condition of the premises, but also friendly and individualized attention by staff. All these features are part of the servicescape and atmospheric features.

The servicescape provides a preview of what the quality of the LTO's actual service is likely to be, and potential customers will be influenced by such atmospheric features as:
- ambient conditions: temperature, lighting, colour, noise, etc.
- spatial layout, furniture and functionality
- signs, symbols and artefacts
- social surroundings, including the friendliness of customer-facing staff such as receptionists.

The importance of atmospherics in attracting customers is demonstrated in Vignette 4.4, in which Silvina, as a 'mystery shopper' in the guise of a potential customer, reports on visits to some LTOs.

Vignette 4.4: Mystery shopper

LTO A: A very old-fashioned building, huge but a bit forbidding; the reception area is not welcoming at all as you go up some steps, meet a porter who ushers you somewhere else, which actually looks like an office in full swing with everybody too busy to deal with a direct sale. The receptionist did not seem to know her products as I tried to ask her how my niece would choose among city centre schools, as I explained we could not tell the difference. She went on to say, 'Well, it is up to you . . .' Nice cafeteria facing the main street, so quite light-filled, with six PCs as well.

LTO B: A rather shabby building but quite full of cheerful-looking students. The classrooms were all quite basic, just desks, chairs and a whiteboard (no appliances visible in classroom). Either doors were open while classes were taking place, or there was a glass classroom door, so that all classrooms were visible. A very rudimentary library with basically nothing in it, and six online PCs. The place is divided into two buildings: one for reception, cafeteria, library and common room, and the other for classrooms only. The receptionist was very pleasant, a native speaker in her mid-20s, very helpful and keen to show me the premises and explain how things worked at her organization: social programme, the library, the city.

> ### *TASK*
>
> If you can, ask a friend to do a 'mystery shopper' exercise, in which she or he visits several LTOs, including your own, and compares them on features of their servicescape and atmospherics from the viewpoint of a potential customer. You could also involve colleagues in mystery shopping at the competition.
> - What are the results of the survey?
> - What improvements may be needed in your servicescape?
>
> A parallel exercise can be done with your website, if your LTO has one. Provide some scenarios to friends or colleagues, have them log onto the site in the role indicated in the scenario, and have them report back on how easy it was to navigate the site and find the information specified in the scenario.

People

It is very clear that in teaching and in service provision, people make a crucial difference. Kotler (1997) argues that service providers can gain a strong competitive advantage by hiring and training their employees better than their competitors do. The better-trained personnel will, according to Kotler, exhibit six characteristics:
- competence: employees possess the required skill and knowledge
- courtesy: employees are friendly, respectful and considerate
- credibility: employees are trustworthy
- reliability: employees perform the service consistently and accurately
- responsiveness: employees respond quickly to customers' requests and problems
- communication: employees make an effort to understand the customer and communicate clearly.

The importance of some of these characteristics for the customer has already been demonstrated in Vignette 4.4, while Chapter 3 has discussed the role of recruitment, induction and training in ensuring that staff have the capabilities and the motivation to meet customers' expectations.

In selling LTO services, it is very useful if the sales personnel actually have experience of language teaching, or, if they do not, to be given the opportunity of shadowing teaching staff to gain an understanding of what their work and the service involve. (Likewise, it is a good idea to have teaching staff shadow sales and other front-line staff.) It is also vital that the LTO sales staff:
- know what they are selling, particularly the benefits to the customer
- know what competitors are selling and how their products compare
- understand the customers' concerns and, if they are selling to corporate clients, the nature of their business.

The combination of knowledge, skills and attributes of a good ELT salesperson is summed up in Figure 4.16 (White et al, 1991).

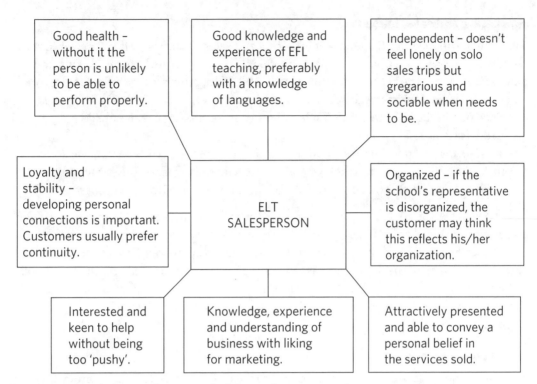

FIGURE 4.16: *The ELT salesperson* (White et al, 1991, p. 222)

Processes

Processes are discussed more fully in Chapter 5, p. 146, which describes EFL service system blueprinting. This involves detailing the various stages of the provision of a service. The blueprint divides activities into 'frontstage' and 'backstage': customers are aware of the frontstage activities since these are involved in their interactions with the service provider. Behind the service provider are the backstage and support activities, and beyond these, management activities.

TASK

Consider the steps involved in making a sale in your LTO.
- List each step in the process, and who is responsible for each step.
- Consider what the customer is expecting as an outcome to each step.
- List what is required in terms of skills and resources for the successful accomplishment of each step.
- Are there any gaps in the existing process? If so, what needs to be done to rectify them?

Marketing and sales budgeting

How much should an LTO spend on marketing and sales? There is no firm answer to this, though 3–5% of sales is a ball-park percentage. So, if sales = €100K, the marketing and sales budget would be between €3,000 and €5,000. Fixing the budget as a percentage of sales is one of the four methods of setting the budget:

- fixed percentage of sales: which sales, past or future? (assumes sales are directly linked to advertising)
- same level as competitors: difficult to estimate, assumes there is a sector average
- task: difficult to do, but the most effective as it is linked to marketing strategy
- residual: what the LTO can afford (there is no connection with marketing strategy).

In principle, the advertising budget should be linked to marketing objectives. So if, for instance, the objective is to increase sales by X% for Course Y in the coming year, the budget can be set according to the amount of advertising spend required to reach both the target consumer and the target increase in sales. So, the solution to calculating how much to devote to sales budgeting is to base it on your marketing plan so that you establish a direct link between what you spend and the effectiveness of the advertising that you pay for.

Monitoring performance

In the previous sections, we have considered a range of marketing and sales procedures. Ultimately, marketing and sales are concerned with achieving targets – volume and profitability – which are part of the annual estimates or budgets for the year ahead, and in the case of strategic planning, over a period of three to five years. Monitoring performance against targets is a vital management activity since it enables corrective action to be taken in time to rectify a shortfall or acquiring extra resources (such as classrooms or teachers) in the event that targets look like being exceeded.

At the operational, day-to-day level, having simple ways of recording performance in such areas as the following is useful:

- website hits
- number of telephone enquiries
- number of drop-in enquiries
- number of responses to coded advertising.

The effectiveness of the advertising can be monitored by, for example, maintaining a tally of the numbers of enquiries received and by asking enquirers to quote the reference code included in the advertisement. Prospects can also be asked how they heard of the LTO by providing a menu of options on the website or on an inquiry or registration form. The sales conversion rate is also important, i.e. the number of enquiries (via different means) which convert to actual sales, as this indicates the value of each channel or mode of advertising.

On a tactical level, the marketing and sales plan will typically set out targets for the year ahead. The targets will usually be expressed in terms of units sold (e.g. student hours or weeks) and income produced. These will be recorded on a database and reported at whatever intervals are regarded as necessary: weekly, monthly or quarterly. To enable managers to monitor performance, the information will usually be presented in a form which enables like-for-like and year-to-date comparisons between the current and the previous year, set against targets for the current year. In advance, management may have agreed trigger points which will activate discounting and other forms of sales promotion in order to build volume in the event of a shortfall, or sales staff may be told to start directing customers to other products if capacity has been reached. Finally, there is another important area which must be monitored: customer satisfaction. This is discussed in more detail in Chapter 5.

MARKETING PLAN

A good marketing plan brings together the various elements we have reviewed in this chapter and it will usually be required as part of the annual planning process. It begins by reviewing your overall strategy, and the business context in which the LTO works. It builds on strengths, compensates for weaknesses, to work out what the strategy should be. The plan also sets clear SMART objectives (see Chapter 10, p. 259) and explains how these will be achieved, and there should be an action plan to ensure that it really does become reality.

The main contents of a marketing plan are:

1 Executive summary
2 Situational analysis
   • Product and market analysis
   • Distribution analysis
   • Competitor analysis
   • Financial analysis
   • Opportunities/Issue analysis – SWOT analysis
3 Marketing strategy and objectives
   • Financial objectives
   • Marketing objectives
4 Tactical marketing programmes. Details and timetables are presented for five key decision areas:
   • Target markets
   • Product
   • Promotion
   • Pricing
   • Distribution
5 Budgeting, performance analysis and implementation. This is the part that will ultimately persuade those who have the power to give final approval. This step consists of three key topics:
   • Marketing budget: presents a clear picture of the financial implications of the plan

- Performance analysis: presents the expected results of the plan including its financial impact
- Implementation schedule: shows timelines and identifies people responsible for performing tasks.

The costed proposal (outlined in Chapter 6, p. 153) and the marketing plan are closely linked, the former being a component of the latter when preparing a full marketing plan. A marketing plan will also be a part of the new product development process outlined in Chapter 8, p. 213.

CONCLUSION

Effective teaching involves understanding the learners: their background, their existing language level, their expectations and motivation, their learning styles and preferences. Marketing involves understanding the same people, but in their roles as customers, consumers and clients. It also involves identifying market segments, and providing services or products which will satisfy the requirements of the customers concerned. Potential customers also have to be informed about and attracted to what the LTO offers, and this involves using appropriate ways of promoting the offer. Engaging in this set of processes will involve all parts of the LTO, which in turn requires co-ordination in the form of a marketing plan. Having converted prospects to customers and consumers, LTO managers face a new challenge: monitoring and maintaining customer satisfaction. This is the subject of the next chapter.

5 Customer service

- BACKGROUND RESEARCH
- CUSTOMERS AND CONSUMERS
- SERVICES
- THE CUSTOMER JOURNEY
- MEASURING PERFORMANCE
- CODES OF PRACTICE
- THE CUSTOMER JOURNEY: POST-PURCHASE
- BLUEPRINTING

INTRODUCTION

This chapter deals with the other side of the coin introduced in Chapter 4. The focus here moves to customers once they have purchased and are using the LTO's services. Although in their professional training teachers are not encouraged to consider themselves as service providers, once they enter the world of the LTO they will find that it is the quality of the service – and particularly the service that they provide in the classroom – which influences customers' satisfaction and which helps to differentiate one LTO from another. Far from deprecating the importance of service, we consider it to be essential for all staff to be aware of their responsibilities as service providers, and to take pride in providing a quality service. Understanding what it is that their clientele wants is, of course, fundamental. What, then, are the customers' expectations of service?

BACKGROUND RESEARCH

The offshore market: New Zealand

Finding an answer to this question has been investigated by John Walker in New Zealand, where LTOs serve a predominantly offshore market, with a nationally diverse clientele. In a focus group-based study, Walker (2001) identified seven broad categories or major issues regarding customers' expectations of TESOL service:
- the ESOL teacher
- English language school milieu
- homestay arrangements
- systems for obtaining client feedback on the service
- servicescape (the settings in which services are provided and where the provider and customer interact)
- effective communication with language school
- procedures for placement in appropriate class/level.

He also analysed the themes that emerged most frequently in four out of five of the focus groups, and he suggested that these could be termed key satisfaction drivers for the participants in the study, which are most likely to influence a customer's decision to recommend a particular LTO (which, in turn, is considered to be a key indicator of customer loyalty in the Net Promoter Score, discussed on p. 133).

- The English language school must be a friendly, comfortable and relaxed place.
- The ESOL teacher should be available to see clients individually outside the classroom.
- The LTO should have effective client feedback systems in place.
- The LTO should communicate effectively and honestly with the client both before and after the client's stay.
- The ESOL teacher should be an effective classroom practitioner.
- The ESOL teacher should be professional.
- The school should be conveniently located.
- There should be access to computers with credible Internet capability.
- The LTO should have good audio/video facilities/equipment.
- Host families should actively encourage and participate in English conversation with the client.

Subsequently, in a large-scale national survey, Walker (2003) compared satisfaction and recommendation predictors, summarized in Figure 5.1 opposite. This shows that there was a correspondence across eight of the nine dimensions. In other words, satisfaction with a service leads to a high likelihood that the customer will recommend the LTO. Walker (2003, p. 300) points out, however, that 'the predictors of satisfaction and recommendation . . . tended to consist of professional skills, organizational issues or management-related aspects associated with effective service' and that 'although teachers were perceived to be friendly, it was not their friendliness but their teaching skills that were most likely to lead to a client recommendation.' This is a very significant finding, as it demonstrates how central good teaching (and teachers) are for achieving high levels of customer satisfaction in any LTO.

The onshore market: Spain

Walker's research focused on the offshore market. What of the onshore market where the customer is already part of the community served by the LTO? In Spain, a typical onshore market, Cristobal & Llurda (2006) investigated the preferences of potential language learners with regard to the different school options available there. Their respondents fell into four groups, ranging from 18 to 35 years of age, 46% of whom were men and 54% were women. The characteristics of the groups, as summarized by the authors, are set out in Figure 5.2 on p. 116.

The last group also stated that one of the reasons they preferred traditional schools, rather than multimedia provision, was that these provide opportunities to meet new people and establish new relationships.

Cristobal & Llurda then identified three factors affecting the characteristics of the 'ideal language school'. These were:

- accessibility, which is related to such factors as location, the appearance and condition of the premises, friendly and individualized attention by staff, and the possibility of making up for unattended sessions

Dimension	Predictors of client satisfaction with LTO service*	Predictors of willingness to recommend LTO*
Teachers	1 availability to help out of class 2 teaching skills	1 teaching skills 2 teacher communication skills
Lessons	1 mix of nationalities in class 2 methods used to teach	1 effectiveness of lessons 2 mix of nationalities in class
Service procedures	1 enquiries procedure 2 placement procedure	1 student feedback procedure 2 complaints procedure
Communication	1 accuracy of information in publicity materials	1 accuracy of information in publicity materials
Administration staff	1 ability to give information 2 communication skills	1 ability to give information 2 friendliness
Homestay	1 opportunity to speak English with host family 2 match between homestay requested and allocated	1 opportunity to speak English with host family 2 match between homestay requested and allocated
Facilities	1 classrooms 2 self-access unit	1 classrooms 2 self-access unit
Activities programme	1 organization 2 information	1 value for money 2 organization
General	1 overall organization of LTO 2 encouragement to achieve goals	1 value for money of programme 2 encouragement to achieve goals

FIGURE 5.1: *Comparison of client satisfaction predictors and recommendation predictors*
Note: 1 = primary predictor, 2 = secondary predictor

- teaching quality, which is defined by the quality of the teachers and teaching, efficiency in developing written and oral skills, and schedule flexibility
- pragmatism, which is related to the possibility that the school prepares students for an officially recognized certificate. It also includes the prestige enjoyed by the school at both local and national levels, and payment conditions and value for money.

They found that their four groups tended to rank these factors differently when considering the choice of a language school. For instance, for working adults, accessibility was a more significant factor than for university students. Cristobal & Llurda (2006, p. 146) conclude that

... multimedia language schools are perceived in a rather positive way, but are also regarded as falling short of what other options can offer to potential 'customers', especially with regard to 'Teaching quality' and 'Pragmatism', interpreted as a series of attributes ranging from 'flexibility', 'prestige', and 'official certification'.

Groups	Preferences
Working adults with little command of English who need to learn the language	Expectation for high-quality teachers, flexibility of schedules, valued personalized attention and direct teacher contact, main goal to learn to communicate rather than obtain a certificate. Less experience as learners than other groups, but higher expectations.
Working women with little interest in language learning	Lower percentage of previous learners of English. Experienced learners valued most the quality of teaching and flexibility, as well as personalized attention. Preferred traditional schools, but also attached higher value to multimedia systems, for their flexibility, as well as opportunities for oral practice.
Young university students and recent graduates with a good command of English	Expressed need for good oral teaching. Opted for traditional schools, followed by private tutoring and study-abroad stays.
Young professional men, with a good command of English, which they use but are no longer learning	The most critical of previous experiences as language learners. Preferences included traditional language schools, study abroad stays, private tutoring and closer contact with teachers, and a perceived higher speed of language learning over other methodologies.

FIGURE 5.2: *Group preferences*

What these two surveys demonstrate is that there are differences between offshore and onshore markets, as well as between prospective customers (Spain) and actual customers (New Zealand). The latter group were in a position to compare current experience with expectations, and since their customer journey was a more complex one than that envisaged by the Spanish group, they paid more attention to service procedures and communication, with homestay necessarily being significant. There was a consensus across both groups regarding the importance they assigned to a key professional area: effective teaching. The reports also raise a question which was discussed in Chapter 4: Who is the customer?

CUSTOMERS AND CONSUMERS

As we noted in Chapter 4, one party may – and often does – occupy the roles of customer, consumer and client. However, these roles may be distributed among a number of different individuals. Likewise, the role of supplier may be spread across a wide range of parties. In this chapter, we will continue to use 'customer' as an all-purpose term covering all three roles, employing the other terms when it is important to differentiate among roles. For the most part, the focus will be on the external customer: the party who purchases services from the LTO. Initially, though, we will consider internal customers.

Internal customers

Whereas external customers are not actually members of the LTO, the so-called 'internal customer' definitely is. All LTO staff can be viewed as internal customers, supplying and receiving services from each other. The really significant customer–supplier relationship is the one involving employees, who supply their work to the employer in return for payment and other forms of compensation.

Employees need to know what the organization sees as its purpose. In other words, they need to have an understanding of the vision and mission of the organization (see Chapter 2, p. 40) and they need to feel a sense of pride in belonging to it. If they do not entertain such feelings, they may not be effective providers of services to external customers.

There also needs to be a determination to 'do it right the first time'; in other words, all staff need to behave competently in line with the organization's service standards and the customers' expectations.

Finally, in order to be able to manage external customers' expectations, internal customers need to have a good knowledge of the services offered. This means that they need to be kept abreast of new developments and services. Indeed, it is important to involve them in the development of new products, as described in Chapter 8 (p. 213).

Achieving the above involves training, communicating with and motivating staff. Given the centrality of staff to successful service provision, the selection and training of all staff are vital in promoting customer satisfaction. The growing importance of Continuing Professional Development in education is indicative of this trend (see Chapter 8, p. 227), while the case study in Chapter 3 (p. 59) illustrates how a DOS responded to the needs of her internal clientele by improving orientation for new teachers.

Internal marketing is, of course, vital in any process of implementing innovation (see Chapter 9) and, given the ongoing need for LTOs to keep abreast of the market, this aspect of marketing and customer services will remain a significant part of the manager's job.

The idea that there are internal customers in an LTO is quite often regarded as unusual, but once the idea is pursued further, it does make sense. A simple example will illustrate. In many LTOs, teachers are required to carry out administrative procedures which they often find irksome. One of these may be submitting a weekly or monthly timesheet in which their teaching and non-teaching hours are recorded. This timesheet will be submitted to a line manager (or to someone performing such a role), and, if teachers are on an hourly-paid contract, the information on the time sheet is used to calculate their pay. In most LTOs, there is a deadline by which such timesheets must be submitted so that the person responsible for calculating pay – usually a member of the administrative staff – has time to do the requisite calculations, prepare a pay slip, and transfer funds to employees' bank accounts. In this exchange, the teacher (provider) supplies information to the administrator (customer). What the customer wants is accurate information presented in a standardized form, and within the deadline.

Once information has been submitted, the provider–customer relationship changes. Now the administrator becomes the provider, by ensuring that the customer (the staff member) receives an accurate payslip and the correct amount of pay by an agreed date. On both sides of this internal customer relationship, accuracy and conformity to deadlines are mutual expectations. A failure on the part of the initial provider – the staff member – to meet the internal customer's expectations can lead to dissatisfaction by both parties, with each critical of the other. Conversely, overly complicated time sheets and deadlines which do not match the constraints of the teachers' schedules can lead to dissatisfaction and a breakdown in the internal customer relationship. Finding out what each party wants and values is really an exercise in internal marketing, and getting it right (time sheets, pay, deadlines) first time is an aspect of total quality management (TQM) which needs to be part of the organization's vision.

The next task is to get you thinking about the way the organization relates to its internal customers – the members of the LTO who are a permanent part of the organization, and who are connected to each other through a network of customer–provider relationships.

TASK

What are the internal marketing practices found in your own LTO?
- List what your LTO already does.
- Suggest what it could do to improve its internal marketing in the following areas:
  1 marketing to employees
  2 communicating a vision
  3 communicating the importance of getting things right first time
  4 communicating customers' expectations.

SERVICES

ESOL as a service

In Chapter 1, we noted that one of the pressures confronting the LTO manager is the emphasis on service. In some LTOs, a student services manager is responsible for an important part of the service package which students (or their parents) purchase: accommodation, a social programme and excursions. These have long been part of what such LTOs provide, and by extension the complete package, including teaching, is now seen as part of a total service although, as the research summarized earlier shows, students as consumers do distinguish between teaching and other parts of the service provision.

Service defined

What is a service? Jobber (2001, pp. 684–5) makes the point that

> *Pure services cannot be seen, tasted, touched, or smelled before they are bought, that is they are intangible. Rather, a service is a deed, performance, or effort, not an object, device or thing... For some services, their intangibility leads to difficulty in evaluation after consumption... The challenge for the service provider is to use tangible cues to service quality.*

This challenge is one that we will keep returning to as we explore customer service management in the context of the LTO.

Characteristics of a service

There are four characteristics which are of particular relevance for LTOs.

Intangibility

One of the great problems for the LTO is that it is difficult enough to provide tangible evidence of service provision (notably teaching) let alone the outcomes (learning) in ways that are meaningful to the customer and consumer. The attempt to solve this problem has led to ever more graphic recruitment literature and the use of video as well as sample classes to inform and persuade customers during the pre-purchase phase (see Figure 5.4, p. 123). It has also led to ways of eliciting customers' views and feelings, and of trying to see things from their viewpoint, some of which will be covered in later sections.

Inseparability

This refers to the simultaneous production and consumption of the service, this being a salient feature of language teaching, as well as most of the other services offered by an LTO. The service provider is a very important part of the process, being an integral part of the satisfaction obtained by the consumer. This means that effectively selecting, training and rewarding staff in the front line are essential to achieving high standards of service quality.

To complicate matters, the consumption of the service in an LTO typically takes place in the presence of other consumers (the exception being 1:1 instruction). Consequently, enjoyment of the service is dependent not only on the service itself, but also on other consumers, so it becomes important to make provision for avoiding inter-customer conflict.

Variability/heterogeneity

Service quality may be subject to considerable variability (or heterogeneity), making standardization difficult. The potential for such variability again underlines the importance of rigorous selection, training and rewarding of staff, while evaluation systems should be developed to provide customer feedback on their experience of both the service and the staff. One way organizations attempt to deal with variability is through the use of technology, particularly computer-based, although there are limits to how far this can be taken in the services provided by an LTO. However, developments in computer-based instruction are such that blended learning solutions will certainly evolve as a way of customizing services to the wants and needs of diverse customers.

Perishability and fluctuating demand

Unlike tangible products, the consumption of a service cannot be stored for the future. In other words, it is perishable. This means that it is important to match supply and demand for a service. For many LTOs, variability in demand, either during the day, or throughout the year, is typically a problem, giving rise to the employment of part-time hourly-paid staff, differential pricing and even the renting of extra classroom space during peak periods. The application of new and emerging technologies may help to store some aspects of language teaching services, but, ultimately, it is impossible to store scheduled lessons. If a class is run at below capacity, the empty places – and income – are lost.

It is suggested that in doing the next task you involve your colleagues, as they are very likely to be involved in providing services with which you have little or no contact, yet from the customer's viewpoint, they are a significant part of the total service 'package'.

> ## TASK
>
> What are the services provided by your LTO? Be exhaustive in making the list. It may help to think of the journey the customer makes (to be discussed further on p. 122), from initial contact to departure, and to list the various services which occur at each stage.
> - Has your LTO found ways of overcoming the inherent constraints brought about by the characteristics of these services? For instance, is there any way of avoiding (or at least reducing) the perishability of language lessons? Or the intangibility of other services that the LTO offers?
> - Which of these services are evaluated by the LTO?
> - On the basis of such evaluation, how is the LTO's performance rated by consumers?
> - Which aspects of the service are regarded as especially important by consumers?

Range of LTO services

When you considered the services offered by your LTO, you may have been surprised at how many there were. In fact, LTO services extend well beyond the teaching–learning acts which take place in the classroom. After all, LTOs provides not only language instruction, but also such services as:
- social contacts
- recreational opportunities
- catering
- cultural experience, information

- access to knowledge resources
- development of desired competencies
- preparation for assessment leading to credentials
- gateway to next step in a career path and potential leadership in chosen career
- access to participation in the global world of business, tourism, popular culture.

The importance which consumers attach to these services will depend on the context and on their significance as far as their needs, wants and aspirations are concerned. For example, in an LTO operating in a society with constraints on social contacts outside prescribed, strictly segregated situations, customer feedback at the women-only branch of an LTO revealed that the coffee bar was very important for them, as it was an acceptable venue for socializing with other women outside their existing social circle. However, the quality of performance of existing provision was not highly rated. This information was used by LTO management to align it more closely with their customers' expectations of the servicescape.

In evaluating the LTO's services, there will be some variation depending on context and circumstances. For example, student registration conventionally takes place at fixed locations and times, so it is perishable. It is a largely intangible process, though with some tangible aspects, notably the documents which have to be completed, the payment which is required, and the paper record of the transaction which is provided to the customer. There will also be other aspects which involve some measure of tangibility, such as placement tests and results. The process as a whole will be characterized by high inseparability in that the provision and consumption of registration usually take place simultaneously.

Student registration is a highly standardized procedure, any variation being related to the range of products or services being purchased (i.e. choice), and the level and placement of individual students. Although registration is highly perishable, there are ways of reducing such perishability by setting up online registration, which, if it includes a placement test, can be carried out at the convenience of customers. (Online teaching is also a way of mitigating the perishability inherent in timetabled lessons.) Another way of reducing perishability is to offer continuous enrolment (which usually means weekly rather than daily registration). From the customer's viewpoint, it will tend to be the intangible aspects of registration which will be important: convenience, clarity, efficiency, courtesy and friendliness will probably be highly-rated intangibles.

Quality

All LTOs offer quality services – or at least that is what most claim. In some countries, in order to operate legally, LTOs have to belong to an accreditation scheme which provides an assurance that the services offered meet the quality standards of the scheme (see p. 136). However, successfully meeting the requirements of a code of practice does not differentiate among the LTOs which have actually met such requirements, since all are accredited and have therefore succeeded in passing a common quality threshold. Differentiation will require applying a further set of standards informed by the principles of Total Quality Management (TQM), which underpin George Pickering's adaptation of the quality framework of the European Foundation for Quality Management (Pickering, 1999b, p. 8) in Figure 5.3.

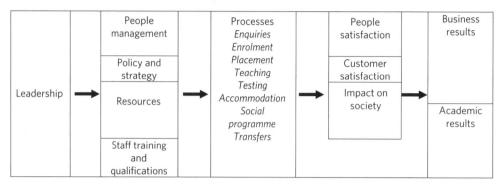

FIGURE 5.3: *The Revised Quality Model* (Pickering, 1999b, p. 8)

In Pickering's model, quality is an attribute of the entire system, which is

> *... based on the idea that Customer Satisfaction, People (Staff) Satisfaction, and Impact on Society are achieved through Leadership driving Policy and Strategy, People Management, Resources and Processes, leading ultimately to excellence in Business Results.* (Pickering, 1999b, p. 7)

Influenced by these principles, we believe in the importance of looking at services from the customers' viewpoint, and of crossing silo boundaries by involving everyone in the LTO in finding ways to develop and improve services so as to provide what the customers tell us they want and like. We also believe that it is important to measure performance and the improvements which we make, as it is by doing so that we can see whether our efforts to achieve quality have been fruitful. Finally, both experience and the principles of TQM demonstrate that this is a continuous, incremental process because, of course, how customers define quality is a constantly moving target, ever changing as they proceed through their customer journey.

THE CUSTOMER JOURNEY

The customer buying cycle

When customers begin their experience of your LTO, they are starting on a journey, and customer journey mapping (CJM) is a way of visualizing how customers interact with and relate to your LTO at each stage of the customer buying cycle (Figure 5.4). CJM considers both the functional and emotional needs of the customer, and plots the interactions that occur and the feelings aroused at each 'touchpoint', that is, any communication, human contact or physical interaction with the LTO.

The customer's journey may begin with a need or desire to buy your LTO's services, and it continues to the point when they purchase and consume the service. The journey may even continue after purchase and consumption and, indeed, given the importance of good word-of-mouth publicity from satisfied customers/consumers, an LTO will try to develop good customer relations after customers have gone. The journey involves a buying cycle, consisting of three main phases and summarized in Figure 5.4.

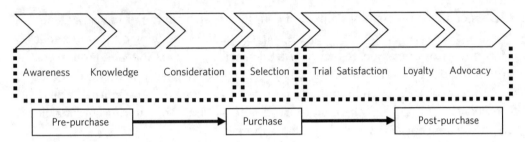

FIGURE 5.4: *Customer buying cycle*

Any occasion when a customer comes into contact with the LTO is an opportunity to form an impression which, famously, Jan Carlzon (1989), president of Scandinavian Airlines in the 1980s, called 'moments of truth'. These occur in the contact between customers and customer-facing staff, as depicted at the top of the inverted organigram (see Chapter 2, Figure 2.3, p. 28).

Some examples of moments of truth in the airline business are:
- phoning or going online to make a flight reservation
- arriving at the airport
- going inside and checking in
- being greeted at the gate
- being taken care of by the flight attendants onboard the aircraft
- being greeted at your destination.

All of these moments of truth involve front-line staff of the airline. Some touchpoints will not involve people, however, as increasingly the customer's first contact will be through a website, and a great deal of expertise and attention is now given to ensuring that websites are effective touchpoints. In an LTO, as in an airline, the customer's journey will involve a number of different people, departments and functions.

Each touchpoint, or moment of truth, is also a voting point, that is, a point at which the customer may pause to consider whether they are delighted, satisfied or dissatisfied with their experience. At this point the customer will 'vote' whether to continue or to leave. This is, in Carlzon's terms, a key 'moment of truth', and if it is a good moment of truth they may vote to stay, but if it is a bad one, they may leave – and a customer is lost.

TASK

When purchasing the services of an LTO, the customer buying cycle will vary in extent and complexity depending on whether your LTO is serving an onshore or an offshore market. In the former, the customers live or work locally, and may simply walk in off the street. In the latter, the customers may live many thousands of miles away, and have to be brought on shore to your LTO through a complex network involving many different parties and services.

Depending on the market context of your LTO, map a customer journey, using the table below. Cover the first four steps in the customer buying cycle: Awareness, Knowledge, Consideration, Selection. As these will involve people and processes in different 'silos', consult with colleagues in these other departments. This is a good opportunity to work together with them to gain an overview of the journey. You may also find it useful to break the journey down into a number of sub-journeys, particularly if you are concerned with an offshore market.

If, for instance, you are considering the Awareness and Knowledge stages, and one of the touchpoints is your website, you need to consider what the customers' needs and wants are when making both an initial and repeat visits to the site. If the site is not a 'hot spot', they may vote by leaving and not returning. Likewise, if they walk in off the street, reception is a touchpoint which should provide an opportunity to create a favourable impression as far as both the physical servicescape, as well as the friendliness, helpfulness and competence of reception staff are concerned.

Journey Step(s)	Touchpoint(s)	Moment(s) of Truth (MOT)	Ways of improving these MOTs
Awareness			
Knowledge			
Consideration			
Selection			

Pre-purchase and purchase phases

Documentation

An important channel via which an LTO and its customers – both internal and external – communicate is printed documentation. Successive stages of the customer journey will require different documentation, some of it to inform the customer, some of it to elicit information from the customer as input to managing the services, some of it to keep in touch after they have consumed the service:

- pre-course: enrolment forms, registration procedures, pre-course information
- during the course: arrival information, inductions, charters, complaints procedure, feedback questionnaires
- post-course: exit survey, follow-up information, new offers and opportunities, newsletters.

Much of this documentation will be produced and used by different individuals or sections in the LTO, so there is the possibility of duplication of effort and information, which can be irksome for customers. Furthermore, the use of computerized databases makes such duplication wasteful and inefficient.

Some documentation will be one-way, from LTO to potential customer, while much will be two-way, involving a response from the customer to the LTO. In an onshore market, documentation will usually be in the customer's native language, whereas in an offshore market, documentation may be in a mixture of languages: English and the customer's own language. Producing multilingual versions of documentation is costly, so LTO practice will depend on the significance of the markets concerned.

TASK

As with many other activities, this is best done as a team with members from the relevant departments or sections of the LTO. Depending on the size and complexity of the LTO, completing this Task is likely to take several hours.

- Assemble all of the documentation which is sent to or received from customers.
- Sort each document into the step in the customer journey to which it belongs: pre-, during, and post-purchase.
- Complete the tables in Figure 5.5 on p. 126. One table is for documents which go from the LTO to the customer, the other for documents from customer to LTO.

Note that it is a good idea to have specific names for each document so that everyone in the LTO knows what is being referred to. It is also important to be clear about the purpose of each document, and what the reader's requirements are. Finally, actual experience of using documents will have revealed how successful they are in achieving their purpose, and in what ways they may need modifying to improve them. Evaluation may also reveal that some documents are redundant, or that they could be merged. Reference to accreditation scheme criteria will also serve as a reminder that publicity material, for example, should reflect clearly the reality of the services that students receive, is accurate in information provided and does not omit key information, especially to do with the cost of services, what is and is not included, maximum group size and so on.

From LTO to Customer

Title of document	Source	Reader	Content	Purpose	Customer's requirements	Evaluation in use
General course brochure	Sales	Potential customer Agent	Course offerings	To inform customer about services, availability and prices To achieve a sale	To obtain sufficient information to make comparisons and choice	Options not clear Large quantity of enquiries to clarify choices

From Customer to LTO

Title of document	Source	Reader	Content	Purpose	LTO's requirements	Evaluation in use
Registration form	Customer	Customer sales administrator	Specification of customer's details and choices	To inform the LTO about the customer, their preferred purchase and other personal requirements	To obtain sufficient information to reserve a place and initiate other downstream actions	High percentage of confusing choices made by customers, requiring follow-up to clarify

FIGURE 5.5: *LTO Documentation*

The outcome of such a document evaluation process should be action points for those responsible for particular documents. Doing an annual document audit is a valuable exercise. Nothing is more important in caring for customers than ensuring that there is good two-way communication, and such annual reviews are a way of fixing flaws and contributing to customer satisfaction at the very start of their journey.

Post-purchase phase

Customer satisfaction

With the move from prospective customer to consumer, the customer begins to make use of the services provided by the LTO. It is during this phase that the customer becomes an invaluable source of information, provided that their views are sought and obtained at opportune moments. It is now virtually the norm to use exit or departure surveys, and while these can provide useful information for LTO managers, essentially they are summative, since nothing can actually be done to repair or improve service for the departing customer, the only potential beneficiaries being their successors. It makes sense, therefore, to use two types of survey:

- formative: in-course
- summative: exit or end-of-course.

The relationship between the two is shown in Figure 5.6. Formative, in-course surveys can be questionnaire-based, provided the surveys are quickly analysed and results made available to relevant staff so that action can be taken in a timely manner. Both types of survey set out to identify gaps in performance compared with customers' expectations.

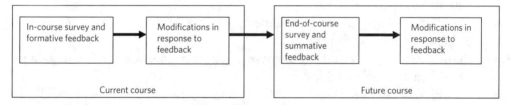

FIGURE 5.6: *Formative and summative feedback*

Parasuraman et al (1991, p. 42) have shown that customers have two levels of expectation:

- adequate: what they find acceptable
- desired: what they hope to receive.

The distance between the two is known as the 'zone of tolerance' (see Figure 5.7, p. 128). In addition, there is also a potential gap between what customers expect, and their perception of what they actually experience as consumers. This is summarized in Figure 5.8 on p. 129. Consumer expectations are influenced by previous experience (as noted, for instance, in the research by Cristobal & Llurda), word-of-mouth recommendation by previous customers (a very powerful influence), and their own needs and wants. These expectations provide a kind of template against which the perceived quality of service is measured. Where the experience falls short of expectation, there is a gap.

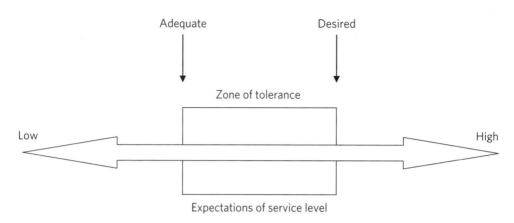

FIGURE 5.7: *The zone of tolerance* (Parasuraman et al, 1991)

Such gaps typically occur at those points in the service that give rise to moments of truth. As Walker (1997) points out,

> *Gaps in the EFL service provision may be responsible for the creation of dissatisfaction among student customers with consequent negative implications for repeat business and word-of-mouth recommendations. Such gaps might be found, for example, in the enrolment procedure or in the internal interaction between support staff and front-line providers.* (Walker, 1997, p. 22)

The 'Gaps' model (Lake & Hickey, 2002, p. 152, adapted from Zeithaml et al, 1988) shows where these gaps can occur:

Gap 1: the difference between customer expectations as consumer and management perceptions of these expectations

Gap 2: the difference between management perceptions of consumer expectations and service quality specifications

Gap 3: the difference between service quality specifications and the service actually provided

Gap 4: the difference between the provision of the service and what is communicated about the service to consumers

Gap 5: the difference between consumer expectations of the service and perception of the service as provided.

In terms of the customer journey, the first indication of a gap between customers' expectations and management perceptions will occur in the pre-purchase phase in communication between LTO and customer. As Walker's research (2001) revealed, there is an expectation among LTO customers that the LTO should communicate effectively and honestly with them before, during and after their stay. A failure to meet these expectations can result in a negative vote on the part of the potential customer.

The following sections consider how to survey customers' expectations and perceptions as a way of avoiding gaps at fail points in their journey, and on p. 147, a service blueprint as the basis for setting up an effective LTO-wide service system is outlined.

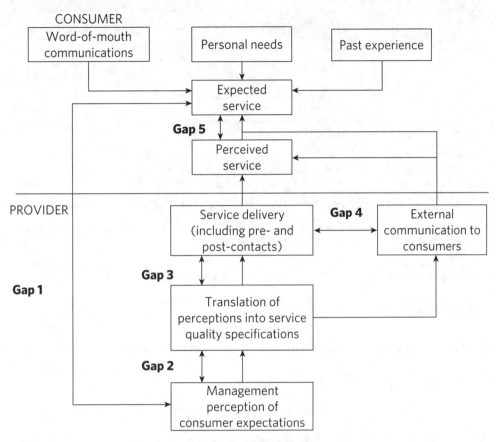

FIGURE 5.8: *The 'Gaps' model* (Lake & Hickey, 2002)

MEASURING PERFORMANCE

Given the intangible nature of most of the services offered by an LTO, and the subjective nature of evaluation, measuring performance is difficult. As LTO services are relatively costly and may involve high stakes for the consumer, LTOs are increasingly treating feedback very seriously, while accreditation schemes also usually require evidence of such customer feedback systems. Although the intention is admirable, the execution is not always as effective as it could be.

To be useful, a questionnaire must not only provide the customer with a way of indicating their satisfaction; it must also give information which provides the basis for action. Unfortunately, the LTO world is full of examples of questionnaires which may fail on both counts, as the example of an exit questionnaire in Figure 5.9 on p. 130 demonstrates.

Although qualitative data, as obtained from interviews and focus groups, can provide extremely useful information for managing customer services, much of the information elicited by this particular questionnaire is of minimal value because it is low on quality and is very difficult to quantify. To be useful, information must be standardized so that, over time, trends can be revealed through analysis and displayed in charts.

1	What are you going to do after you finish your English course?
2	Are you doing another course after this course? If yes, what is the name of the course?
3	Are you happy with classrooms and facilities? If no, why not?
4	Are you happy with the library? If not, why not?
5	What do you think about the Independent Learning Centre? Was it useful for you?
6	Are you happy with the Language Laboratory? How often did you use it?
7	Were you happy with your course? If no, why not?
8	Is there anything you would like to change in the way the teachers teach you?
9	Are you happy with your teachers? If no, why not?
10	Did you get enough out of your course for the time you were here? If not, why not?
11	Is there anything we should change to make it better?

FIGURE 5.9: *Customer satisfaction questionnaire*

Expectation/performance

The gap between expectation and experience is usually identified using a client satisfaction rating scale, such as the one used by Walker (2003, p. 295) in his national survey referred to on p. 114.

Rating	Scale designation	Indication	Interpretation
1	Far worse than I expected	Strong dissatisfaction	Disappointment
2	Worse than I expected	Dissatisfaction	Disappointment
3	About what I expected	Satisfaction	Mere satisfaction
4	Better than I expected	Strong satisfaction	Delight
5	Far better than I expected	Very strong satisfaction	Delight

FIGURE 5.10: *Client satisfaction rating scale*

The analysis of questionnaires using such a scale for key satisfaction drivers can be displayed in a graph from which significant trends can be identified. The graph opposite (Figure 5.11) illustrates the output from such a survey based on scores from the two extreme points of the scale in Figure 5.10. On the basis of such data, the management of the LTO could then identify areas which needed attention and those which did not.

Where the strong dissatisfaction score exceeds the strong satisfaction score, as in value for money and nationality quota, LTO management would need to give some attention to these areas. Where, however, satisfaction levels exceed dissatisfaction scores, as in the social programme and excursions, there would probably be no need to put even more resources into that aspect of the service. Fortunately for the LTO, key areas of the service – notably teaching, study facilities and friendliness of staff – have very high satisfaction scores, indicating that management and staff actually delighted their customers. Such positive feedback motivates continued effort in these areas, and acts as a morale boost for staff – provided the information is communicated to them.

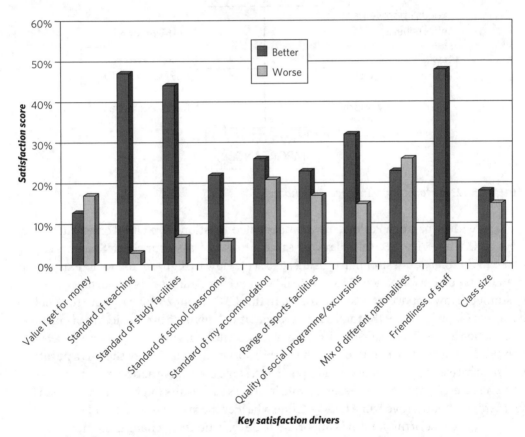

FIGURE 5.11: *Survey output*

Performance/Importance (PI) surveys

This is a type of survey which can be used to answer two questions:
- How well has a given service been performed?
- How important is this for each customer? (This enables customers to tell you what they really value; in short, how they define quality.)

Although PI surveys can take more than one form, they consist of at least three main elements:
- area or point to be evaluated
- 5-point scale: for 'Importance'
- 5-point scale: for 'Performance'.

By combining measures of importance with the performance scores for each question, a PI matrix will highlight the most significant areas for performance improvement as far as the customer is concerned.

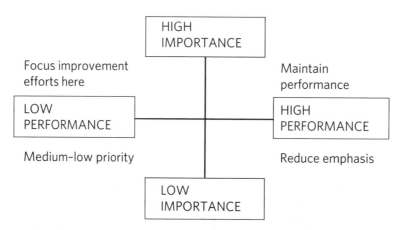

FIGURE 5.12: *Performance/Importance matrix*

Figure 5.13 is part of a Performance/Importance questionnaire based on one used in a large LTO, while Figure 5.14 displays the same information as a bar chart. Students are asked to complete a questionnaire, using a 1–5 scale (low to high) to rate various aspects of their course on performance ('How well did we perform?') and on its importance to the customer ('How important is this to you?'). In this LTO, about 250 surveys are routinely collected (approx 22% of the total student population), giving a broad picture of customer satisfaction levels. The academic director analyses the data, which, together with a brief commentary, is then distributed to staff for appropriate action. Where there is a negative variance between performance and importance, some corrective action may be necessary. In some cases, no action is necessary, while in others the results might indicate a need for further investigation over time to determine whether there is a general trend.

In any exercise of this kind, it is important to be realistic about changes or improvements that can be made. For example, the location of an LTO is not something that can be easily changed, although the effects of inconvenient location might be mitigated by offering a benefit, such as subsidized parking. Areas requiring improvement need to be ranked not only according to their importance, but also in line with feasibility, since some things cannot be improved quickly or even at all. It is important to make this clear to customers, and a response to their efforts in completing a questionnaire indicates that their views are being taken seriously, even if, in some cases, there are constraints in meeting all of their desires.

	Performance	Importance	Variance
Did the course meet your expectations?	3.5	3.7	−0.2
Did you find the course content useful?	3.7	4.2	−0.5
Did you find the coursebook useful?	3.85	4.12	−0.27
Did you find the supplementary materials useful?	3.78	3.81	−0.03
Was the level appropriate?	4.15	4.2	−0.05
Was the pace appropriate?	3.91	4.12	−0.21

FIGURE 5.13 *Performance/Importance questionnaire*

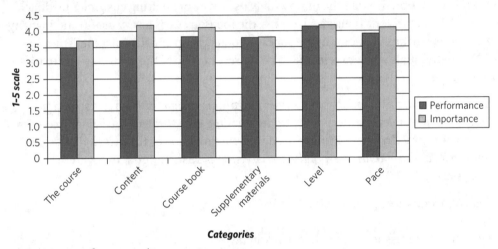

FIGURE 5.14: *Performance/Importance survey*

Net Promoter Score (NPS)

This is a relatively new methodology developed by author Fred Reichheld, Satmetrix Systems, and Bain & Company. It claims to be the best predictor of customer loyalty (and therefore, a good indicator of how effective you have been in not just satisfying, but exceeding customers' expectations). The methodology is simple: customers are asked the question: 'How likely is it that you would recommend (*name of LTO*) to a friend or colleague?'

Customers can be categorized according to their answer to this based on a 0–10 point rating scale with 0 representing the extreme negative and 10 representing the extreme positive end.

- Promoters (those who answer 9 or 10) are loyal enthusiasts who keep buying from the LTO, and encourage their friends to do the same. These are 'advocates' on the relationship ladder (Figure 5.17, p. 143) or the 'zone of loyalty' in the customer loyalty grid (Figure 5.18, p. 143).
- Passives (those who answer 7 or 8) are satisfied but unenthusiastic customers who can be easily wooed by the competition (see 'zone of satisfaction', in Figure 5.18).

- Detractors (those who answer 0–6) are unhappy customers trapped in a bad relationship.

The formula to calculate the NPS is as follows:

$$\text{\% of Promoters} - \text{\% of Detractors} = \text{Net Promoter Score (NPS)}$$

The range of NPS for good companies goes from 50–80%, while a score of around 10% indicates a considerable need for improvement. Since willingness to recommend was so significant in Walker's studies reported on pp. 113–14, NPS could be regarded as a very useful key performance indicator (KPI).

Focus groups

Although questionnaires are the most widely used way of eliciting customer feedback and, from the data, identifying service gaps, the focus group is a very useful and in many ways superior means of obtaining feedback. A focus group consists of a small number (8–12) of individuals who are selected to be representative of the customer group you wish to survey.

> *Focus groups are particularly well suited for gaining insight into what instructional issues are most relevant to students, understanding how students are being affected by a change in practice, or assisting in the development of surveys by identifying issues most relevant to potential respondents.* (Division of Instructional Innovation and Assessment 2007)

Preparing a focus group requires some care, including:
- clarifying the purpose
- identifying the issues you wish to investigate
- writing clear, succinct questions, which avoid bias and take account of the capability of the people in the focus group
- piloting: if possible, test questions on people similar to those who will be in the focus group to make sure that the questions are clear and that the participants will be able to answer them
- choosing a moderator who is familiar with the topics to be covered, and who is good at managing such groups so as to involve all participants.

After the meeting, write a summary that includes findings and interpretations on key issues, themes and sub-themes. The depth and complexity of data analysis will depend on the ultimate purpose of the focus group survey and the resources available. If the purpose is exploratory, a brief analysis and summary of key trends and themes will be sufficient, but if the intention is to gain an in-depth understanding of issues, a much more detailed analysis of transcripts will be required.

Focus group surveys involve more than having a cosy chat with some students (valuable though that may be for other reasons). Nor is it necessary to use focus groups with the same frequency as with exit questionnaires. They are a valuable way of identifying and clarifying issues of concern to customers, and informing strategic planning rather than operational, day-to-day action. Developing the capability within the LTO to use focus groups effectively may involve staff training. Alternatively, an outside consultant can be commissioned to do customer service research using focus groups as part of their methodology. This, in fact, is what happened in the English Language Institute, reported in the case study below.

Case study: ELI

The English Language Institute (ELI) operates with a large amount of autonomy in a large college, which has a stated mission to develop the skills and improve the life of its students. The director of the ELI, encouraged by the senior management of the college, has a strategic plan to increase student volume substantially, with 50% of ELI students proceeding to regular courses in the college. Currently, customer satisfaction is surveyed by means of Student Feedback forms and 'Have Your Say' forms. Although such feedback is useful for routine operations, to inform their strategic planning, the ELI commissioned an outside consultancy to do more extensive and in-depth research, which was done through focus groups, and surveys of the students, agents and staff of both the college and the ELI.

Their findings demonstrated a need to make improvements by helping students improve their spoken English through providing opportunities to meet local citizens, engaging students in co-curricular activities, and providing better student and administrative support.

The survey concluded that ELI could add more value for their customers by:
- providing specialist English courses
- offering degrees
- providing more information on formal courses
- creating a 'buddy' system
- helping students learn English through role playing
- providing more guided leisure activities.

Making use of feedback

Customer satisfaction survey data is of little value unless it leads to action. Formative feedback at an early stage or during service provision can – and should – lead to immediate action. Summative feedback, or the type of in-depth survey data in the case study above, will inform medium- and long-term actions at a tactical or strategic level.

Survey data are classified according to the following criteria:
- urgency: does it need immediate action, or can it be deferred, and if so, for how long?
- importance: how important is this to customers? How will it affect future recruitment and satisfaction?
- feasibility: what constraints and opportunities are there for taking action? Do we have the capacity and capability to act? If not, consider the resource and training requirements involved.

- area: facilities and equipment, additional services, systems and processes, teaching and learning, etc.

Then action plans are devised for those areas prioritized. In Chapter 10, p. 261, there is a template for an action plan and an example of a Gantt chart: two project management tools for taking follow-up action to a survey. By adopting a systematic approach to dealing with customer feedback, you will ensure that their concerns really are at the heart of the services you offer.

REFLECTION

Review the customer satisfaction procedures and documentation used in your LTO.
- How useful is the information in customer feedback?
- How is the information processed and interpreted?
- Who is responsible for collecting, processing and disseminating the information?
- Who is responsible for taking action prompted by this information?
- How are the effects of such actions measured?
- What improvements do you identify as being needed to improve the total process?

CODES OF PRACTICE

A code of practice is a statement of the key principles and standards which an LTO, as a service provider, is expected to follow and uphold. Codes of practice are at the basis of accreditation schemes. Members are bound by the code, compliance being evaluated through inspection. Government agencies may also lay down codes of practice to be followed by providers. For example, the New Zealand Ministry of Education has published a Code of Practice for the Pastoral Care of International Students, while the European Association for Quality Language Services (EAQUALS) has developed codes of practice for students, staff and information.

The EAQUALS code of practice provides a basis for an inspection, as well as a framework to guide LTO management in setting up and operating the systems and processes required. In the scheme handbook the code of practice and criteria are set out in a table, an extract from which appears in Figure 5.15 opposite. This includes examples of the clauses of the code, with points for verification and examples of good practice, and possible sources of evidence for assessment. These provide an overview of the different, most common possible manifestations of good practice in different types of institutions. They do not claim to be exhaustive lists; neither do they mean that inspectors should observe all the listed points or find all the listed evidence in all types of institution.

The table in Figure 5.15 could be adapted to provide a scheme for specifying service standards, beginning with the customer's requirements in the left column, procedures for meeting these requirements in the middle column, and the outcomes specified in measurable terms in the right column, as shown in the second version of the table (Figure 5.16).

STUDENT CHARTER	
Academic Management: Delivery of Courses	
1.5.1 (g) accurate placement testing to determine language competence	
Focus points	Possible sources of evidence
Placement testing • coherence of content and form • appropriacy (students' needs and age range) • credibility and reliability	review of sample tests, interview guidelines, alternative placement procedures (e.g. self-assessment), discussion with academic manager(s) and teachers, focus group meeting with students
Placement administration • efficiency • use of its results for appropriate group formation • homogeneity of groups • systems for dealing with students'/teachers' concerns over placement	as above + discussion with administrative staff involved in placement testing, review of current group lists in relation to scores on placement testing, class observation, review of class change procedures

FIGURE 5.15: *Extract from EAQUALS Inspection Scheme – Version 5.3*

Customer's requirements	Procedures	Outcomes
to be assigned to a homogeneous group in which they can learn effectively	• an up-to-date and time-efficient system for placing individual students at the beginning of courses, involving diagnosing levels of language knowledge, language skills (including oral), and previous experience of language learning	• 100 % of students take placement test on day 1 • 100% of students assigned to appropriate level of class on day 2 • 90% of students correctly assigned to classes by level
	• results used to group students in reasonably homogeneous groups, in which effective learning can take place	• 90% of students satisfied with placement
	• system for dealing with student or teachers' concerns about placement (e.g. when students perceive level as 'too easy')	• 100% of students' complaints of misplacement resolved satisfactorily within 24 hours

FIGURE 5.16: *Adaptation of scheme to indicate service standards for student placement*

In Figure 5.16, Code of Practice item 1.5.1 is translated into customers' requirements as far as placement is concerned. The procedures list ways of handling this aspect of the service, while the outcomes indicate the desired level of performance in measurable terms.

TASK

If your LTO is already a member of an accreditation scheme, use the code of practice and inspection criteria to review those parts of the system which are central to achieving a high level of customer satisfaction.
- What systems do you have in place?
- How do you measure outcomes to demonstrate that the systems are working?

If you are not a member of an accreditation scheme, visit one of the following sites and download accreditation scheme codes of practice or guidelines (URLs are given in the References & further reading section starting on p. 277):
- Commission on English Language Program Accreditation (CEA) (US)
- European Association for Quality Language Services (EAQUALS)
- Accreditation UK, run by the British Council and English (UK)
- National ELT Accreditation Scheme Limited (NEAS) (Australia)
- New Zealand Qualifications Authority
- Advisory Council for English Language Schools (Ireland)

Apply the criteria or guidelines applicable to a significant aspect of the services offered by your LTO.

Handling complaints

In the Accreditation UK handbook (Accreditation UK, 2008, p. 23), one of the quality assurance criteria states that 'on joining a course, students will be given in writing a procedure for complaints. All complaints and the action taken will be recorded.' The existence of such a procedure is important because, as Walker's New Zealand survey showed, this is one of the predictors of willingness to recommend an LTO.

Complaints, being an expression of dissatisfaction, whether justified or not, are face-threatening acts (Brown & Levinson, 1987, p.60) in that they challenge claims to expertise and competence on the part of a service provider. Not surprisingly, then, the party to whom a complaint is addressed may feel threatened and upset. The party making the complaint may also feel uncomfortable, as performing a face-threatening act is something which is avoided in many cultures. So, handling complaints is an area which requires careful management, particularly as failures in service recovery can increase dissatisfaction and bad word-of-mouth reports to agents and potential customers.

Far from regarding complaints as a threat, we should view them as an opportunity in that the customer is prepared to go to the effort of making a complaint. Furthermore, there is plenty of evidence that having an opportunity to vent a complaint has a positive effect on the customer's perception of the whole experience. However, for venting to be positive, the provider needs to handle the complaint positively and there needs to be evidence of repair.

Firstly, the LTO must have a complaints handling policy which should make it clear that complaints are welcome and will be attended to. All staff should be trained in complaints handling so that they have the confidence, as well as authority and competence, to deal with them. The organization must also have the capacity to deal with complaints from whatever source they come. In order that the LTO can learn from the experience, there must be a complaints log as a basis for analysing complaints, as repeated patterns of complaint will indicate gaps and fail points which must be dealt with effectively.

Secondly, it is essential to have guidelines for dealing with complaints, such as the following:

1 Put yourself in the place of the customer. This is a key step in being truly customer-focused.
2 Start with the view that the customer has a valid point as this will help identify a solution.
3 Thank the customer for complaining.
4 Apologize. This does not mean that you are accepting liability or responsibility, but it is good manners, and may be sufficient repair.
5 Listen to what the customer is saying. Avoid a mechanistic response.
6 Get all the facts. Encouraging the customer to give all relevant information helps you to understand the situation. It also gives the customer a chance to vent his or her feelings and calm down.
7 Find out what you can do to repair (or recover) the situation. Be clear about what this service recovery will involve and how long it will take, particularly if you have to consult with colleagues or clear decisions with senior management.
8 Fix the problem, making sure that your definition of the right repair is the same as the customer's. Service recovery is a vital part of dealing with complaints.
9 Log details of the complaint and action taken.

Vignette 5.1 (p. 140) is an account of a complaints handling and recovery procedure in a small, family-run LTO in Japan, as told by Joshua, the teacher concerned. Although the service recovery was successful, the limitations of the school's placement procedures were not actually addressed, so the kind of problem he dealt with would probably occur again.

Vignette 5.1: Joshua's LTO

About five months ago the customer service manager approached me and told me of an adult student, Sanae, who had signed up for classes once a week, and was going to try my intermediate-level class. The manager told me of the importance of a 'good classroom experience' for her, because Sanae had originally been placed in an elementary-level class. After that class, Sanae had complained that this class was below her level. The school, as an attempt at recovery, had offered her next class free, and put her in a pre-intermediate level class. After attending, Sanae had decided to quit, but the staff had been able to persuade her to try one more class.

Before attending my class, I arranged for Sanae to complete a needs analysis which I use for private students. I observed on the needs analysis that her profession is 'proofreader'. A simple look at her needs analysis (and common sense) showed me that she is a high-achiever, and most likely has an advanced level of English reading, writing and grammar, but not speaking. The current placement system, which is a 15-minute interview with a foreign teacher, did not recognize:
- the difference between speaking, listening and grammar ability
- prior learning experiences
- student goals and interests.

Most of the school's main competitors do not suffer from such service setbacks because they have clearly defined measures for level/class placement.

After attending my class, Sanae decided to join, and has attended regularly for the last five months.

Duty of care: health and safety

As pointed out in Chapter 6, p. 173, LTO managers have a duty of care to many stakeholders, including, from the viewpoint of customer services, two groups:
- internal customers, i.e. the staff
- external customers, i.e. the students and their sponsors.

The duty of care to both will usually have to conform to regulatory requirements. Failure to do so will lead to a fine – or worse, such as suspension of licence to trade. Non-compliance may also affect membership of an accreditation scheme. So, quite apart from good practice, there are significant commercial reasons why such duty of care obligations are met.

The health and safety systems of an LTO can be blueprinted following the same procedures as those outlined for customer services on p. 145. First, you may find it instructive to complete the following quiz and to do some follow-up for any questions you are unable to answer.

TASK

Below is a quiz from a UK Health and Safety training manual. See how many questions you can answer with reference to your own LTO.

Company Health & Safety Quiz

1. Where is your nearest fire exit from the building?
2. What is the company policy on smoking?
3. Name the first-aider(s) in your department.
4. Employers do not have to be concerned about the health and safety of temporary workers: True or False?
5. Who is the company health and safety manager?
6. Where would you find the first-aid box?
7. You do not have to wear personal protective equipment if you do not want to: True or False?
8. To whom should you report health and safety problems?
9. Where would you find a written statement of the company's commitment to health and safety?
10. What is the procedure to follow if you have an accident at work?

Duty of care also involves managing risk. There are risks which affect customer services and, as with other risks, these should be listed in a risk register, which will include:

- a description of the risk
- who is responsible for dealing with it (the owner)
- when the risk was first identified
- the probability that the risk will occur
- the impact of the risk should it occur
- counter measures (or mitigating strategies) and who the owner is
- residual impact once counter measures have been put in place
- an outline contingency plan
- current status.

TASK

Make a short list of risks which could affect customer services.

Check the LTO risk register to see if these risks are entered. (If there is not a risk register, you should discuss this with senior management.)

If you have identified a risk which is not present in the register, bring it to the attention of senior management, following the specification given above.

THE CUSTOMER JOURNEY: POST-PURCHASE

Relationship marketing

The LTO's relationship with customers does not necessarily cease once they have finished their course and moved on. As noted in Chapter 4, relationship marketing, unlike transaction marketing, is directed towards repeat sales and long-term performance and contact. Increasingly, organizations are putting their effort into retaining existing customers rather than only attracting new ones, as was illustrated in Vignette 4.3 on p. 80. For the LTO, there are considerable benefits in developing and maintaining strong customer relationships through:

- increased purchases
- lower cost
- lifetime value of the customer
- word-of-mouth publicity
- employee satisfaction and retention.

There are also benefits for the customer:

- risk and stress reduction arising from trust built on a consistent level of service quality
- higher-quality service derived from the service provider's knowledge of the consumer
- avoidance of switching costs
- social and status benefits though developing relationships founded on repeated encounters
- relationship-building.

Relationship-building does not happen overnight, however, but takes time. The successive steps in building a relationship have been depicted by Payne et al (1977, p. 8) in a 'relationship ladder' which shadows the phases and steps in the customer journey.

The type of relationship on this ladder depends on the frequency and depth of contact between the customer and the provider. At the lower levels – prospect and customer – the connection between the customer and the provider is transactional rather than relational. A provider may try to convert the client into a supporter and then into an advocate – that is, someone who will recommend the organization to others (a very important feature of word-of-mouth recommendation). It should be kept in mind that though a partnership is a relationship of mutual advantage, it may not be appropriate for all organizations and their clientele.

Customer loyalty

Building customer loyalty is at the heart of the customer journey, especially during the purchase/consumption and post-purchase phases. The stages involved in this process have been summarized in the customer loyalty grid in Figure 5.18.

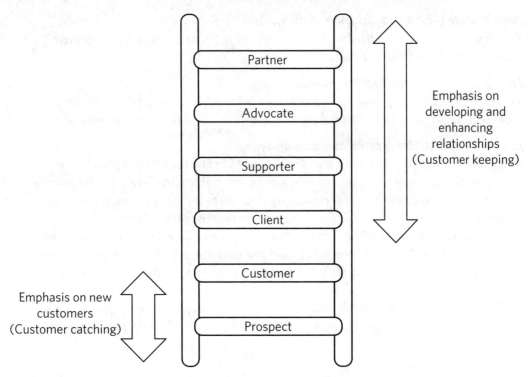

FIGURE 5.17: *The relationship ladder* (from Payne et al, 1997, p. (viii))

Zone 1: Unstated/Expected: the zone of indifference

This zone includes all those customer needs and wants that are basic to meeting the unspoken contract between you and them. The best that can be hoped for is indifference if the LTO meets these needs.

	Expected	Unexpected
Stated	Zone of satisfaction	Zone of delight
Unstated	Zone of indifference	Zone of loyalty

FIGURE 5.18: *Customer loyalty grid* (Affinity Consulting 2002–2006 in Ward, 2007)

Zone 2: Stated/Expected: the zone of satisfaction

This is where customers actually tell you what is important to them. Meeting their requirements leads to satisfaction.

Zone 3: Stated/Unexpected: the zone of delight

This is where customers hope for something, ask for it, but do not really expect you to provide it. This is an area for special attention in building a loyal group of customers.

Zone 4: Unstated/Unexpected: the zone of loyalty

This is an area where expertise in the services provided by the LTO, and the lack of expertise of the customer, can have a real pay off. Providing benefits above and beyond what customers are even aware of can create loyal customers. Providing such benefits requires imagination and devising innovations that are of real benefit to customers.

All zones are important. To reach the zone of loyalty, it is necessary to cover all the other zones. If the LTO is really good at innovations (a major factor in creating loyalty), but struggles at reliability (a key factor in creating satisfaction), then it will end up struggling in all four zones.

The notion of customer loyalty has recently been given a piquant twist with the introduction of the concept of Lovemarks (Figure 5.19) by Kevin Roberts of Saatchi & Saatchi.

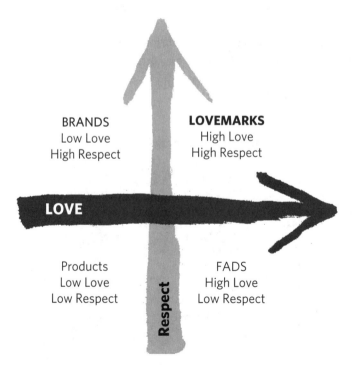

FIGURE 5.19: *Love/respect axis*

The proposition is that there are goods and services which inspire both high respect and high affection. The elements of respect are as follows:

Performance	**Trust**	**Reputation**
• Innovation	• Reliability	• Leadership
• Quality	• Ease	• Honesty
• Service	• Openness	• Responsibility
• Identity	• Security	• Efficacy
• Value	• Commitment	

Love adds an emotional dimension: mystery, sensuality, intimacy. While it is relatively easy to see how these can be applied to such brands (or marks) as Camper shoes, The New Yorker magazine or even a city, it is more challenging to see how they could apply to the services of an LTO, yet it is precisely through inspiring such emotional commitment that an LTO will really be able to convince prospects that it has the qualities of a 'lovemark'. Nothing could be a more powerful way of promoting the LTO's services, of retaining existing customers and attracting new ones, and of building a competitive advantage.

Customer retention strategies

Because of the benefits deriving from long-term relationships, it is worthwhile for an LTO to develop customer retention strategies. Since not all customers are worth retaining because they may give priority to exploiting the relationship, or maybe do not want to be retained, an LTO needs to identify those who really are worth retaining. This means finding out why customers leave or stay, what creates value for them, and what their profiles are. Decisions can then be made about devising appropriate retention strategies.

There are three main types of bond used to strengthen the relationship between the customer and the supplier:

- financial incentives, such as discounts and special offers
- social bonds, promoted through frequent communication and customization of the service
- financial, social and structural bonds by designing solutions to customers' problems into the service provision system.

BLUEPRINTING

In Chapter 2, we drew attention to the limitations which departmentalization or 'silo-ization' can impose on an LTO. Chapter 8 (p. 213) proposes an approach to new product development which involves cross-functional teams from different organizational silos, and on p. 121 of this chapter, the importance of involving everyone in managing quality is noted. The rationale behind blueprinting is based on such TQM principles, and involves describing, in detail, the various stages of the provision of a service.

Shostack (1984) uses a simple example of a shoeshine operation to illustrate the approach:

1 The shoes are brushed.
2 Polish is applied.

3   Polish is buffed off.

4   Money is collected.

Each activity has a time associated with it, e.g. brushing might be estimated to take 30 seconds.

Shostack introduces two useful concepts:

- 'fail' points: stages at which things can go wrong and the identification of remedial action necessary to correct them (i.e. service recovery)
- 'line of sight': some activities can be seen by the customer and others cannot. In teaching, pre-class preparation (a backroom activity) by the teacher is outside the line of sight, whereas actual teaching is within the line of sight, because, as noted earlier when discussing services, the student/consumer participates in the teaching–learning process. There are many other backroom activities, however, which go into providing an LTO service, including those involved with marketing and sales. Many of these will underlie the various LTO services which you listed in the Task on p. 120.

The Blueprint matrix

Figure 5.20 illustrates the basic scheme for a service system blueprint, separating 'frontstage' and 'backstage' functions by the 'line of visibility', with the activities witnessed and participated in by customers above and those out of sight below the line.

Customer		
Line of interaction		
Service Provider		Frontstage
Line of visibility		
Set-up Functions		
Line of internal interaction		Backstage
Support Functions		
Line of implementation		
Management Functions		

FIGURE 5.20: *Service System Blueprint Matrix* (Shostack, 1984, from Walker, 1997)

Preparing a service blueprint

Shostack outlines the key steps in preparing the service blueprint as follows:

1   Identify the activities involved in providing the service and present these in diagrammatic form. The level of detail will depend on the complexity and nature of the service.

2   Identify the 'fail' points. The actions necessary to correct things that have gone wrong must be determined, and systems and procedures developed to reduce the likelihood of them occurring in the first instance.

3   Set standards against which the performance of the various steps might be measured. Frequently, this is the time taken.

4   Analyse the profitability of the service provided, in terms of the number of customers served during a period of time.

Walker (1997) has applied Shostack's blueprint concept to service provision in the LTO (see Figure 5.21, p. 148) and, 'assuming that the system is already in place and that the blueprint is to be used in a quality assurance rather than a planning mode' (Walker, 1997, p. 19), he suggests a number of ways for the manager to gather the data required to chart an LTO service system:

- observation and analysis of workflows. This involves an on-site review of the entire service provision, similar to that involved in CJM (p. 122). This is a task that is likely to involve several people from different departments or silos.
- interviews with service providers. These will involve front-line service providers, since they are most likely to be most in touch with and best informed about customers' attitudes and perceptions of the quality of the service provided (see Chapter 2, p. 28). In particular, 'teachers are likely to be able to provide key information about actions, events and processes affecting the quality of the service provision' (Walker, 1997, p. 19).
- focus groups of providers/users. The benefits and procedures involved have already been summarized on p. 134.
- document analysis, as noted on p. 124.
- participation as consumer of service. This can involve taking on the role of 'mystery shopper' which can provide valuable insights into service provision from the customer's perspective, as illustrated by Vignettes 4.4 (Chapter 4, p. 107), and 5.2 (p. 149).

Creating an LTO service blueprint

Having gathered such data, the manager can begin to create the service system blueprint, following the steps suggested by Walker:

1 Decide which actions occur frontstage and which occur backstage.
2 Identify the start activity.
3 Flowchart the process above the line of visibility, separating consumer and provider actions at the line of interaction.
4 Identify the end activity/outcome and any repeat participation.
5 Identify and flowchart the backstage functions and actions.
6 Link the backstage and onstage activities with lines of interaction.
7 Identify any onstage–backstage feedback line.
8 Check for fail points ('F' in Figure 5.21) and wait points.

His diagram (Figure 5.21) depicts a service system blueprint of a typical LTO. The entire process followed by the customer is flowcharted above the line of visibility, while below the line of visibility the management structure and the six support teams are identified, and lines of interaction running vertically indicate how the organizational structure relates to the backstage and frontstage activities. On the right-hand side, a feedback loop from providers to management conveys information on the customer's and provider's perceptions of the success of the programme.

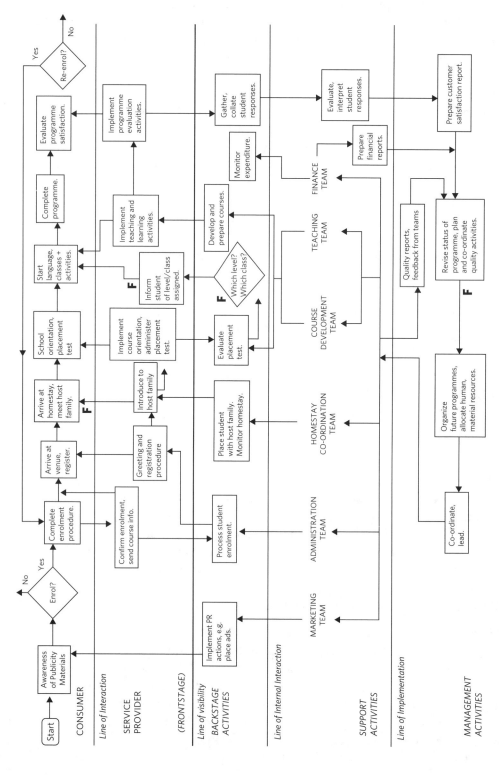

FIGURE 5.21: *EFL Service System Blueprint (Walker, 1997)*

> **Vignette 5.2: Mystery shopper**
>
> While on a business trip to London, Silvina enquired about Intensive English courses for a fictitious 18-year-old niece from Argentina. She visited a number of LTOs, and commented on the attitude towards direct sales in the LTOs concerned.
>
> 'I was really shocked by the way direct sales are tackled and how little attention they give a potential customer who contacts them directly. Probably the fact I was Argentinian made them think I would then contact a potential agent in my area, though no mention of agents was made. When I asked "How do I hear from you? Can you send me a quote by email?", all of them just referred me to their website and "user-friendly online application form", and went on to say that once the application was sent a member of staff would contact me immediately to process/confirm the booking and discuss forms of payment. The receptionists obviously did not work on a commission basis as they seemed indifferent as to whether the sale happened or not.'

Blueprint applications

Walker goes on to suggest a number of applications for such a blueprint:

1 As a planning tool:
   - visualizing the service from start to finish, and identifying potential fail and waiting points in advance
   - determining the likely level of resourcing required in terms of front-line teaching staff, support staff, materials and equipment.
2 As an organizing tool:
   - preparation of job descriptions/employee selection criteria
   - development of rational work flows
   - equipment design and selection
   - conceptualizing the visual environment of the service
   - creation of tangibles (such as textbooks, newsletters, certificates, etc.)
   - creation of 'scripts' for verbal interactions.
3 As a communication/training tool:
   - providing visualization of the overall service
   - communication of service details
   - identification of customer contact personnel.
4 As a control tool:
   - identification of gaps in service provision
   - facilitation of quality control through analysis of fail points
   - development of monitoring/feedback systems
   - staff appraisal.

Walker notes that LTO managers 'will find that merely going through the process of developing a service system blueprint will provide them with a number of useful insights into improving the quality, productivity and effectiveness of their own EFL operation'.

CONCLUSION

Once the customer has purchased the service, the LTO needs to monitor their satisfaction and to make adjustments to align provision with expectation. All LTOs have a duty of care to customers, both external and internal. Any risks affecting the well-being of customers should be entered in a risk register which will record the actions taken to mitigate such risks.

When customers reach the end of their journey, it is worthwhile maintaining the relationship, as retaining loyal customers has many benefits for both the LTO and the customer. Not all customers will want to maintain a close relationship, and it may not be in the interests of the LTO to retain some customers. While developing customers' respect for your services is necessary, encouraging a positive relationship can transform the standing of the LTO and give it a significant competitive advantage.

Managing customer services is a complex operation which is aided by service blueprinting. This involves distinguishing between frontstage and backstage in the service encounter, and identifying the various roles and processes involved in preparing and providing the service. Implementing customer service management procedures may, in some LTOs, represent a significant innovation, the management of which is the subject of Chapter 9.

TASK

Keeping in mind the limitations of the questionnaire in Figure 5.9 (p. 130), and the use of either expectation/performance or performance/importance scales, adapt an existing questionnaire in your LTO or devise a new one.

- Decide whether a new one is to be a formative or a summative survey.
- List the aspects of the service you wish to obtain feedback on. Remember that items should be connected to actions which can be taken to fix any gaps identified, and that you should avoid trying to cover too many areas in the survey.
- Consider how the quantitative data will be analysed and presented, and what level of results will trigger follow-up action.
- Draft a questionnaire and pilot.

TASK

Apply the service blueprint to service management in your own LTO. This will mean involving colleagues and it may take some time to collect and analyse information and prepare the blueprint. Such an exercise could be a useful professional development exercise involving staff across different departments or silos.

Strategic financial management

- STRATEGIC PLANNING: FINANCIAL OUTCOMES
- PLANNING AND ANALYTICAL TOOLS
- STRATEGIC PLAN IMPLEMENTATION
- INVESTMENT DECISIONS
- BENCHMARKING
- FINANCIAL STATEMENTS
- DUTY OF CARE

INTRODUCTION

The term 'financial management' makes many people nervous. The reasons for this are two-fold: there is a tendency to equate financial management with accounting, and many people are uncomfortable with the idea of working with numbers. Financial management is not the same as accounting, however. It involves looking at the financial impact of decisions, using financial information to make informed business decisions, and managing financial resources. Although it involves working with numbers, the numbers are not an end in themselves. Rather, it is the information that is contained in the numbers which managers can use to inform their decision-making.

Chapters 6 and 7 will explore strategic (organization-wide, long-term) and operational (routine) financial management, which have different applications at different levels of LTO management. An LTO director will have strategic responsibilities including the overall financial picture, long-term organizational growth and stability, and possibly debt financing or investment opportunities. This means that an LTO director is likely to use strategic financial management concepts and tools. Directors of studies (DOS), in comparison, have a different set of responsibilities primarily connected with the day-to-day operation of the LTO, so they will be more likely to use operational financial concepts and tools.

This chapter will explore strategic planning, whose focus is long-term planning and goal-setting, and we will consider how financial management is a vital component of the process. In addition, we will look at some tools that aid in the creation of strategic plans.

Decision-making and communication

What, then, is strategic financial management? It is a set of financial managerial decisions and actions aimed at the achievement and/or maintenance of the financial health of an organization. As financial management is one aspect of overall management, financial outcomes are also one aspect of informed decision-making. In for-profit LTOs, the financial outcomes may be a significant driver in decision-making. In NFP or social sector LTOs, the most significant driver is the mission of the organization; the financial outcomes are not a measurement of profit but of how effectively resources are employed to achieve the goals of the LTO.

In virtually any LTO, some questions that concern managers are:

- How are offerings in a target market to be expanded, or enrolment on a particular course to be raised?
- Should course sections or classes be consolidated?
- How does an LTO grow its total student population by 10% in one year?
- What are the minimum and maximum enrolments for a particular course?
- What will be the effect of changing the ratio of contract, non-benefited to regular, full-time teachers?

All of these questions have financial implications and impact. In making decisions and finding solutions, a manager should use the financial data available to make sound decisions. In addition, it is important for a manager to know who can contribute data and information, who should participate in decision-making, and who is affected by the decisions.

For example, an LTO has been running a Saturday ESL course for young learners. This course has been successful and there seems to be a growing demand. A manager might have to decide whether the growing demand for this course is sufficient to justify opening a second class. In order to make this decision, the manager must know how to calculate:

- maximum class size based on the type of course and facility resources
- student to teacher ratio to justify additional labour costs
- average class size
- break-even enrolment for a course section
- how this course fits into the overall revenue and profitability picture of the LTO.

In addition, the manager must understand the market and how likely reaching break-even will be for a second class.

In making decisions such as this one, it is important to communicate with other staff. A manager may need to consult some staff who will contribute information toward the decision or those who must participate in, and share responsibility for, making the decision. Finally, a manager will need to communicate the decision to staff and others who need only to know the outcome. In the preceding example, the DOS could gather financial data from the accountant and work with the marketing or admissions staff who are familiar with student applications, and with the classroom scheduler. The eventual decision would need to be communicated to all those who contributed and to any staff who would be involved in implementing the outcome.

STRATEGIC PLANNING: FINANCIAL OUTCOMES

Where do you want to be and how do you get there? Those are the basic questions asked in long-range/strategic planning process. In any line of business, management must look not only at where the enterprise is in the current year, but where management wants it to be in three or five years. Strategic planning can have many different outcomes such as overall growth, restructuring of the organization, repositioning it in the marketplace, or a combination of these. Strategic plans look closely at where the LTO management wants to be in terms of market share, course capacity and design, and financial stability or growth. In order to achieve the desired outcomes, a clearly defined plan with identified resources and measurable outcomes must be put in place. The following discussion approaches strategic planning in a financial management context.

Business plan models

A business plan is a form of a strategic plan. It outlines the business structure and activity, and provides market analysis data and financial data. It has specific objectives and timelines for achieving those objectives. It also presents pro-forma financial statements: a series of projected financial statements (Block & Hirt, 1994). The detailed financial information shows why a business is or will be profitable. It outlines any necessary financing the business needs and is usually created when approaching a funder or lender (such as a bank). Business plans can provide an overview of all aspects of a business from management structure to proposed market share to expected income. For an LTO, this can provide a written, documented plan to follow over a specific period of time.

Costed proposal outline

A costed proposal is a request to someone for funding for an activity with intended outcomes. Managers may encounter many situations in which the creation of a costed proposal will be a valuable tool for them and their enterprise. The proposal should lay out the required inputs, the intended outputs, and the processes and resources involved in achieving the latter. Costed proposals can be used to present the manager's ideas to a variety of audiences including the line manager, the governing board and potential funders. It is an efficient way to present design, research and financial data. While some funders will have their own proposal format that they want applicants to complete, the basic elements of a costed proposal are fairly universal.

Figure 6.1 on p. 154 uses these elements and provides a basic framework for you to follow in creating a costed proposal.

Assumed audience

As you develop your proposal, it will be generally most useful to keep your assumed audience in mind. This could be senior management in your LTO, a governing board or an external funder. For this reason, you should not constrain yourself to the section headings named here. In fact, you should give the headings the names that will be most useful in terms of communicating with your audience. In addition, if your audience is completely external to your organization, you may wish to add a section to your proposal that

Proposal part (sample heading)	Function	Format and length (approximate)
Executive summary	brief statement highlighting main points: • need • capacity • programme • amount requested	prose: 1 page
Needs assessment	assess needs explain programme environment (risks and opportunities) to owners/funders in a way that builds from their world view(s)	prose: 2–5 paragraphs 1–2 pages
Proposal	explain proposed activity with special attention to the clients to be served	prose: limit to under 10 pages, if possible
Work plan/timeline	explain key personnel roles and key steps they will take to create the activity	organize information graphically: 1–2 pages • bullets and/or annotated diagram of key steps, e.g. Gantt chart, process map, flow chart
Key personnel	brief bio-statements of key personnel	1–2 paragraphs per person
Evaluation plan	explain how you will evaluate the project	prose: 1–2 pages
Budget	pro-forma income statement pertinent to the activity, including: • revenue • direct costs • indirect costs (ratio estimate) • taxes (if pertinent) • earnings • notes on budget lines	spreadsheet
Conclusion	brief summary and closing paragraph	prose: 1–2 paragraphs less than a page
Appendices (optional)	as needed	as needed

FIGURE 6.1: *Specification of a costed proposal*

describes the organization and its capacities. This is often called an 'organization statement', 'capacity statement' or 'capabilities statement'. It can either be one of the last sections of the proposal or an appendix.

Each part of the proposal defined above is discussed in more detail below.

Executive summary

Generally, the executive summary is a one-page synthesis of your proposal. It should be clear and succinct, conveying the essence of the proposal by itself: your audience, the need, a summary of your activity, and a statement of the amount you are asking for. A funder wants to see the main points before reading the whole proposal, and the executive summary is sometimes detached and circulated. Indeed, it is frequently the only part of the proposal that some people read. If you cannot capture your audience with the executive summary, they may not read any further.

Needs assessment

As you structure your section, keep your audience in mind. It must make sense from the standpoint of these potential stakeholders.

In this section, identify the audience to whom the request is addressed, show understanding and respect for their world views, and briefly sketch the relevant environment (context of your proposal). Your LTO is probably the main environment of the activity, and the LTO mission is certainly a relevant world view. However, it may not be the only one.

Your emphasis should be on the risks and opportunities presented by the current environment of your LTO and your LTO's strengths and weaknesses. Briefly analyse the competitors and important demographic, economic and/or technological trends that are creating the needs that you see. Do this using a STEP analysis (see Chapter 9, p. 234). If you are going to propose a modification of an existing course, product or service, then briefly describe the existing activity. This becomes the status quo for your proposal.

Proposal

Other possible names are 'proposed course', 'proposed scope of work', 'proposed product', etc. Present your proposal in a brief verbal model. Explain its rationale in the context provided by your needs assessment. Whether your objective is a new programme, a modification in standard procedures, or improved in-house training, define it from a business perspective.

Explain the scope of the activity, its time frame, and your expected return on investment. Choose a time frame that will help your audience understand and support your proposal. Some typical time frames are one quarter (three months), one year, and three years.

You might propose a 'one-shot' project, or a new course that you expect to run many times. In either case, you need to declare two things in this section very clearly:
- what key benefits its clients will receive
- how your activity is to make money (or accumulate assets) for the stakeholders.

Work plan

Explain how the proposed activity will be done, when, and by whom. Focus on the key personnel and the steps that they will take. Create a diagram or structural model of the main steps involved. Here is where you might use a Gantt chart or some form of work flow diagram, similar to those employed in project management (see Chapter 10). It is not necessary to chart every step, only the keys ones to achieve the scope of work. The structural model allows your audience to better understand your plan and the costs that you project in your budget to complete the planned activity.

If you are proposing an activity in which steps will be taken only once (e.g. the design of a curriculum or development of a new product), then your work plan should focus on this one-shot project. If you are proposing an activity which is to be replicated many times, such as a new course, then your work plan explanation should focus on the recurring steps, that is, the new standard procedure or work flow. New product development is discussed further in Chapter 8, p. 213.

In this section, also explain any assistance (either one-time or ongoing) that you expect from the LTO and/or funders that will not appear in your budget. In effect, such assistance can be seen as potential costs of your proposal that you are expecting someone else to pay. Thus it is better to be explicit about this from the beginning.

Key Personnel

List the key personnel to be involved in the work being proposed. For each major role, provide the name, position/role in the proposal and a brief biographical paragraph. You can provide additional information, such as curriculum vitae, as appendices to the proposal.

Evaluation plan

How are you going to measure the success of your project? What tools will you use? What does success look like both financially and programmatically? Explain in a paragraph or two what your evaluation plan is, how often you will implement an evaluation process, and what tools you will use.

Budget

This is the financial model upon which your proposal is based. It can take the form of the profit and loss (P & L). This kind of management report is also known in some companies as an 'income statement', 'income and expense statement', or 'statement of profit and loss'.

What is required in support of your proposal is not a historical document, but rather a projection of the future financial performance of your proposed activity. As suggested above, you should select a scope and time frame that clarify and substantively support your proposal. If you are including a multi-year budget, remember to restrict start-up costs to the first year only, as these are not ongoing costs. Your budget should include the following financial components:

Revenue   This will typically be course tuition and fees or sales revenue from your products. Look closely to see whether your activity builds capacity for your organization. Building capacity positively impacts on future P&L statements by decreasing costs and/or expanding revenues. If some capacity-building might be involved in your proposal, think about selecting a scope and time frame that demonstrate this benefit.

Your activity may also increase the intangible assets of your organization, such as intellectual property and goodwill among your clients. Such potential benefits are notoriously difficult to project. It is probably best to mention these possibilities to your audience but not to project a financial impact (unless you already have a track record to refer to).

Direct costs   These are the expenses which are directly linked to the volume of activity, and need to be classified functionally into an appropriate number of categories (e.g. Instruction, Material, Supplies). Remember that much of the credibility of your proposal rests on how completely you have done this part of the costing and what strategies you have come up with for minimizing direct costs.

Indirect costs   These are the costs which are generally fixed, regardless of the level of activity, and need not be classified, but if you can and wish to, limit them to 3–5 categories at most (e.g. Occupancy, Marketing and Advertising, Management, Employee Benefits).

Indirect costs are very often estimated using a formula that is standardized within the organization for this purpose: percentage of revenues and percentage of direct costs. If possible, do what your organization does and provide a short note to this effect.

If you wish to establish a different approach to costing indirect costs or if your proposal will significantly impact indirect costs, explain this in the body of the proposal itself. Provide a reasonable approach to the new costing, do the numbers in the budget, and explain the numbers in your notes.

Taxes   Include if relevant to your institution in your country.

Earnings   This is the famous 'bottom line' of the budget. It is also known as 'contribution to corporate margin', 'net earnings', 'net income', or 'net profit'.

Notes   Along with the categories and numbers in your budget lines, notes are necessary on any line that is not absolutely self-explanatory. Since it is best to err on the side of clarity, we recommend that you consider explaining every line in your budget by a brief note. Whether the notes are on the same page as your numbers or on a separate page, the budget line that they refer to should be very clear.

Conclusion

This should be brief; less than a page. You will need to explain how you are measuring outcomes and success or failure. What is your continuing plan for the future? This should also include a succinct statement summarizing your proposal.

Appendices

Appendices help keep your proposal brief yet substantial and persuasive. They allow the readers to 'drill down' to a deeper level of analysis. Such analysis may be essential if your proposal involves complex technical issues, relevant professional research, historical information, and so on.

Provide an appendix on any point that is essential to your proposal and that requires a level of detail that would interrupt your main argument. Some examples might be descriptions of the status quo, market research findings, a programme or position description, a competitive analysis, a standards document, a sample course outline or lesson plan, or another pertinent budget. Beware of using the appendices as a 'dump' for information which may be only marginally relevant – or even not relevant at all. Nothing is more irritating to a reader than having to read large amounts of material which adds nothing to the writer's case.

This is also where you might add your capacity/capability statement. Even if your audience is an internal one, some form of capacity or capability statement could be useful, especially if launching a new line of business, course or project that is not immediately connected to past or existing areas of work for the LTO. Helping your audience to connect the institutional, departmental and personnel capabilities to the work you are proposing adds to the persuasiveness of your proposal.

Resource inventory

'Resource' is a term much used in any discussion of LTO management, referring to anything available to an enterprise to achieve its goals. This means that resources include not only tangible items, such as equipment, but intangibles, such as skills, systems, knowledge and intellectual property.

A successful strategic plan must not only be clear in its articulation of the goals and objectives of the plan, but there must be a clear outline of the resources needed to achieve those goals and objectives, as further discussed in Chapter 8, p. 216. Therefore, a strategic or business plan should have a clear statement of the resources required. A resource inventory will help an organization understand what resources it already has that can be allocated to the plan. Matching the needs specified in the plan with existing LTO resources helps identify the resource gaps that must be filled for the plan to be successful.

Some types of resources that would appear in such an inventory are:
• facilities
• personnel
• technology
• financial assets
• funding sources
• intellectual property of courses/activities.

A resource inventory might be as simple as a spreadsheet or table outlining the categories and listing the specific LTO resources within those categories. Alternatively, it might be as sophisticated as a portfolio of documents, photos, appraisals, etc. or an online/electronic resource inventory tool. However the LTO decides to display its resource inventory, it is important that managers understand what the inventory says in relationship to the strategic plan goals and outcomes. It is important to consider which resources are allocated to each goal or outcome and which goals need new resources to be successfully implemented.

Long-term goals/plan outcomes

The goals of a strategic plan must be clearly documented. Strategic financial goals are usually stated in terms of revenue growth by amount or percentage, e.g. $10,000 or 10%. The eventual outcomes must be measurable and comparable to the goals identified. One method of measurement is by setting key performance indicators (KPIs). For example, a $10,000 increase in net revenue in Year One might have a KPI of an increase in revenue of $2,500 per financial quarter.

Another component of strategic financial goals is defining the responsibility for achieving those goals and the consequences of not achieving those goals. In the example of the $10,000 increase in net revenue, the plan should identify which unit(s) or activity/activities are expected to yield a specified portion of that goal. Also, if monitoring reveals that those KPIs or targets are not being achieved, alternative strategies, such as cutting costs or eliminating certain investment spending, will need to be in place. For example, a strategic plan for an LTO might include the goal to purchase new furniture as an investment in improving the premises of the LTO. Should the purchase of the furniture be contingent upon achieving some or all of the increased revenue target? If the purchase of the furniture is scheduled for the third quarter, then by that point, the LTO should know how well it is doing towards achieving its increased revenue goal. If the LTO is not going to achieve that goal, then the purchase of the furniture can be suspended or altered (e.g. purchase less furniture). It is important not only to have clear, measurable goals, but also to link relevant goals to one another, and to have fall-back plans in place should any of the goals not be met.

Defining success, improvement and failure

To have a successful strategic plan, an LTO must clearly define the success, improvement and failure of all the goals in the plan. These definitions must be accepted and considered realistic by all managers so that the goals are obtainable and measuring progress towards achieving the goals can be done as accurately as possible. If the LTO is not clear about what constitutes successful achievement on the one hand, or failure on the other, then measuring achievement will be difficult.

In addition, the definitions should be placed within specific time frames; they should be quantifiable/measurable, and the consequences of each outcome should be understood by all. For example, if the strategic goal is increasing revenue by $10,000, the parties involved should understand what their role(s) are in achieving this goal. The goal should be laid onto a timeline, in this case over the course of a fiscal year. The achievement of the goal should be measurable and quantified by specific times and the individual(s) responsible for achieving the goal should be clearly identified. In this example, it is decided that the revenue will be increased by at least $2,500 each quarter and it is further planned that the $2,500 revenue will be achieved by the Adult Advanced English course and the Teen Language and Culture course. The adult course will increase revenue by $1,500 and the teen course by $1,000 during each quarter. The goals will be measured by an analysis of the revenue achieved at the end of each fiscal quarter. This is the picture of success.

The LTO must also decide what are the measurements of improvement and failure. Improvement can be defined broadly as any improvement towards the final goal. How, though, will an LTO define failure? Is it at the $9,999 mark? Or is there more latitude in the goal? It could be that any revenue below $7,500 is considered a failure, and the strategic goal must be re-examined and/or its implementation rethought.

When the strategic goals have their outcomes clearly defined, an LTO can then best manage the implementation and analysis of those goals. If the progress does not meet the definition of success, then LTO management can take appropriate corrective actions to further improvement towards gaining success.

REFLECTION

Does your LTO have a strategic plan?

> If so, obtain a copy of it and look at the goals of the plan.
> • Are the goals clear and measurable?
> • What are the measures used in the plan?
> • Are they all financial?

Measures could include student enrolment, financial performance, course review, stakeholder satisfaction, among others. Are the measures for your LTO clear and explicit?

> If your LTO does not have a strategic plan, what are the areas of your LTO that you would like to see addressed in strategic planning?

PLANNING AND ANALYTICAL TOOLS

Analytical tools are important in both planning and measuring strategic goals. Financial management plays an important role in any strategic planning process and many of the tools that you would use in analysing an idea or an issue can also be used for financial analysis. Then there are some tools that are specific to looking at the numbers. The tools that we will explore are:
- worksheet for strategic goal implementation
- budget as analytical tool
- break-even
- modelling.

The first tool helps you look at the whole picture for planning and implementation of strategic goals. The last three tools let you specifically look at the numbers connected to your goals.

Strategic planning tools such as STEP and SWOT analyses, used to identify internal and external factors affecting an organization, are described in Chapter 9 (pp. 234 and

236), where their use as tools in managing innovation is covered. Since financial management is not just about the numbers but also all the factors that go into the numbers, the STEP and SWOT analysis tools are excellent ways to view a topic with both internal and external lenses. Doing a SWOT analysis itself does not produce a set of numbers for a manager to analyse. However, it does identify areas that will help a manager to know what financial information is needed to inform the implementation of the strategies created by the analysis.

Strategic goal implementation

The following worksheet is an implementation tool. As described in the section on objectives in Chapter 10, p. 259, an organization's objectives must be SMART (Specific, Measurable, Agreed, Realistic and Time-bound). By completing the worksheet for strategic goal implementation (Figure 6.2) for each strategic goal, an LTO has a firm plan, with concrete steps, a fixed timeline and lines of responsibility for its completion. This information is important from a financial management perspective because if financial resources are to be allocated or obtained to implement a strategy, this worksheet will make that information apparent and transparent, and the financial elements needed to succeed in implementing the strategy can be incorporated into the plan.

Strategic goal What is the goal?
Time frame When will we do this?
Steps to achieving goal How will we do this?
Accountability Who will be responsible for what?
KPIs/Measurements of success How will we know if we've achieved our goal?
Outcome of goal Success/failure/improvement?

FIGURE 6.2: *Strategic goal implementation worksheet*

This is a generic template that is easily adaptable to the specific needs of an LTO. For example, you might want to divide accountability between those employees in Finance and those in Programmes so that you are representing cross-organizational teams. In smaller LTOs, accountability for Finance and Programmes might already rest with one person. The purpose of accountability for this template is to identify those who will be responsible for seeing the goal to completion, whether it is one person or a team of people. Your timeline might then be more in the form of a Gantt chart (see Chapter 10, p. 261, for an example). The tool is flexible enough to meet an LTO's planning needs.

Budget as analytical tool

A budget is a plan of revenue and costs for a department, unit, activity or organization that is usually for the year ahead. As a budget is a plan, monitoring is used to identify any deviations from the plan so that corrective action can be taken, if necessary. A budget is a vital aid in strategic financial management in the following ways:

- it can help you set up a schedule of financial benchmarks
- it provides information for comparison with actual revenues and costs over the defined period of the budget
- it can provide a model for creating long-range, multi-year budgets.

Detailing revenue and cost plans through budgets will also provide managers with an understanding of current plan information at the LTO, unit or activity level that is required for formulating financial strategic plans. Managers can identify course profitability and potential growth sectors, which helps to shape the financial growth strategy of the LTO. In the next chapter we will explore the creation of budgets in some detail.

Break-even analysis

Break-even analysis is a modelling or analytical tool. The break-even point is the point at which all costs are covered and you neither make a profit nor lose money. The net, which is revenue less cost, equals zero. In the LTO context, the break-even point is usually expressed as a student enrolment number, though it could be used for a number of student groups for a course or number of courses offered in a programme as well. Break-even analysis is useful when looking at new courses or course redesigns. It can also be helpful when looking at costing out sections for a course, e.g. how many students do we need to enrol in a section to make it profitable to run another class?

First we will look at the components of break-even analysis, then the formula, the steps for conducting a break-even analysis, and finally an example of a break-even model in Figure 6.3. Break-even is based on the per student revenue including tuition and fees. The costs are broken into two main types of cost: 'variable' and 'fixed'. Variable costs are those costs that change with enrolment, usually budgeted on a per student basis. Fixed costs are those costs that stay the same regardless of changing enrolment. When calculating the break-even point, you look at how much the per student net or margin is and then what your fixed costs are. You will need to make your per student net enough times to cover your fixed costs.

The formula is: $\text{Break-even point} = \dfrac{\text{fixed costs}}{(\text{unit revenue} - \text{unit cost})}$

When an LTO looks for the break-even number in a course, it involves calculating the per student revenue less the per student variable costs and then dividing the fixed costs by that amount. That number is the break-even number of students.

1   Identify the total fixed costs for the course (i.e. teaching salaries, marketing, overhead, teaching materials). This becomes the top of the equation.
2   Identify the tuition and fees being charged per student or total revenue per student.
3   Calculate all of the per student costs or variable costs (i.e. books, copying/materials, activities/outings, lab fees).
4   Subtract the total per student variable cost from the total per student revenue. This becomes the unit (per student) net on the bottom of the equation.
5   Divide the fixed costs by the per student net amount and you should get the total number of students required to break even for the course.

Figure 6.3 looks at the break-even enrolment level for a language course. The market analysis has determined that the maximum tuition for this course should not exceed $1,000.

Account	Rate in $
Revenue	
Tuition	1,000
Total per student	1,000
Costs	
Variable costs per student	
Books	150
Copying	25
Outings	50
Total variable costs per student	225
Gross Profit	775
Fixed cost(s)	
Teaching salaries/benefits	1,200
Institutional Support	3,000
Total fixed costs	4,200

Divide the fixed costs ($4,200) by the per student net amount ($1,000 – $225 = $775) and you should get the total number of students required to break even for the course (5.42). In practical terms, you cannot have a partial student so you should round up to the nearest whole number, i.e. 6.

FC:	Fixed costs	$4,200
Unit Revenue:	Unit revenue or price/unit	$1,000
Unit VC:	Unit variable cost	$225
BE:	Break-even point in units	5.42

FIGURE 6.3: *Break-even example*

TASK

Select one course your LTO offers.

For what purpose would you need to perform a break-even analysis for this course (e.g. opening a new section of the course, determining tuition increase)?

- Identify the variable and fixed costs for this course.

(Variable costs might include: staffing, classroom supplies, course marketing, course activities, etc. Fixed costs might include: rent, utilities, support staff, furniture, general supplies, LTO marketing, etc.)

- Try setting up a simple break-even analysis. What does it tell you about enrolment or price?

Once you have determined your break-even point for the course, and given the course and your market, will you increase your minimum enrolment target, increase the tuition price of the course, or a combination of the two, in order to achieve financial viability for the course?

Modelling

A model is a conceptual tool that shows the relationship between various elements of revenue and costs for a department, unit, activity or organization, and allows users to forecast how any change in those elements will affect the whole. Modelling is a way of looking at and manipulating a set of data. In terms of financial management, this usually means looking at financial activities and how change may affect the outcome. So, an LTO manager might want to create a model that looks at how changing class size impacts on the staffing of a course or how enrolment affects the net return of a course. A model will help a manager decide on the minimum number of students a course needs to enrol in order to be profitable to the LTO. At a higher, strategic level, modelling can assist the management of an LTO in making business decisions such as closing an activity, beginning a new activity, investing in resources such as facilities or personnel, etc.

This model is a very simple example, but models can be much more complex and they help in making long-term strategic decisions around pricing, marketing and allocation of resources. For example, using the scenario in the case study, a manager could then build a model to visualize a pricing structure whereby the volume of courses a corporation buys would reduce the price of each course. A corporation agreeing to purchase three courses in a year would have to pay $10,000 per course, but if they agreed to purchase five courses in a year, the price per course could drop to $8,000. A model would tell a manager exactly where the price shift that is most advantageous to the corporation and the LTO should happen.

Case study: Freeman LTO revenue strategy

Freeman's Board has decided that as a long-term revenue strategy it should market language classes to corporations within the region. The reasons for this strategy are:
- There is a strong corporate presence within the region in need of language classes.
- Freeman has a successful curriculum and a well-trained, stable teacher force.
- Freeman has strength and a successful reputation in adult courses.
- The courses would be conducted onsite at each corporation so no LTO facilities resources are required.
- The revenue can be calculated on a per course fee rather than on enrolment. The corporation pays for a course that is priced for a maximum enrolment of 15.
- All direct costs for the course would be fixed, based on the maximum enrolment limit.
- Institutional costs are kept at a minimum, maximizing the net revenue.

The Board would like this strategy to yield approximately 25% of the net income of the LTO by the third year of operation; this would be approximately $125,000. A model will help Freeman know how many corporate courses they must sell by Year Three to reach that target. The manager would create a financial model using a 'spreadsheet' software program, with interlinked cells so that it is possible to see the effects of alterations in input cells, such as number of courses. This is an example of what that model might look like:

Model of corporate courses

Number of courses: 10

	# Courses	Price per	Total
Revenue:	10	$10,000	$100,000

	# Courses	Cost per	Total
Costs:			
Instruction	10	$3,000	$30,000
Travel	10	$500	$5,000
Materials	10	$250	$2,500
Indirect	10	$1,000	$10,000
Total costs	10	$4,750	$47,500
Net:	10	$5,250	$52,500

This model shows that 10 courses would yield a net of $52,500. So, how many courses would be needed to yield a net of $125,000? The only area on this model that would have to be modified is the highlighted box for the number of courses. All other areas of the model will change according to what number you input in that box. As the next example shows, 24 courses will yield a net of $126,000. So, we know that by Year Three, the LTO must sell 24 corporate courses to meet this strategic objective.

Model of corporate courses
Number of courses: 24

	# Courses	Price per	Total
Revenue:	24	$10,000	$240,000
	# Courses	Cost per	Total
Costs:			
Instruction	24	$3,000	$72,000
Travel	24	$500	$12,000
Materials	24	$250	$6,000
Indirect	24	$1,000	$24,000
Total costs	24	$4,750	$114,000
Net:	24	$5,250	$126,000

STRATEGIC PLAN IMPLEMENTATION

In the previous sections of this chapter we explored how thorough strategic planning includes a resource inventory, an implementation plan, a budget and possibly a model for strategic activity. In this section, we will explore how these tools tie into the actual implementation of the strategic plan.

Resource allocation

When an organization implements a strategic plan, it requires resources to achieve its goals. As mentioned earlier in this chapter, it is helpful to create a resource inventory of existing resources in the organization. The next step is to tie those existing resources to the defined goals and allocate different types of resources toward the same priorities. This is a logical but often overlooked step when implementing a plan. Too often money is raised for one goal while staff and space are focused on another goal. The result is that none are fully accomplished or are not accomplished as quickly as they might be. Sometimes this means reassigning staff, fundraising, reallocating space or investing existing net revenue from one course into another.

All decisions have a financial impact, not just on the one course/activity, but on others. While these management decisions must be made, the consequential impact should be recognized. Any decisions should be made with the main focus towards the top priorities, while retaining an eye on the others affected by those decisions.

As an example, in the strategic goal of increasing the annual revenue by $10,000, the LTO has made the decision that the increase would come from adult and teen courses. It is decided to open and fill new sections of these courses rather than dramatically increase the enrolment in existing courses, which are at capacity. The LTO must therefore decide whether it already has the human resources it needs to add new classes of the courses concerned, or whether this is an area where financial resources need to be allocated to take on new staff. It could be that the resource inventory indicates that there are teachers who are available for these new classes. It might be part of the strategic plan to close other courses while opening these new ones, and therefore those teachers can be reallocated to the new course classes. If the resource inventory indicates that teachers are not available, then the LTO must decide whether the new teachers are hired on a contractual basis or whether they become full employees of the LTO. These decisions are governed not only by financial factors, but also by the recruiting practices and legal obligations imposed on the LTO by the region/country they operate in. Some countries do not allow for short-term contracts but insist on teachers becoming full-time employees, whereas in other countries, employing contractual teachers is a legal and acceptable practice (see Chapter 3, p. 59, for more discussion on contracts).

Measuring success, improvement and failure

As previously discussed, for a strategic plan to be achieved, progress towards the goals must be defined. On a financial level, this could be provided in periodic reports reflecting the financial impact to date. The financial goals of an LTO are measurable and quantifiable numbers. Other strategic goals of an LTO might have more room for interpretation, but financial goals are clear and explicit. Actual posted activity such as the amount of money from fundraising activities, programme revenue growth, spending within budgets or money saved, can be used to measure progress towards these financial goals. These can be measured in actual amounts or in percentages against the total for the goal. Another measurable outcome is the overall growth in the net assets of the LTO. Net assets are the amount by which the value of the assets of an enterprise exceeds its liabilities. A change in net assets represents a change in value of the organization. In corporations, this is the change in equity of capital of the business.

Defined benchmarks and timetables should be laid out and agreed to by all parties involved. The consequences of meeting, exceeding or failing to meet these goals should also be clear to all. At specified points in time, if little improvement is shown, the result should be analysed to see what factors need to change. New KPIs and possibly new goals might be established and the process started again.

INVESTMENT DECISIONS

All investment decisions share common traits such as the impact on the organization and potential cost. Some are major investment decisions such as entering a new market, purchasing facilities or premises, improving parts of the LTO infrastructure driving future programme and financial growth. Others may be smaller, such as new courses or office furniture. At all levels of management, most investment decisions are made by a group of people looking at various aspects of the investment. Consensus is usually arrived at and can be important for the staff directly affected by the decision. Investments are not just money committed, but time and resources as well.

Investment criteria

At all levels of investment, there are certain criteria that should provide a framework for making decisions. All aspects of a decision should be considered, such as mission impact, market position, programme growth, and future potential for other programmes. This section will focus on the financial criteria and measures. These include:

- timelines for both the investment and the activity
- expected return on investment (ROI)
- what resources will be committed
- risk involved.

Both the return on investment (ROI) and the internal rate of return (IRR) have two main components: the rate of return, and the expected time frame of the return. The rate of return is the percentage of the investment that is made in revenue over time. This is easily calculated in a spreadsheet program with built-in formulas. The time frame is how long it takes until a profit is made on the investment. A commitment of funding for one year for a new course might be expected to pay for itself in the next three years. This provides a timeline for the expected return, for the resources such as staff and space committed, and sets benchmarks for evaluation. Another factor might be potential growth if the course is successful. For example, what is the maximum course size achievable based on existing LTO resources and on the target market?

The last criteria we will look at are 'opportunity costs' and 'sunk costs'. Opportunity costs are the revenues lost by choosing to take this opportunity and not do something else. The activity not done may have had a profit which was not realized; this is the opportunity cost of the activity that was done instead. For example, if a second section of course A and not course B is offered, the opportunity cost of course A is the unrealized profit from course B. An LTO might choose to run the less profitable course to build up a certain market segment. The opportunity cost should be considered when making this decision.

Sunk costs are those costs incurred in exploring an activity whether or not it is done. It is the money spent whether or not the activity goes ahead. This might be a market study, work hours/salaries to develop a new course, or other such costs. LTO management may set limits on how much they are willing to spend in sunk costs when setting new course criteria.

BENCHMARKING

A benchmark is any standard or reference by which something can be measured or judged. Benchmarking is a process used in strategic management in which organizations evaluate various aspects of their processes in relation to the best practice of their own sector. It allows organizations to develop plans which incorporate selected best practices to increase the performance of the enterprise. Benchmarking may be a one-off event, but is often a continuous process in which organizations regularly seek to challenge their practices and assumptions.

Case study: Fitch Language Academy

Fitch Language Academy has autumn, winter and spring classes, but closes over the summer months and would probably not have financial benchmarks that fall during the months that the Academy is closed.

Fitch Language Academy's goal is to achieve a gross revenue target of $500,000 during Year One.

The highest gross revenue achieved in any one year in the last three years was $450,000. To achieve a $50,000 increase in revenue, Fitch Language Academy has chosen to offer more courses. Classes are offered from September–June and the Academy is closed in July and August. An analysis of the revenue patterns for the last three years yields the following information about average revenue:
- September–November = $200,000
- December–February = $100,000
- March–June = $150,000

Fitch Language Academy decides to set the following revenue benchmarks for their strategic goal:
- September–November = $225,000
- December–February = $100,000
- March–June = $175,000

Enrolment patterns suggest that there has been growth in the autumn and spring courses, but that enrolment for the winter courses stays pretty much the same. Winters are generally very cold and snowy and the Academy believes that these are factors influencing lower but steady enrolment in the winter. Therefore, they believe they can realize growth in enrolment by offering more classes in the autumn and spring.

Benchmarking connects the budget to the implementation plan and it allows managers to map and then track the progress of their strategic goals. In financial management terms, this is often tied to revenue or cost targets to be achieved by specified dates. Such targets may also be specified as key performance indicators (KPIs). When setting benchmarks (or KPIs), it is important to tie them to the flow of the activity being tracked.

A manager would use these benchmarks or KPIs to do quarterly checks to monitor progress towards the strategic financial goal. The benchmarks could be further broken down by months within each quarter so that a manager could track monthly progress. This gives even greater flexibility to take corrective action if the progress is not sufficient. To set the monthly benchmark, the manager would need to know past revenue performance by month to make appropriate monthly benchmarks for the new plan.

FINANCIAL STATEMENTS

Financial statements are a way to present financial information consistently to investors, shareholders and the public. They give basic financial information about a business or NFP organization. Standards and regulations for presenting financial information and reporting vary by country and geographic region. For example, in the US some of the information presented is different for a publicly-held company than for a private NFP organization. It is important to know and understand the requirements in your country. For smaller LTOs with few managers, it is also helpful to have the accountant prepare these for you. As a manager, you should know on what accounting basis your LTO operates and whether your financial statements are prepared on a cash or accrual basis. Cash basis recognizes income only when the cash is received. It also recognizes costs when the payments are made. Accrual basis recognizes income when the activity happens, such as tuition bills sent to students. It also recognizes costs in the period the activity occurs. In accrual basis accounting, revenue and cost must match in relation to one another, so costs related to income are recognized when the income generating activity happens. This does not mean that revenue and cost must equal.

In this section we will look at the following financial statements:
- profit and loss statement (income statement)
- balance sheet
- statement of cash flow.

Profit and loss statement

The profit and loss (P&L) statement is also known as the 'income statement'. This is an illustration of the financial activity that is bounded by a certain period of time – a month, a quarter or a year – which should be clearly specified on the statement. The P&L statement shows revenue (money coming in), cost (money going out), and the net or 'bottom line.' In the US and the UK, NFPs do not have a net profit or loss, but instead have a surplus or deficit. The main purpose of the income statement is to show by what categories or ways an LTO obtains and expends money. This statement is useful to analyse the proportion or distribution of revenue and cost by category.

Sometimes in a large LTO, the information may be shown by different lines of business or by different branches (as in a chain). However, there is usually also an income statement showing the whole LTO. Another difference may be in showing three fund types: permanently restricted, temporarily restricted and unrestricted funds. These designations refer to gifts or other funds that are given to the LTO and must be used according to the designation they fall under. Permanently restricted funds are always restricted and are usually investments. The interest income from the investments is used to fund activities. Temporarily restricted funds are monies given for a specific purpose such as donor or grant funds and spent only for that purpose. Unrestricted funds can be either money given to the organization with no specific intent or revenue from activities. Financial reports may show these separately as well as combined, since other reporting related to the use of restricted funds may be required.

Language Institute Statement of Activities Year ended August 31, 2008	
Revenue	**$**
Class fees	1,741,290
Total operating revenue	1,741,290
Operating expenses	
Personnel costs	783,600
Office expenses	12,300
Materials	37,625
Marketing	63,500
Equipment	78,400
Total operating expenses	975,425
Change in net assets	**765,865**
Indirect expenses	479,250
Total change in net assets	**286,615**

FIGURE 6.4: *Example of US-based NFP LTO P & L*

Balance sheet

The balance sheet shows the growth of a business in net worth or net assets. The purpose of this financial statement is to share the overall financial picture of an organization with shareholders, stakeholders and investors. The balance sheet for a corporation or business shows assets, liabilities and equity. For NFPs the equity is replaced by net assets. Assets are things, tangible or intangible, owned by the LTO. This may include cash, investments, property, some equipment and intangibles such as goodwill or trademarks. Liabilities are things owed by the LTO such as accounts payable, outstanding tax payments, or loans. The net, or net assets, is the difference between the total assets and the total liabilities. The 'balance' in 'balance sheet' refers to the accounting equation:

$$\text{total assets} = \text{total liabilities} + \text{equity (net assets)}$$

Figure 6.5 on p. 172 is an example of a US-based NFP LTO balance sheet. For illustration purposes, the total assets are shaded. The total liabilities are highlighted in a box. The net assets are the difference between the shaded total assets and the boxed total liabilities. The total liabilities and net assets, which needs to equal the shaded total assets, are also shaded.

Statement of cash flow

The purpose of the cash flow statement is to illustrate when money has come in and gone out of the business, i.e. the flow of cash for the business over time. It will show revenue, such as tuition or fee payments, coming in, and money, such as monthly rent cost

Language Institute
Statement of Activities
Year Ended August 31, 2008

Assets	$	$
Current assets:		
Cash	5,000	
Accounts receivable	10,000	
Inventory	2,000	
Total current assets		17,000
Property, plant & equipment		30,000
Total assets		47,000
Liability and owners equity		
Current liabilities:		
Accounts payable	7,000	
Notes payable	2,000	
Total current liabilities		9,000
Long-term debt		30,000
Total liabilities		39,000
Net assets: Unrestricted		8,000
Total liabilities and net assets		47,000

FIGURE. 6.5: *Example of US-based NFP LTO balance sheet*

Language Institute
Statement of Cash Flow
Year Ended August 31, 2008

Cash flows from operating activities	$	$
Net income	25,421	
Changes in operating assets and liabilities:		
Decrease in accounts receivable	200	
Increase in accounts payable	850	
Total adjustments		1,050
Net cash flows from operating activities		26,471
Cash flows from financing activities		
Increase in notes payable	6,000	
Net cash flows from financing activities		6,000
Net increase (decrease) from cash flows		32,471

FIGURE 6.6: *Example of US-based NFP LTO statement of cash flow*

payments, payroll cost or loan payments, going out. It is usually presented in a summary form. Potential funders may look at a statement of cash flow to see if an LTO can sustain itself or if it needs to use credit at times to cover costs. Figure 6.6 on p. 172 is an example of a US-based NFP LTO statement of cash flow.

Note that a statement of cash flow may not reflect all the same information as an income statement. Since this reflects the actual cash or cheques coming into the business, it will not reflect money moving from restricted funds to offset cost or it may reflect timing differences. A more complete discussion of cash flow at a detailed level will be provided in the next chapter.

DUTY OF CARE

'Duty of care' means that an organization has a responsibility, often legally defined, to protect employees, customers and other stakeholders from unnecessary risk of damage or injury to their well-being. Duty of care extends not only to health and safety (see Chapter 5, p. 140), but to protecting an organization from financial risk.

Different level managers have different levels of duty of care and different stakeholders to whom they are responsible. The director of an LTO has a duty of care for the entire institution and is ultimately responsible to all stakeholders, while also probably reporting directly to a board or other governing body, including a governmental agency. The DOS has a smaller sphere of management and is closer to the stakeholders directly involved than the director: the management staff of the LTO, the teaching staff and participants. The stakeholders that the DOS might be directly involved with would be the management staff of the organization and possibly teaching staff and participants. The DOS is usually accountable to the director. A departmental manager has an even smaller, more focused sphere of management and is more directly connected to the majority of stakeholders, such as instructors, staff and participants. This manager might report to the DOS or some other intermediary management personnel.

In all management positions, duty of care is a responsibility that should be conscientiously attended to. There are three main areas that managers must be responsible for:
- financial risk management
- responsibility to stakeholders
- legal and contractual compliance.

Financial risk management

Financial risk management is the practice of creating value in an organization by using financial tools to manage exposure to risk. While similar to general risk management, financial risk management:
- identifies the source of potential financial risk
- identifies ways to measure risk
- creates plans to address risks.

Financial risk management focuses on using financial instruments to determine how to minimize costly exposures.

The type of financial risk that directors of LTOs guard against is often at a broader level than managers at other levels. The director might need to be concerned with investment strategies of the organization and keeping an eye on the assets and financial resources and responsibilities undertaken by the LTO. Also, the director might be the one responsible for, or be part of a team that looks at the liability of an institution in terms of legal compliance with laws and regulations around health and safety to protect the institution against situations that could result in lawsuits or financial settlements.

The DOS reports to the LTO director and is responsible for the management decisions and oversight at the next level of operation. The DOS must be on guard against the risks of over-expenditure while also reviewing/analysing the revenue trends and factors that could impact negatively on the financial health of the institution. The DOS is also responsible for the policies and procedures of the LTO as set by the director, board, Human Resources, Finance, etc. which are there to protect the LTO from abuse and misuse.

Department managers have similar responsibilities to the DOS but their sphere of management is more restricted and the DOS is dependent upon the risk management skills and vigilance of the department manager. Department managers would have a closer connection to the revenue and costs of a course. Their reviews/analysis could suggest management decisions to put a course back on track if it was underperforming, thus lessening the financial risk to the institution. In addition, department managers are often the first in line of bottom-up reporting in terms of questions or violations of LTO policies and procedures. Teachers, staff and participants are more likely to report issues or concerns to the department manager, who is often an LTO's first line of defence for some of these types of risks.

All levels of management have a share of the responsibility of ensuring the financial health of an institution, and managing this financial risk serves the LTO and all its stakeholders.

Responsibility to stakeholders

A stakeholder is any party (individual or corporate) who affects or is affected by the actions of an enterprise. Part of the duty of care of an organization will be safeguarding stakeholder interests. The stakeholders of an LTO can be as follows:

- participants
- parents of participants
- teachers
- staff
- board
- investors
- creditors
- vendors
- governing body/agency
- community where the LTO operates.

An LTO has an overall set of responsibilities for operating a fiscally sound, ethical organization in the interest of all stakeholders. However, at a more practical level of responsibility, an LTO and the levels of management within the LTO have differing amounts of responsibility to different stakeholders. At all levels of management there are levels of direct and indirect responsibility to stakeholders both up and down the hierarchy of stakeholders.

REFLECTION

Consider your own LTO.
- Who are its stakeholders?
- Who are the stakeholders to whom you are directly responsible?
- How do you report to your stakeholders?
- What are the interests of the stakeholders to whom you are directly responsible?
- Do their interests differ from the interests of the other stakeholders of the LTO?
- How do you know what your stakeholders' interests are?
- Do you meet with your stakeholders directly?
- How often do you meet with your stakeholders?
- Is there some other form of communication you employ to stay current with your stakeholders?
- Is information funnelled to stakeholders through another layer of management at your LTO?

Legal and contractual compliance

The duty of care in terms of legal and contractual compliance has strong financial implications. For example, funds obtained by the LTO through either a government agency or an investor might have legal or contractual limitations as to its use. All levels of management at an LTO must be acquainted with these limitations because, if their funds are used for costs not in compliance with the contractual stipulations, not only could the LTO lose the funding but could find itself responsible for covering those costs and jeopardize future funding by being out of compliance.

In addition, there are accounting board standards that must be followed. The LTO's accountant or financial officer is responsible for making sure that the LTO is in compliance with the accounting standards used in the country of the LTO. However, management is responsible for knowing that there are standards to be followed and that the activities of the LTO reflect compliance with these standards. For example, in the US the accounting board standards are governed by FASB (Financial Accounting Standards Board). The IASC (International Accounting Standards Committee) is another standards body which applies to most of Europe and Japan. Similarly, the accountant should be following a set of accounting principles such as GAAP (Generally Accepted Accounting Principles). These principles give guidance on the type of documentation an organization needs for different types of transactions. It is good for managers to have a basic understanding of the principles being followed by the LTO in relation to their own responsibilities. For example, if you are responsible for signing off on reimbursements or expenditure, it is important to understand what documentation (invoice, receipt, statement, etc.) is needed by the LTO accountant to validate the transaction.

There are other levels of legal and contractual compliance such as taxes or registration to do business in a country that are the direct responsibility of higher management levels such as the LTO director. Contractual compliance issues, such as ensuring that a fifteen-hour language course actually offers fifteen hours of instruction, are ones that a programme manager would be responsible for. It is important for an LTO manager to understand the compliance responssibilities at his or her level of management. Such understanding is crucial to avoiding financial risk and to fulfilling responsibility to stakeholders and the overall stability of the organization.

CONCLUSION

In this chapter we have looked at the elements of strategic planning in financial management terms and with the duty of care for which managers are responsible. The tools discussed in this chapter should be useful in the strategic planning, implementation and evaluation process. A clear strategic plan helps set the stage for operational financial management. This in turn feeds the implementation and evaluation stages of planning. In the next chapter we will explore various elements and tools of operational financial management.

7 Operational financial management

- TYPES OF BUDGETS
- BUDGET COMPONENTS
- OPERATIONAL ISSUES
- CASH FLOW
- SYSTEMS

INTRODUCTION

In the previous chapter we explored strategic financial management. In this chapter we will explore operational financial management, which delves into daily financial management tasks and responsibilities and looks at some of the tools that managers use on a regular basis to understand the operational financial performance of the LTO. Depending on the size and management structure of the LTO, managers may find themselves in the position of having to create budgets for a specific activity or course, a division or an overall organizational budget. Whether it is their specific responsibility to create budgets or not, managers should know how budgets are created so that they understand in what way the area they are responsible for managing is viewed financially. Note that this chapter is not intended to teach double-entry bookkeeping, the focus being on the budgeting process.

TYPES OF BUDGETS

In managing the finances of any LTO, it is necessary to have sound financial plans in the form of budgets. Typically, budgets are set during a planning period which precedes the beginning of the next financial year. A budget will draw on history (i.e. performance during the current and preceding years) and projections (i.e. predictions of income and expense based on sales forecasts and commitments or agreements already undertaken).

Budgeting creates a framework within which individuals, departments or sections, and whole organizations can work. According to Brookson (2000, p. 9), there are six main aims of budgeting:

- planning: to aid the planning of an organization in a systematic and logical manner that adheres to the long-term business strategy
- co-ordination: to help co-ordinate the activities of the various parts of the organization and ensure that they are consistent
- communication: to communicate more easily the objectives, opportunities and plans of the business to the various business team managers

- motivation: to provide motivation for managers to try to achieve the organizational and individual goals
- control: to help control activities by measuring progress against the original plan, adjusting where necessary
- evaluation: to provide a framework for evaluating the performance of managers in meeting individual and departmental targets.

It is common to prepare budgets for a three- to five-year term, with an annual rollover so that the final year of the plan is always three or five years ahead of the current year. There are two main approaches to budgeting: baseline (or incremental) budgeting and zero-based budgeting. These processes can be used to create annual budgets for organizations, units of the organization and/or activities within the organization, project budgets and capital budgets. The first approach takes last year's budget or actual income and costs as the starting point, while the second approach builds a budget from scratch based on income targets and the costs needed to fulfil the LTO's activities. In this chapter we will explore the following types of budget:

- annual operating budget: a budget built on an annual basis which outlines the revenue and costs connected to the planned activities of the LTO
- Life of Project budget: a budget built specifically for a project's income and costs
- capital budget: a separate budget developed for capital expenditures such as large equipment purchases, buildings, or other depreciable assets.

Baseline, also known as incremental, budgeting is an efficient way of creating an annual operating budget for an entity or activity that is stable and non-changing. Enrolments, staffing and all general costs would be the same as for the previous budgeting cycle, but with a percentage increase to account for inflation of costs. The difficulty with inflation rates is that often the rate is not uniform across the different costs. For example, wage inflation might have a very different basis from the inflation rate for materials, travel or fuel. Generally, the inflation rate will be dictated at the highest LTO level. If you are a manager at that level and having to set the inflation rate, there are several factors to take into account.

The average inflation rate in the economy of the country is the most common place to start. Another factor is that a regional inflation rate may need to be the basis for the LTO's inflation rate. One could also look at the inflation trends of the last several years for the LTO. The inflation rate would then be based specifically on the inflation trends of the LTO.

Even if a baseline inflation rate has been set for the LTO using one of these methods, management may wish to employ a different inflation rate for certain costs within a budget. For example, if the LTO is located in a country or region that has been seriously affected by higher fuel prices, that could influence the inflation rate to be set for certain costs, such as travel, utilities and vehicle costs. Whichever way management calculates the inflation rate, they should always look to both the outer and inner environments for inflation impact.

A baseline budget may have several different inflation rates, based on the type of revenue or cost in the budget. However, these rates should be defined and a clear rationale for their use provided with the budget. If you are a mid-level manager who does not have the responsibility for setting the inflation rates for your institution/programme, it is still important to understand what the rates are and how they were determined so that as you create your budget you understand the impact on your programme.

Figure 7.1 is an example of a basic baseline budget with several different inflation rates and their rationale.

Description	FY07 OPERATING BUDGET $	Inflation Rate $	FY08 FINAL OPERATING BUDGET $	Rationale
REVENUE		5%		
Tuition: Adult ESOL	150,000	7,500	157,500	A 5% revenue increase is standard for the market.
Tuition: Young Learners	75,000	3,750	78,750	
Application fees	9,000		9,000	No increase in application fees.
		10%		
Materials fees	10,000	1,000	11,000	Average increase of books is 10%.
Subtotal revenue:	244,000		256,250	
COST		4%		
Teaching: salary	50,000	2,000	52,000	Annual salary increases expected at 4%.
Teaching: adjunct (fixed-term contract)	25,000	1,000	26,000	
Programme: salary	30,000	1,200	31,200	
Distributed fringe	26,250	1,050	27,300	
		2%		Other general costs avg. 2%.
Guest lecturers	3,000	60	3,060	
Postage	1,500	30	1,530	
Courier	750	15	765	
Supplies: office	1,000	20	1,020	
Supplies: educational	1,000	20	1,020	
Printing/copying	4,000	80	4,080	
		15%		Fuel/energy increase of 15%.
Domestic travel	15,000	2,250	17,250	
International travel	35,000	5,250	40,250	
Subtotal costs	192,500		205,475	
NET	51,500		50,775	

FIGURE 7.1: *Baseline budget example*

> **REFLECTION**
>
> Examine this budget.
> - What are some of the things you notice?
> - What is the net income for the new fiscal year as compared to the previous year?
> - Is the variance between the two acceptable?
> - If not, how would you propose increasing the net?

Two things that should stand out are, firstly, the significant increase in travel costs due to the increase in fuel/energy prices, and, secondly, the projected net is lower than the previous net.

Questions to ask in terms of whether this is an acceptable variance are:
- Is it temporary, confined to this one year?
- Is it likely to continue at this rate?
- Can the institution sustain the financial impact?

If the variance is not acceptable, one thing you might consider is increasing the revenue. In increasing revenue, you will have to decide if this is to be done by increasing tuition, enrolment, or both. If enrolment is to be increased, then you will have to revisit your direct costs as well.

Another consideration might be in the cost area of the budget. Instead of a 4% increase in salaries, you might want to consider lowering that percentage. In doing so, what impact might that have on the variance? Also, consider what impact that might have on your staff, bearing in mind that, as pointed out in Chapter 3, pay is such a significant issue.

Basically, one can look at either increasing the revenue, decreasing the costs, or both. However, in a baseline budget process, that would most likely mean revisiting the inflation rates rather than the actual costs since the premise of this budget process is that none of the factors in the budget has changed, neither enrolment nor cost categories. The variance is the difference between a projection and an actual (revenue, cost or net) or the difference between past performance and current or projected performance. The variance between the net for the two successive years might be perfectly acceptable. However, if the trend continued, then stability becomes stagnation and eventually decline.

Very often, what the market can bear in terms of increased tuition costs is less than the actual increase in costs. Therefore, LTOs have to determine a strategy to make their offerings more cost effective or find new revenue streams/areas of business to diversify revenue levels. This means that an LTO should no longer be using baseline budgeting, but will need to do some form of zero-based budgeting.

Zero-based budgeting is a complex and comprehensive approach to budgeting. A zero-based budget is built from the ground up. Income or enrolment targets are set and costs are built around the costs needed to conduct the activity based on those targets. In a zero-based budget, the manager can revisit all aspects of an activity's income and costs. For instance, in a course that has a history of meeting enrolment targets, the manager has the opportunity to look at increasing this or at modifying the costs of the course by revisiting the course design. One way might be to increase average class size, thus reducing instructional costs, or to reduce the number of contact hours. While it is never an ideal situation to modify a course design simply to meet a financial target, this is often the reality which confronts managers. So, managers have to look at the financial impact of course design. This can be done through a zero-based, but not a baseline, budgeting process.

A zero-based budget also allows programmes to reallocate funds within a course. For example, if a course's financial statements show that the cost of photocopying has consistently exceeded the budget projections while the cost of postage is consistently underspent, then a programme manager could decide to reallocate some of the postage funds to photocopying. In addition, by examining line item costs individually, a manager can make better-informed course decisions. In the case of photocopying costs, a manager might want to examine why they consistently exceed the budgeted amount. Who is making photocopies? Can it be tied to instructional costs or to a per student basis? In researching this area, a manager might decide to make changes to photocopying policies, thus reducing the cost of photocopying for the course.

Figure 7.2 (pp. 182–3) is an example of a zero-based budget which shows that the manager had to consider not only the income/enrolment target, but all the costs associated with that course. The example is for an annual budget for an LTO branch office. Note that on salary, there is a 20% levy for benefits, i.e. the social security or comparable charges which an employer is required to contribute. The actual percentage varies widely from country to country. An LTO as part of a larger, 'host' institution may also be required to make a contribution to central institutional fixed costs. In this example, this overhead is levied at a rate of 20%. Again, there will be local variations on such institutional overhead rates.

TASK

Study the budget in Figure 7.2.

Look at the institutional costs total and percentage. What is the percentage of institutional costs that this budget needs to support? Assume that this rate cannot be altered.

Your supervisor has asked you to increase your net profit from 9% to 12%.
- What will you do to attain this return?
- Will you increase the tuition price? Will you increase enrolment?
- What are the other consequences of increasing enrolment? Will you cut costs? If so, which ones?

With the institutional costs percentage rate at 31% of income unalterable, you will need to consider other options for increasing the net profit to 12%. Currently, the net profit is 9%, so you will need to look at your revenue and costs to determine how best to increase this by 3%.

If you decide to increase enrolment to obtain a higher revenue, you must look at the costs that will be affected by the increase and adjust accordingly. If you are considering a tuition price increase, you will need to examine your marketplace to see if it can bear an increase and if so, how much of an increase. You also need to consider if there are any

INCOME						
Tuition-based income		Course fee $	Students		Total income $	Percentage of income
Juniors age 7–12		500	500		250,000	15%
Teenagers age 13–18		750	795		596,250	35%
Examination classes		400	355		142,000	8%
Adults: general		750	425		318,750	19%
Adults: business		1,000	275		275,000	16%
Corporate class-based income		Course fee		Courses		
In-company (per class)		12,000		10	120,000	7%
TOTAL INCOME					**1,702,000**	**100%**
COSTS						
Teaching salaries	Pay	Benefits = 20%	Total	No.	Total	Per cent
Course Director	80,000	16,000	96,000	1	96,000	12%
DOS	65,000	13,000	78,000	1	78,000	9%
Teachers: senior	50,000	10,000	60,000	2	120,000	14%
Teachers: full-time	42,000	8,400	50,400	5	252,000	30%
Teachers: part-time hours	50	—	50	3,807	190,350	23%
Total teaching salaries					736,350	88%
Administrative salaries	Pay	Benefits = 20%	Total	No.	Total	
Admin/secretary	45,000	9,000	54,000	100%	54,000	6%
Registration secretary	35,000	7,000	42,000	100%	42,000	5%
Total administrative salaries					96,000	12%
TOTAL staff costs					**832,350**	**54%**
Office costs		Cost	No. of Months			
Communications		300	12		3,600	31%
Copying		200	12		2,400	21%
Postage		400	12		4,800	41%
Office supplies		75	12		900	8%
TOTAL office costs					**11,700**	**1%**
Equipment		Cost	No.			
Video cameras		1,000	18		18,000	23%
TV/video recorders		800	8		6,400	8%
Computers with software		3,000	18		54,000	69%
TOTAL equipment					**78,400**	**5%**
Materials		Cost	Units			
Teaching materials						
Books		200	24		4,800	7%
Videos		250	24		6,000	8%
Miscellaneous		125	24		3,000	4%
Total teaching materials					13,800	19%
Student materials						
Reading folders		25	2,350		58,750	81%
Total student materials					58,750	81%
TOTAL materials					**72,500**	**5%**
Publicity		Cost Per	Units		Total	
Print advertising		400	80		32,000	47%
Radio advertising		2,000	10		20,000	29%
Brochures		0.75	20,000		15,000	2%
Posters		15	100		1,500	2%
TOTAL publicity					**68,500**	**4%**

Institutional overhead costs			Cost	Per cent	Total	
Administrative salaries & Social			800,000	20%	160,000	33%
Institutional promotion/ publicity			75,000	20%	15,000	3%
Maintenance			120,000	20%	24,000	5%
Utilities			150,000	20%	30,000	6%
Rental: school			1,080,000	20%	216,000	45%
Insurance			75,000	20%	15,000	3%
Property tax			96,250	20%	19,250	4%
TOTAL institutional costs					**479,250**	**31%**
TOTAL COSTS					**1,542,750**	**100%**
NET PROFIT or (LOSS)			(Percentage of Income)		**159,280**	**9%**

FIGURE 7.2: *Zero-based budget example*

costs that could be reduced or eliminated. For example, is the video equipment a necessary cost for this year? Could it be reduced or cut completely?

A Life of Project budget is usually a zero-based budget that often has a defined funder or source of funding, a clear set of activities and outcomes, and a set period of time for which it will operate (see Chapter 10, pp. 257–265). The length of the project determines the length of the budget and can be any length of time from a month to multi-year. These budgets often operate outside of the annual budgeting process, but nonetheless relate to the operational budget, either in terms of additional resources the institution might allocate to carry out the project and/or in terms of the net revenue that the project will contribute to the annual revenue picture of the LTO.

A capital budget is an annual budget that is created in addition to the annual operating budget. The purpose of the capital budget is to plan for major expenditures such as construction, land/property purchases, vehicle or major equipment purchases. Most items in a capital budget (with the exception of land and property) must be depreciated over time. The concept of depreciation relates to an asset's loss of value over its expected life. For example, a vehicle is assumed to have a lifespan of a set number of years, by the end of which it will no longer function. Each year, the vehicle depreciates in value. This depreciation must be recorded in the account records of the LTO. Like the operating budget, capital budgets are often based on a three- to five-year plan. Most organizations have a capital policy and depreciation schedules based in part on government tax depreciation guidelines.

BUDGET COMPONENTS

To be proficient at budgeting, modelling and pricing, we strongly recommend that all managers get some training in using spreadsheet software. Some organizations use database software for creating budgets, and so gaining an understanding of databases would be important. If you do not already know how your institution creates budgets, you should find out so that you are following the same processes. As the majority of institutions use some kind of spreadsheet software for one or more of the processes mentioned above, the examples that follow are in the form of spreadsheets.

Revenue

Revenue is the amount of money an LTO earns from its activities over a certain period of time. In Europe, including the UK, the term for this is 'turnover'. Revenue does not necessarily appear in all budgets. Often a manager does not have the same control or input over revenue as costs. One of the reasons for this is that it depends on whether the manager is responsible for a cost or profit centre. An example of a cost centre within an LTO would be a library or accounting office. It is generally a support function of the LTO and does not usually generate revenue. If you manage a cost centre, you will not necessarily have enough revenue to cover the costs of your centre, or even any revenue at all. Examples of a profit centre would be a programme office offering courses, a bookstore, or a catering or accommodation office. For profit centres, the revenue projections are kept at a macro (higher) level within the organization or else are dictated as a projection target for managers and therefore are not a component of the budget that the manager administers. For the purposes of this section, we are going to assume that revenue is a component of the budget. For an LTO, there are many different possible sources of revenue. These might include but are not limited to:

- individual tuition
- participant costs not covered by tuition (i.e. room and board, books and fees, cultural programme)
- programme sponsorship.

Tuition is usually the amount charged to cover the costs of providing a course. Student fees are sometimes charged for such items as course materials, student access to an LTO's library, computer lab, recreational facilities or social programmes. These fees are sometimes covered by the tuition charged or can be charged as a separate fee or fees. Tuition does not normally include room and board, so this income is usually charged as a separate revenue stream. Some revenue streams such as room and board may not appear in the same budget as the revenue for tuition and other course costs. In some organizations, certain types of revenue are handled in the department most closely connected to that revenue. So, the revenue for room and board might be budgeted for in the Housing or Facilities Departments rather than the Programme Department.

The case study opposite shows an example of a revenue calculation.

Costs/expenses

Costs, also referred to as expenses, are all those to be incurred by the programme or activity for which a budget is being created. There are many categories of costs but for the purposes of creating an LTO-related budget, we will be concentrating on three major types of costs: direct, indirect and start up. Not all budgets will have all three types of costs.

Direct costs

Direct costs are the costs directly linked to the volume of business. These costs can be either variable (i.e. based on enrolment) or fixed (i.e. unchanging when enrolment changes). Direct costs could include the following:

- teaching or course provision
- materials (textbooks)
- copying materials
- communications
- postage
- food service.

These costs are calculated on a basis that is connected to any or all of the following: the number of students/participants, number of teachers, number of months for the course, number of events. These numbers are variable because if the basis for the calculation is changed, the cost amount changes. For example, if you budget for a course to have a maximum enrolment of 15 students, many of the costs might be connected to that enrolment figure. Copying might be calculated as $25 per student and so your total budget for copying would be $375. If you enrol 10 students, then your copying line will be reduced to $250 ($25 per student × 10 students).

Case study: Revenue calculation

The revenue is for one course offered twice a year. The enrolment target for the course is set at 15 participants per semester for a total of 30 for the year. There is an application fee that all participants must submit for their enrolment applications to be reviewed and each student is charged a fee for the required texts, which the LTO distributes to them.

	Amount	Enrolment	Total for Semester 1	Total for Semester 2	Grand total per course
REVENUE					
Application fee	$25	35	$875	$875	$1,750
Tuition	$500	15	$7,500	$7,500	$15,000
Books	$50	15	$750	$750	$1,500
TOTAL REVENUE			$9,125	$9,125	$18,250

While the enrolment projection is for a total of 30 participants for the year, the application fee has a projection of 35 per semester. This will depend on the practices of your institution but commonly, application fees are charged and collected upon the submission of a participant's application, so it is often the case that the course will receive more applications than it has slots to fill. Or there are applicants who do not qualify for or fit the course. Some organizations make the application fee refundable if enrolment is not accepted, but many charge the fee as a way of defraying the cost of reviewing applications.

Teaching or course provision is also tied to enrolment, but probably less on an individual student basis and more on the basis of a threshold, such as class size or student–teacher ratio. If your LTO says that the maximum permitted class size is 15 and there are 20 students who wish to enrol, you will need to either deny enrolment to five students or divide the class into two sections with a teacher for each section. Of course, in making the decision to do this, you must look at the revenue those five students generate and the additional costs they generate. Figure 7.3 shows an example of what that analysis might look like.

REVENUE	Cost $	No.	TOTAL $	No.	TOTAL $	Basis
Tuition	500	15	7,500	20	10,000	Students
Application fees	25	15	375	20	500	Students
Subtotal revenue			7,875		10,500	
			TOTAL		TOTAL	
COST						
Teaching: salary	2,500	1	2,500	2	5,000	Teachers
Distributed fringe: 25% of salary	625	1	625	2	1,250	Teachers
Copying	25	15	375	20	500	Students
Food for breaks	10	15	150	20	200	Students
Postage	5	15	75	20	100	Students
Books	25	15	375	20	500	Students
Teacher materials	100	1	100	2	200	Teachers
Subtotal cost			4,200		7,750	
NET			3,675		2,750	

FIGURE 7.3: *Additional cost analysis*

Figure 7.3 shows that by enrolling the five extra students, the LTO will realize a net income of $925 less than if there were only one class with 15 students.

There are also direct costs that are fixed. All costs which do not significantly vary according to the level of business, and, indeed, have to be covered regardless, are fixed costs. Some examples of a fixed direct cost you would have in your budget might be communication (phones/faxes/Internet), advertising, and office supplies. These costs would not necessarily be directly affected by enrolment and thus would not vary.

Indirect costs
In addition to direct costs, an LTO manager must also consider indirect costs, sometimes referred to as 'overhead'. Some of the overhead costs that might be included in this category are:

- rent
- utilities
- administrative costs (management salaries and costs)
- insurance
- property tax
- maintenance.

For some LTOs, these costs are calculated as an overhead rate or percentage to which all courses and activities must contribute from their income in order for them to be covered. For other LTOs, indirect costs are defined in budgets as pro-rated or allocated costs tied to the activity of the budget. Figure 7.2 (p. 182) includes an example of institutional overhead.

Start up costs

The last category is start up costs. These are costs that must be incurred on a one-time basis to initiate a course or activity. In subsequent budgets for these same activities these costs would not be incurred. Some of the costs that might be included in this category are:

- marketing and promotion
- course development
- teacher recruitment.

When you are budgeting for these costs, it is usually a good idea to keep them together in a 'start up costs' category so that they can be easily removed in subsequent budgets for that business or activity.

Notes

Budget notes are a critical component of any budget an LTO manager creates. They serve to explain to the reader the assumptions under which the budget was created and to clarify any budget item that is not obviously self-explanatory. Notes are as important for the author as for the reader. After several months, it is all too easy to forget why a cost was included in a budget or what the cost was intended to be used for. Having detailed notes helps the author of a budget to explain and manage a budget and to replicate it in the future if necessary. Notes are also an important tool for the budget manager, who may or may not be the same person as the author. The notes serve as a framework for the planning of a business or activity and thus provide a guide for managers who are charged with executing and/or monitoring that business or activity.

General budget notes apply to the entire budget and help the reader of the budget to form their own frame of reference as they examine it. For example:

- This budget assumes that the start date is 'X' and the end date is 'Y'.
- This budget assumes no inflation for the time period of the budget.
- This budget presents a minimum net income of 33% of revenue.

Detailed budget notes explain the purpose of the cost and how the cost (or total for the cost) was calculated. For example:

- Salary: 1 teacher $\times$ $2,500 for the course for a maximum of 15 students.

- Printing/photocopying: $25 per student x 15 students, for course readings and materials.
- Indirect costs: calculated at a rate of 33% of the projected gross revenue.

Budget notes can be a separate document that is attached to the budget or they can be written in next to each line item on the budget. The form of the notes is not as important as the completeness and clarity of the information they contain. LTO management may have their own preferred way of displaying notes.

REFLECTION

Go back to the annual zero-based LTO budget (Figure 7.2). Examine the revenue and cost projections. Detailed though the budget is, what questions do you have about these figures that should be answered by budget notes? For example:
- How many classes does enrolment represent?
- How big is the class size for each type of class?
- How many hours is each course?
- What is the rationale for the video equipment?

OPERATIONAL ISSUES

Now that we have looked at how to develop a budget, we will look at how that budget is used during the year. This includes how to monitor the budget activity and make any necessary changes. Remember, a budget is a financial plan. What happens when the course plan changes or the actual activity deviates from the plan?

Budget monitoring and control

Monitoring financial performance and making appropriate adjustments are major management responsibilities. In order to do this, management at all levels must have regular, accurate financial information. We may need information to make informed decisions about enrolments or to adjust spending priorities when necessary. A DOS or LTO director may need information for each programme to make investment decisions or to seek funding. A course director will need to know what that course's financial picture looks like. Budget monitoring is a way to look at measurable outcomes achieved. This will be illustrated again in the section on budget reports.

Most monitoring looks at activity after it has happened. Another form of monitoring is cost approvals on a daily basis. Someone with authority over the budget should approve costs before they are incurred. The purpose is to be sure that spending is in line with the budget as it has occurred and that deviations really are necessary. If approval is after the fact, it is much more difficult to prevent cost overruns and keep a positive net margin.

For many managers, monitoring a budget is supposed to be a regular part of their responsibilities. However, it is all too common to look only on the cost side. It is much better to monitor both the revenue and the cost activity against the budget. This is true whether it is at a higher, macro level or a detailed, line item level. When revenue shifts occur, they may affect how costs are to be controlled. If revenue is higher than expected, it would be helpful to know why. The obvious answer is that enrolments were higher than envisaged, but it may also be that fewer scholarships or discounts were given out. Have you received funding from an unexpected source? Is this likely to happen again? What effect, if any, does this have on costs? If revenue postings are lower than expected, what can you do to control costs? Are there natural cost reductions from lower enrolments, such as course materials? Budget monitoring can inform many different decisions, not just how much money you spend.

When monitoring cost budgets, it is important to look not only at spending against budget, but also at timing or phasing issues in certain budget lines. Are there costs such as taxes that are paid quarterly, not monthly? Have one-time purchases such as furniture or new computers been planned for in the budget? If these costs have not yet been incurred, the total budget picture may look better than it really is. The solution is to add any future costs to your current activity, then compare that total against the budget. The next task invites you to consider a scenario which continues over the next few tasks.

TASK

At one LTO, course enrolments have come in under budget. This LTO also offers reduced fees to students in need. For the current semester, the LTO director had planned to purchase new video equipment for ten classrooms in addition to normal costs. The director knows enrolment is low and would like to make the same net profit regardless of enrolment.
- What programme-related questions should the director ask? For example, is the need for the video equipment immediate?
- Can the purchase of equipment be reduced or delayed?
- What other budget lines would you look at?
- What are the controllable costs?
- Since enrolment is down, which variable costs tied to enrolment can be reduced?

There are certain categories of costs that should be monitored more closely, either because overspending may be likely in your organization or because there are greater consequences for overspending. The biggest investment and cost for educational organizations is payroll. It is important to be sure that all pay and associated benefits are budgeted and covered. If a course has high enrolments and an extra section, what is the additional cost for teaching hours? There may be different ways of handling this that have different cost factors, such as giving a current employee additional work instead of hiring another teacher for just that one course.

As we step back and look at the whole budget for a course or for a programme, monitoring over time should also help us see trends emerging. This may be in enrolments, tuition levels, the amount of aid or scholarships given to students, additional pay to faculty or staff, increased materials cost, or lack of investment. For example, when looking at tuition revenue, we may see the revenue for one course growing over time. If tuition rates have stayed constant, then the enrolment data should show the same growth pattern. This information can be used to determine marketing strategies as well as tuition rates. Is the LTO staying competitive or can it charge a higher tuition and still meet enrolment targets? Is the LTO better off financially with lower tuitions and higher enrolments? How can the use of scholarships affect this decision? Conversely, if there are certain courses not making their budgeted revenue, is this lowering overall net income? Are there other courses making up the difference? If there is money to invest, how would this information influence management's decisions? Cost monitoring is important not only for trend analysis, but also the daily management of money.

Things to watch for in budget monitoring:
- trends reflected in actual activity
- trends informing better budgeting
- correct activity posting
- over spending
- allocation of budget in correct categories.

Budget adjustments

What happens when enrolments are 20% higher and therefore both revenue and cost are higher? Since a budget is a plan or estimate, it can be adjusted to reflect changing circumstances. In order to distinguish the difference between where you started and where you have adjusted, budget adjustments are not made to an opening budget, but to a current budget. In this way, managers can see at the end of a budget period where things have changed, possibly leading to more informed budgets next time. Since most smaller budgets are consolidated at a higher level or roll up to an overall budget, budget adjustments will also roll up to a macro level to give a more accurate picture for a whole programme or organization.

Continuing with this example of higher enrolments, enrolments for one course in a programme were expected to be 20 students but are actually 24 students. This means not only more revenue but also additional costs for faculty salaries, benefits and taxes, and course materials. In order to see how costs are tracking against the expected higher amounts, it would be easiest to see an adjusted budget in the budget report. It is also helpful to see how the adjusted budget for this course affects the whole programme budget. If other courses are under-recruiting, the additional net here may help offset their losses. Changes in programme activity could also lead to reallocating the cost budget. When there are shifts in programme activity, the budget should shift as well to reflect these changes. This is known as a budget reallocation: the total stays the same, but the distribution between categories or lines is different.

TASK

The LTO director has asked your opinion but still really wants to invest in the video equipment. There were ten planned full tuitions at $1,000 and three discounted tuitions at $900. You have said that with lower enrolment, certain costs such as materials and class activities will go down and that maybe a smaller investment is a better idea. The director asks you to put your recommendations on paper and include an adjusted budget.

	Budget $	Actual activity $	Future activity $	Total $	Adjusted budget $
Full tuition	10,000	9,000	—	9,000	
Discounted tuition	2,700	900	1,800	2,700	
Total revenue	12,700	9,900	1,800	11,700	
Salaries and benefits	5,000	2,000	3,000	5,000	
Student materials	1,300	900	300	1,200	
Equipment	2,000	—	2,000	2,000	
Class activities	1,300	—	1,200	1,200	
Other costs	500	200	300	500	
Total cost	10,100	3,100	6,800	9,900	
Net	2,600	6,800	(5,000)	1,800	

Figure 7.4 shows one possible scenario, with the adjusted column in bold.

	Budget $	Actual activity $	Future activity $	Total $	Adjusted budget $
Full tuition	10,000	9,000	—	9,000	**9,000**
Discounted tuition	2,700	900	1,800	2,700	**1,800**
Total revenue	12,700	9,900	1,800	11,700	**10,800**
Salaries and benefits	5,000	2,000	3,000	5,000	**5,000**
Student materials	1,300	900	300	1,200	**1,100**
Equipment	2,000	—	2,000	2,000	**600**
Class activities	1,300	—	1,200	1,200	**1,100**
Other costs	500	200	300	500	**400**
Total cost	10,100	3,100	6,800	9,900	**8,200**
Net	2,600	6,800	(5,000)	1,800	**2,600**

FIGURE 7.4: *Adjusted budget with reduced expenditure*

This scenario assumes that there will be no new full tuitions and that one more discounted tuition will be accepted. The recommendation is to reduce the equipment expenditure from $2,000 to $600, thus achieving the same net as originally projected.

Another possible scenario is to cut the equipment line completely and thus leave some margin for unexpected costs.

A third scenario might be to accept a smaller net for the year and increase the amount to be spent on equipment by the acceptable amount of deficit. For example, if it has been decided that a net of $2,000 is acceptable, which is a $600 variance from the projected net, then the equipment line can be adjusted back up to $1,200.

TASK

Refer to the budget in the previous Task. What are some of the ways you can suggest of making approximately the same net?
- Are you better off taking the students with reduced tuition and keeping the costs for them, or foregoing the revenue and further decreasing costs?
- What ways do you suggest cutting costs?
- Can you postpone or eliminate certain costs?
- What would you suggest to the director?

Figure 7.5 shows a scenario with full tuition revenue as originally budgeted and actual discounted tuition revenue.

	Budget $	Actual activity $	Future activity $	Total $	Adjusted budget $
Full tuition	10,000	9,000	—	9,000	**10,000**
Discounted tuition	2,700	900	1,800	2,700	**900**
Total revenue	12,700	9,900	1,800	11,700	**10,900**
Salaries and benefits	5,000	2,000	3,000	5,000	**5,000**
Student materials	1,300	900	300	1,200	**1,100**
Equipment	2,000	—	2,000	2,000	**700**
Class activities	1,300	—	1,200	1,200	**1,100**
Other costs	500	200	300	500	**400**
Total cost	10,100	3,100	6,800	9,900	**8,300**
Net	2,600	6,800	(5,000)	1,800	**2,600**

FIGURE 7.5: *Adjusted budget with full tuition revenue*

Figure 7.6 shows another scenario with actual full tuition revenue and discounted tuition revenue as originally budgeted.

	Budget $	Actual activity $	Future activity $	Total $	Adjusted budget $
Full tuition	10,000	9,000	—	9,000	**9,000**
Discounted tuition	2,700	900	1,800	2,700	**2,700**
Total revenue	12,700	9,900	1,800	11,700	**11,700**
Salaries and benefits	5,000	2,000	3,000	5,000	**5,000**
Student materials	1,300	900	300	1,200	**1,200**
Equipment	2,000	—	2,000	2,000	**700**
Class activities	1,300	—	1,200	1,200	**1,200**
Other costs	500	200	300	500	**400**
Total cost	10,100	3,100	6,800	9,900	**8,500**
Net	2,600	6,800	(5,000)	1,800	**3,200**

FIGURE 7.6: *Adjusted budget with full discounted tuition revenue*

As you can see, taking in more students, even at a reduced tuition rate, has a positive impact on the net profit. This provides you with greater options for equipment expenditure and margin for unexpected costs.

Budget adjustments are handled in different ways in different organizations. Some LTOs may decide adjustments at a higher level of management such as the school director or DOS, then give them to course directors to manage. In others, course directors may be involved in planning decisions and therefore be part of the budget adjustment process. If you are responsible for a budget, it is helpful to know how adjustments are made and the factors influencing those decisions in your own organization. The one occasion when managers should not adjust budgets is at the end of a course or year when the activity is completed. Adjusting after the fact, when the activity is over, creates unnecessary work as well as losing useful information. Remember, a budget is an estimate or a plan. It is helpful to know how you did compared to that plan in order to make improvements during the next budget cycle. If budgets are adjusted after the fact to reflect reality, managers lose an important learning and planning tool.

Budget reporting

Budget reports are the mechanism to show what the picture looks like. The periodic report is a useful – indeed, essential – means to these ends. Budget reports are hierarchically organized to provide an appropriate amount of information to the various levels of management. There are generally three levels in this hierarchy:

- the highest, or macro, level presents the LTO revenue and cost either by the financial statement categories or by the major business units within the LTO

- the secondary level presents the revenue and cost by each course within a major business unit
- the lowest, most detailed level presents the revenue and cost by line items within each course.

For example, an LTO director might want to see a higher level such as the financial statement categories, a DOS might want a secondary level of reporting, while a course director would need the most detailed level showing the line items within a course.

Most budget reports are prepared monthly. However, other time periods such as quarterly, yearly or course length may be used based on specific needs. In a business, it is common to have quarterly reports which go to the board of directors. In tracking grant funds, a budget report may be created to look at monthly activity and multi-year activity for the entire length of the grant.

A monthly report can be arranged to present performance from two perspectives:
- budget for the month concerned compared with actual performance for that month
- budget for the year compared with cumulative performance up to that month.

TASK

	Original budget $	Current budget $	Current month $	Year to date $	% complete
Revenue:					
Tuition	10,000	10,000	3,000	13,000	130%
Materials fees	500	500	150	650	130%
Total revenue	10,500	10,500	3,150	13,650	
Cost:					
Salaries	3,000	3,000	1,200	2,100	70%
Benefits	600	600	240	420	70%
Materials	500	500	150	650	130%
Supplies	100	100	25	50	50%
Advertising	400	400	0	397	99%
Total cost:	4,600	4,600	1,615	3,617	
Net	5,900	5,900	1,535	10,033	

Above is a sample budget report. The original budget was planned for a course with three sections and a teacher for each. This budget report is halfway through the cycle. Study the report and then answer the following questions:
- What happened to enrolment expectations?
- What resulting costs do you think will be different?
- What types of costs will still be paid out over the length of the course?

Enrolment expectations exceeded the projections by 30%, while, as a variable cost, the materials line will definitely increase. With a 30% increase in enrolments, there has been an increase in the number of sections and instructors. This is reflected in the additional cost in salaries and benefits, which are at 70% spent at the midpoint of the course. Costs which will still be paid out over the length of the course include salaries, benefits and supplies. It is unlikely that more materials or advertising costs will be incurred.

An alternative approach to budget reports is to display activity for different courses at a higher level, showing, for example, how one LTO branch is performing. It may show only the course revenue and cost or it may show general cost categories such as salaries, materials, etc. It may show a variance against budget instead of showing a per cent spent against budget. Figure 7.7 is an example of a higher-level budget showing a variance column.

	Original budget $	Current budget $	Current month $	Year to date $	Variance $
Revenue:					
Adult course tuition	10,000	12,000	3,000	9,000	**3,000**
Teenager course	4,400	4,000	2,000	3,000	**1,000**
Weekend course	2,000	2,000	250	1,750	**250**
Materials fees	3,000	3,500	1,800	2,600	**900**
Total revenue	19,400	21,500	7,050	16,350	**5,150**
Cost					
Salaries	4,000	4,800	1,200	3,000	**1,800**
Benefits	600	960	240	600	**360**
Adult course	3,000	3,750	—	1,275	**2,475**
Teenager course	2,000	1,800	25	200	**1,600**
Weekend course	1,500	1,600	52	402	**1,198**
Total cost	11,100	12,910	1,517	5,477	**7,433**
NET	8,300	8,590	5,533	10,873	**(2,283)**

FIGURE 7.7: *Budget with variance column*

As the activity happens, the variance to budget gets smaller. When the year-to-date amount is greater than the budget, the variance is negative. In looking at revenue, this means there is more income than expected. This is a good outcome. When looking at cost, a negative variance means a budget has been overspent. These two reports illustrate ways to measure financial outcomes and quantify results. They do not necessarily explain the reasons for the outcomes.

CASH FLOW

Looking at a budget only tells part of the financial story. Looking at cash flow will tell another part. Cash flow tracks the cash coming into and going out of the business. Cash coming in would include all revenue payments. Other inflows might be donor gifts, grant payments, or refunds from merchants or suppliers. Cash outflow includes merchant or supplier payments, loan payments, tuition refunds, payroll and tax among others. It is important to know the LTO's cash position as well as profit/loss. A business can be profitable, but have cash flow difficulties because of an excess of payments going out over receipts coming in at a given point in the financial year (a common problem in a seasonal industry). A balance sheet may look healthy while the cash flow is negative. Circumstances where this would be seen are semester, annual or seasonal breaks when there are no tuition payments coming in and one-time cost payments are due, making the cash going out higher than normal.

The common way to track your cash position is on a statement of cash flow. This information can be presented in two different ways, one giving an overview and one providing more details. The overview is usually presented with other financial statements. The detailed view is used more frequently as a daily management tool to help an accountant track how much money is in the bank at any given point in time. This ensures that the LTO has sufficient cash to pay bills when they are due or to make major purchases.

For example, you want to purchase 30 new classroom desks. The best time is between sessions, in either August or January. In looking at your projected cash flow, you see that there is cash coming in from tuition payments at both times of the year. However, in January quarterly payroll tax is due and there may not be enough cash left, requiring you to incur finance or bank charges on the purchase. In August you will have enough cash to pay for the desks. The September tax payment will be covered by tuition and book purchases in that month. Overall, it is more cost-effective to pay cash in August and avoid the potential finance charges.

Some income and costs, or expenses, such as salary payments, utility bills, VAT or other tax payments, may happen on a monthly basis. Others, such as grant income payments, rent, and employment tax, may happen quarterly. The expenditure for equipment is unlikely to be evenly distributed across the 12 months of the year, but is likely to peak at the beginning of the year as illustrated above. Tuition or other course fees will be cyclical depending on the LTO's calendar. Figure 7.8 shows an example of a cash flow over a 12-month period.

TASK

Look at the cash flow worksheet in Figure 7.8 and answer the following questions.
- In which months is there a negative cash flow (as indicated by bracketed figures)?
- In which months is there a positive cash flow?
- In which months is there no income?
- In which months are the greatest amounts of tuition income received?
- When is the highest cash balance?
- What possible problems is the cash flow highlighting?

CASH FLOW PRO FORMA

Month	1	2	3	4	5	6	7	8	9	10	11	12	Totals
Fees received	201,000	185,000	174,129	174,129	174,129	174,129	174,129	174,129	174,129	174,129	—	—	1,779,032
Payments	164,029	146,841	128,029	155,529	225,241	128,029	128,029	128,029	128,029	128,029	128,029	128,029	1,715,869
Net cash flow inflow (outflow)	36,971	38,159	46,100	18,600	(51,112)	46,100	46,100	46,100	46,100	46,100	(128,029)	(128,029)	
Opening cash balance	—	36,971	75,130	121,231	139,831	88,719	134,819	180,919	227,020	273,120	319,220	191,192	
+/- Net inflow (outflow)	36,971	38,159	46,100	18,600	(51,112)	46,100	46,100	46,100	46,100	46,100	(128,029)	(128,029)	
Closing cash balance	36,971	75,130	121,231	139,831	88,719	134,819	180,919	227,020	273,120	319,220	191,192	63,163	
Assumptions	Marketing expense paid in Month 1 and Month 4												
	Equipment purchased in Month 5												
	All other expenses the same each month												

FIGURE 7.8: *Example cash flow*

As is quickly apparent, there is a negative cash flow in months 5, 11 and 12, yet these are also the months in which there is a combination of reduced or no income and unchanged outflow, while the bulk of income is received in the first two months. Such fluctuations are typical of educational institutions as it is rare to have income and expense evenly spread throughout the financial year. Indeed, there are probably very few lines of business which are immune from seasonal fluctuations, so it would be unusual to find an enterprise without negative cash flow at some point in the fiscal year.

While this does not appear to be a problem, it does present some potential difficulties. At the end of the cycle as the cash balance drops, a negative cash balance could occur, requiring debt financing to cover expenses until the next cycle begins. When a cash balance becomes negative, it means the business has run out of money and may not be able to pay its bills. If a business has run out of money, it is insolvent and under many financial regimes can no longer continue trading. To avoid this problem sufficient cash balance could be carried over from the previous year. Another solution would be to have a financial arrangement with the bank to cover this cash deficiency until tuition payments come in. The bank would then be repaid and the relevant sum added to the payables. The opposite may be true as well, when the business has a very high cash balance. Rather than retain cash in the operating bank account, it might be better to move some of this into an interest-bearing account so that the money is not standing idle but is generating more income.

Payment practices will vary, of course, and in LTOs with continuous enrolment there may well be a variety of payment periods, which will complicate cash flow analysis, particularly forecasting. Some LTOs may encourage up-front payment for a whole year or part of the year by offering a discount. Depending on the percentage of customers who take up this option, there could be a very large lump of income at the start of the year or period, with correspondingly lower income during the rest of the year.

Performing a cash flow analysis is important because it will alert us to periods of the year when there may be negative cash flow, a negative cash balance or a very high positive cash balance. Such information can then contribute to decision-making regarding tuition payments and the payment of bills. If the forecast reveals a really serious negative cash balance, we should take action ahead to avoid such a situation, or to make advance arrangements to deal with it.

SYSTEMS

In this chapter we have dealt with various ways to manage money and to plan for the financial impact of activities. As you read through this material, we hope that you are thinking of your own organization's systems to accomplish these tasks and how they work. Understanding how they work is an important step to working with them and within them. It is common to find that programme staff and business staff have very different perspectives and even different languages and have trouble understanding one another. As we come to understand how our own LTO works, we are ready to build our own systems that can be integrated into the whole.

Understanding organizational systems

Every organization has different ways of doing things and different responsibility levels. It is important to understand the culture and ways of our own organization when it comes to money. Some managers may have a bigger role in budget development, adjustments, and setting spending priorities. If you are running a small LTO, you have a defining role in setting priorities and responsibility for creating overall profitability. If you are a manager within a larger LTO, those decisions may be guided by higher levels of management which determine the strategic priorities for the year and spending allocations. For example, a branch of an LTO may have an amount given to them to work within or a target market and expanded course funding for that market segment. It is important to understand the role different management levels play in your own organization and how much discretion and responsibility each level has for setting and achieving targets.

Another role that is important to understand is that of support offices. In larger organizations, it is common to find a finance office that must work with programme staff. In smaller organizations, one person may perform all the support functions and work with an outside accountant. In any situation, it is important to understand what role support people have and what they can do for you. The flip side is to help them understand your role and what you need to provide to them.

In larger organizations, this can be difficult. Support units may speak in financial terms that are not yet clear to you. They may or may not be interested in the courses which they support. Dialogue with support people can narrow the perceived gap. Ask questions and ask what you can provide to help them. At the same time, ask them to explain any terms or language that you are not familiar with. Frequently this also means educating them about your courses so they understand what you are trying to accomplish. After all, you work for the same organization and are working towards the same goals of providing profitable courses.

Creating or aligning your own systems

There are really two types of budget systems: one is the mechanical process of creating and maintaining a budget using some kind of software program; the other is the operational side of creation, monitoring and adjusting at regular intervals. Most LTOs use a basic spreadsheet program to create or adjust budgets. There are budget software packages available as well and some financial systems have a budget module within them. There are certain tasks discussed earlier that need to be defined no matter what technology is used to create or modify a budget.

Organizations have a schedule for developing the annual budget at a specific time of year. Knowing when that happens and understanding deadlines is very important, as it gives managers lead time to plan and prepare the budget, including any factors that may change during preparation.

After the budget is created and approved, it is necessary to develop a systematic approach to monitoring based on the activity timeline. The scheduling of course activity, such as course registration, semester mid-points and final course dates, is usually known well in advance. Budget monitoring should follow the same calendar. It is advisable to monitor some activities frequently, such as monthly or weekly. Course directors should look at the programme calendar and develop a budget-monitoring calendar based on following the same activity points. Different levels of management may have different budget review dates. For example, the LTO director may have a bi-monthly review of all courses to ensure overall profitability. No director or manager wants to be surprised by budget shortfalls.

TASK

Write out a schedule of activity for your own courses. Note the points when major financial activity happens.

Based on that information, create a budget-monitoring calendar for your course. The budget monitoring calendar should be tied closely to when financial activity happens. Include notes of when it would be most appropriate to make any budget adjustments necessary.

CONCLUSION

Financial management is often the most feared and dreaded part of any manager's position. In the previous chapter we considered how strategic financial management inevitably becomes part of a manager's role. Strategic planning is a periodic exercise that happens at a set point in the LTO calendar, and it determines what path the LTO will travel for the next few years and where management want it to be at the end of that period.

Operational financial management is part of a manager's daily or weekly responsibilities. Managers will find that many decisions they make have financial impact, and need to seek financial information as part of making fully informed decisions. While we are not suggesting that financial impact should be the only determining factor, it is one facet of a multi-faceted decision-making process. Financial considerations are also part of marketing and selling the LTO's services, while academic management, to be covered in the next chapter, involves resource management, and estimating and paying for a key resource without which an LTO will cease to operate: teachers and their time.

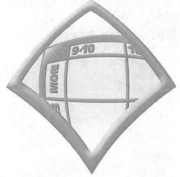

8 Academic management

- ACADEMIC MANAGEMENT
- CURRICULUM MANAGEMENT
- MANAGING RESOURCES
- PROFESSIONAL DEVELOPMENT
- MANAGING QUALITY

INTRODUCTION

In this chapter, academic management will be considered from the viewpoint of two complementary roles: that of CEO or leader and manager of the organization, its people and resources, and that of the leading professional, focusing on the educational and pedagogical core of the LTO's language teaching service. In fact, academic management faces in two directions: towards students and teachers on the one hand, and, on the other, towards the organizational systems and processes which make effective provision of teaching and learning possible. Such a dual viewpoint means that the academic manager is often called upon to reconcile two sets of interests: those concerned with the commercial success of the LTO, and those prioritizing its responsibilities as an educational provider.

The emphasis in this chapter is on quality management, beginning with clarity of the goals of the LTO, expressed in its mission statement (see Chapter 2, p. 40), and realized in the policy documents and guidelines which inform course planning and development, assessment and placement, and the teaching and learning which occurs in and out of the classroom. Facilitating the progress of the student/customer through their journey involves effectively managing resources, which range from consumables to the intangibles that are an important part of what makes the LTO special.

Ultimately, it is through organizing and managing integrated systems and processes, as summarized in Figure 8.1 on p. 202, that quality outcomes will be achieved. Devising agreed-upon key performance indicators (KPIs), which establish measurable goals, is an important part of effective academic management in particular, and of the overall management of the LTO.

ACADEMIC MANAGEMENT

What is involved in academic management? What, in brief, does an academic manager do? The work of the individuals described in the vignettes on pp. 202–4 illustrates both the range of institutions in which academic managers work, and the kinds of responsibilities which they carry.

FIGURE 8.1: *LTO management*

Vignette 8.1: *Managing a new branch*

Loraine is the manager of a branch of a long-established not-for-profit (NFP) chain of LTOs which operate on a commercial basis. She was appointed to help turn around a city centre branch which had been underperforming, and her job was to:

- motivate staff suffering from low morale
- work with a business development manager in devising new courses appropriate to the market
- meet and exceed the quality expectations of clientele
- help develop a technology-enhanced language learning (TELL) policy for the chain.

On accepting the appointment, she was told by the head of the chain that the lease on the current premises was coming to an end in six months, and that consequently a significant addition to her responsibilities would be helping to set up and fit out new premises, to manage a set-up budget, and to ensure a seamless transition from one location to another. Advice and help in carrying this out would be available from the central administration of the chain.

Vignette 8.2: Managing a programme

Hassan is a co-ordinator of the writing programme in the English department at a technical university in the Middle East. As a writing course co-ordinator, most of his work involves:

- making decisions about teaching hours
- assigning classes and offices to the teachers he supervises
- timetabling with the collaboration of the registrar
- dealing with students' queries, grievances and requests.

The courses for which he is responsible prepare students for academic writing and entry into their degree studies. Having learnt from his colleagues in the university that students were poorly prepared for using computers in writing classes as a study and work tool, Hassan, who is highly computer-literate, initiated the development of a programme to develop such skills among both English department staff and students. Achieving this called for an understanding of the decision-making processes and resource allocation authorities within the university, and adeptness in obtaining their support in introducing new facilities and in extending teachers' skills as facilitators in developing students' word processing, search and study skills using the computer.

Vignette 8.3: Managing a department

Astrid is head of English as well as head of the Languages department in a very large, publicly funded college of further education. There are nine departments, eight of which provide courses, while the ninth, Central Services, includes HR, the IT department, course registration, the Finance department and PR. At an institutional level, the heads of all nine departments, as well as one elected representative of the department, are members of a college decision-making committee. As head of English, Astrid reports to the head of Languages, but as she occupies both posts, she reports directly to college management. As head of English, she decides who to employ as teachers, and she is responsible for assigning teachers to courses. All teachers are employed on an hourly basis. Her main responsibility is programme planning and development, which includes making decisions about:

- the coursebook series to be used
- the kinds of courses to be taught
- innovations to be introduced
- maintaining the levels of quality of service expected of her college.

In terms of strategic planning, she is responsible for deciding upon aims for the following year and finding ways of achieving them.

Vignette 8.4: Managing a training programme

Rob is the manager of Foundation Training for a communications company on a Ministry of Defence (MOD) contract with the military of a foreign country. The company provides the necessary hardware, software and management support for operational systems throughout the country. As part of the contract the company trains soldiers to be competent technicians and operators of equipment. Most training takes place at the military's school in the capital, although additional regional training is scheduled and so trainers need to be mobile.

The school in the capital is overseen by the head of Training, who manages four departments: Training Facilities, Training Development, Foundation Training and Equipment Training; and liaises with the MOD and the military about the quality of service provision.

Rob is supported by the Foundation Training co-ordinator. He is responsible for the content and provision of general and ESP English language training as well as basic technical training and he reports to the head of Training. Needs analysis, material approval, timetabling, testing and course evaluation are administered separately by the Training Development department to be consistent with the institution-wide approach to military training.

The English trainers are employed on a full-time basis. As well as teaching soldiers in the capital and on occasion in the regions, they contribute to the continual modification and improvement of the company's in-house materials, liaising with Equipment Training instructors.

The dual roles of the academic manager

The range of responsibilities of these managers covers the dual roles of educational leadership proposed by Law & Glover (2000, p. 6): those of chief executive and professional leader (see also Chapter 1, p. 15). The former involves internal and external roles:

Internal:
- curriculum management (including teaching)
- assessment and evaluation
- articulating the organization's strategic focus and direction (strategist)
- allocating and co-ordinating a range of organizational functions (manager)
- acting as organizational broker and referee (arbitrator).

External:
- being accountable to the governing body, educational authorities, accreditation agency, government (executive officer)
- articulating the mission of the school (diplomat)
- undertaking public relations with stakeholder communities and external bodies (publicist).

The role of professional leader likewise involves internal and external roles:

Internal:
- developing staff and guiding them professionally (mentor)
- demonstrating personal teaching skills and technical competence (educator)
- supporting students, parents, clients, etc. (adviser).

External:
- representing the school in external professional activities (ambassador)
- acting as institutional spokesperson vis-a-vis educational and professional matters (advocate).

As managers, Loraine, Hassan, Astrid and Rob perform many of these roles. In their executive role, they are responsible for managing the resources of the organization, or their section of it, in pursuit of its organizational goals or mission. Managing these resources calls for the skills of human resource management, financial management, marketing, and customer relations management. In their leading professional role, they make use of the skills which are part of their training as teachers and educators, including those involved in curriculum development, teacher education and professional development (PD). As a subset of educational leadership, effective LTO management calls for both executive and professional skills, whether these are embodied in one individual, such as Loraine, Hassan, Astrid and Rob, or in a team of people, such as the branch or department in which they work and for which they may have overall responsibility.

Levels of academic management

The range of skills and responsibilities and the time perspective of the academic manager will, as shown in the vignettes, vary according to the status of the manager within the organizational hierarchy, as we noted in Chapter 1, Figure 1.8, p. 19.

Both Loraine and Astrid, as heads of a branch and a department respectively, are concerned with strategic as well as tactical management, while Hassan, as a co-ordinator, focuses on medium-term tactical and short term operational responsibilities and decisions. Although he is a head of department, Rob's strategic responsibilities are constrained, as these are determined by the head of Training, but he is responsible for the tactical management of his department and for liaison with other departments, particularly Equipment Training. As branch and departmental heads, Loraine and Astrid make decisions which affect everyone in their part of the organization. As a co-ordinator, the scope of Hassan's authority and decision-making is circumscribed, being largely restricted in its impact to the people who come under his area of responsibility. Likewise, Rob's decision-making extends to the members of his department and the activities for which they are responsible.

Typically, the following are the core responsibilities of an academic manager:
- curriculum management
- assessment and evaluation
- staff development
- quality assurance.

It is to the first of these that we will now turn.

TASK

Analyse the jobs of Loraine, Hassan, Astrid, Rob and yourself, following the educational leadership roles summarized on pp. 204–5 and using the following framework.

Yes if present
No if not present
Not sure if uncertain

Role	Loraine	Hassan	Astrid	Rob	Yourself
Strategist					
Manager					
Arbitrator					
Executive officer					
Diplomat					
Publicist					
Mentor					
Educator					
Adviser					
Ambassador					
Advocate					

When you have done that, assess the percentage of each role for your own job by saying:

- how much time and effort it occupies
- how important it is (time and importance may not coincide, of course).

Then complete the table below for your own job. Refer to Figures 1.5–1.7 on pages 17–19 in Chapter 1 for examples.

Job title	
Focus	
Through	
Leadership	
Management	
Administration	

Finally, in what ways has the analysis helped to clarify aspects of your job which you were unclear or uncertain about?

CURRICULUM MANAGEMENT

Like the three levels of management – strategic, tactical and operational (see Chapter 1, Figure 1.8, p. 19) – there are three levels in curriculum management:

Level	Content	Management level
1	Vision, mission, values	Strategic
2	Academic policies, schemes and frameworks	Tactical
3	Specific courses	Operational

FIGURE 8.2: *Levels of academic management*

Level 1: Vision, mission, values

It is easy to deride vision and mission statements, but, as noted in Chapters 1 and 2, it is important for everyone in an LTO to have a shared understanding of and belief in what the organization exists for and where it is going. The significance of this becomes obvious when such attributes are absent. Although profitability will undoubtedly be a goal as far as shareholders or owners are concerned, from the viewpoint of other stakeholders – notably the clientele and employees – educational and personal goals will be more significant, particularly as the quality of what an LTO offers should be aligned with the claims and aspirations expressed in its mission statement. Ultimately, this means that curriculum management is to be seen as a significant way of making the mission tangible.

Although for some accreditation schemes a published LTO mission statement is mandatory, as any web search will reveal, LTOs can be surprisingly reticent about publishing their mission statement so it is not always clear to what extent the claims made in their offer are part of the vocation and espoused values of the organization.

> ### *REFLECTION*
>
> In Chapter 2 (p. 41), you were asked about the mission statement of your LTO. In this activity, we will consider the link between the mission statement and academic management.
>
> - What is the mission statement of your LTO?
> - What are the aspirations and values stated or implied by the mission statement?
> - What expectations of the LTO is the mission statement likely to give rise to in the minds of your clientele?
> - In what ways are the services or products offered by your LTO aligned to the mission? For instance, if part of the mission is 'to promote international communication and understanding', how is this realized through nationality mix in student intake and class composition?
> - To what extent is an academic manager's work influenced by the mission of the LTO?

Statement of principles

As far as curriculum management is concerned, the mission, vision and values will be realized through a statement of principles, such as those cited by Richards (2001), describing the teaching philosophy supporting a secondary school EFL English programme. The statements were produced through discussion involving teacher trainers, curriculum planners, and teachers and served as a reference for materials developers, teacher trainers and teachers. As Richards notes:

> Articulating a teaching philosophy in this way can help clarify decisions relating to choice of classroom activities, materials, and teacher evaluation. (Richards, 2001, p. 216)

Richards lists this statement of principles as follows:
- There is a consistent focus throughout on learning English in order to develop practical and functional skills, rather than as an end in itself.
- Students are engaged in practical tasks that relate to real-world uses of English.
- Realistic and communicative uses of language are given priority.
- Maximum use is made of pair and group activities in which students complete tasks collaboratively.
- There is an appropriate balance between accuracy-focused and fluency-focused activities.
- Teachers serve as facilitators of learning rather than as presenters of information.
- Assessment procedures reflect and support a communicative and skill-based orientation to teaching and learning.
- Students develop an awareness of the learning process and their own learning styles, strengths and weaknesses.
- Students develop the ability to monitor their own learning progress and ways of setting personal goals for language improvement.

(Richards, 2001, p. 216)

Level 2: Frameworks and guidelines

The existence of an articulated philosophy underpins decisions at the next level, that of frameworks for course development and provision. Level 2 represents a tactical level of course development; in other words, it is here that there will be:
- policy statements or guidelines on approaches to teaching and learning
- syllabus checklists
- procedures for applying the above to the planning and preparation of specific courses.

All of these take place in a series of developmental stages involving decision-making roles which have been summarized by Johnson (1989, p. 3) in Figure 8.3 opposite. Note that the professional and managerial roles of the LTO manager come together in this sequence and that managers will be drawing on professional knowledge and expertise, either their own or that of their colleagues.

Developmental stages	Decision-making roles	Products
1 curriculum planning	policy makers	policy document
2 specification: • ends	needs analyst	syllabus
• means	methodologists	
3 programme implementation	materials writers	teaching materials
	teacher trainers	teacher-training programme
4 classroom implementation	teacher	teaching acts
	learner	learning acts

FIGURE 8.3: *Decision-making roles* (Johnson, 1989, p. 3)

An academic manager may be involved at all stages in this sequence, not necessarily at a 'hands on' level, but as a receiver of products (such as a policy document) or as someone responsible for their production – which means, of course, that other people may well be involved with doing the actual work under instruction and support from their academic manager.

TASK

It is routine for accreditation schemes to require LTOs to have 'a structured course of studies divided into levels and appropriate to students' needs' (the European Association for Quality Language Services [EAQUALS] Accreditation Scheme); i.e. the 'products' listed in Figure 8.3. Figure 8.4 opposite is a list of what is required in this particular accreditation scheme.

Use this to survey the documents or guidelines available in your LTO for all staff who are responsible for the development and provision of courses.

If there are gaps or limitations in the guidelines and procedures outlined for academic and administrative staff, it will be necessary to fill them or improve the guidelines and procedures. If, in fact, the management is constantly involved in monitoring actual performance against agreed standards, such updating and improvement will already be part of good practice. It is possible, though, that the organization operates on automatic pilot, and that very little attention is given to guidelines and procedures – until something goes wrong or until an accreditation inspection is imminent.

When problems occur in the design and provision of the LTO's services, it is very likely that at least some will have arisen from Level 2 gaps; i.e. there are inadequate or out-of-date guidelines and procedures. At a time of change in the market, it is possible that existing guidelines and procedures have lagged behind contemporary practice and need substantial revision. As Graddol (2006, p. 91) shows, there are changes occurring in what he terms 'Global English', for which the focus will be international intelligibility, rather than a specific variety. Learners, he suggests, will be largely instrumentally motivated, learning English to get jobs in their own countries and to communicate with non-native speakers from other countries. He suggests that content will often be related to another curriculum area, as in Content and Language Integrated Learning (CLIL). He also suggests that existing exams will often not be appropriate, with task- or job-based assessment being used to indicate candidates' actual English skills. Potentially, such developments have significant implications for academic management at all levels.

Level 3: Specific products or services

The last level is that of specific courses provided on specific occasions to specific customers. This is the level that directly involves the customer (as consumer), since the teaching and learning events cannot take place without their involvement. This is also the trickiest level of the three because of the unpredictable nature of the events themselves. It is also the level at which the dual functions of an LTO are revealed: as teaching institute and service provider. Finally, this is the level of operational management at which systems and resources, planned and installed as part of tactical management, support and facilitate the provision of the services which the LTO provides its clientele.

What is required	Is it present?	Who is responsible for providing it?	Who uses it?
Structured course of studies • curriculum – an overall description of objectives, with reference to the levels of the Common European Framework of Reference including a framework of levels and general statement of means used to achieve these objectives			
• syllabus and/or means of specifying appropriate course content, aims and learning outcomes for teachers and students (e.g. through description of courses); statements of content to be covered in a certain period of time and specification of what language knowledge and skills will be covered at what level			
• schemes of work or other forms of appropriate lesson planning which enable teachers to implement course content and structure and which are available to and understood by students, and make pedagogic sense in the institution's context			
• records of work covered			
Levels • a comprehensive, written description of levels available to students and known to staff including basic 'descriptors' and specifying students' abilities and when these are attained			
• reference to the Common European Framework of Reference			
Students' needs • guidelines/support to implement curriculum and syllabus documents to meet the needs of specific groups of learners			
• rationale for grouping (level, age, gender, nationality quota, occupation)			
• means of reviewing and updating the course description/curriculum/syllabus documents			

FIGURE 8.4: *Course requirements* (adapted from EAQUALS, 2007)

TASK

At this level, the focus in accreditation schemes is on the standard of teaching and the use of appropriate and effective teaching methods. Adapted from the EAQUALS scheme, Figure 8.5 is a list of such requirements.
- Apply this list to Level 3 provision in your own LTO.
- How useful is such a checklist in evaluating this aspect of academic management in your LTO?
- If limitations are revealed, what, as academic manager, will you be able to do about them?
- What will be the resource requirements which have to be met in order to improve this aspect of academic management?

What is required	Is it present?	Who is directly responsible for ensuring that it is?
Teaching methods • efficient planning and organization of lessons, transparent to students so that they understand what they are doing and how it will help them learn		

• effective class management:
  – teachers' ability to use a variety of techniques and to organize students in different working groups (i.e. to use whole class, group and pair work as appropriate)
  – teachers' ability to present information, monitor, provide support, manage changes of activity efficiently and clearly		

• effectiveness and appropriacy of methods in relation to students' age, level, aims and needs		
• effective and appropriate (to the age, level and type of the group) use of resources such as textbooks, boards, handouts, audio and video equipment, etc.		

FIGURE 8.5 *Teaching standards* (adapted from EAQUALS, 2007)

Course and product development

While the academic and pedagogical qualities of course provision are quite properly prioritized in accreditation schemes, there is another important commercial aspect of course provision: product development, or New Product Development (NPD). In an LTO, NPD tends to be less common than 'refreshing' existing products (or courses) as part of the evolutionary changes referred to in the punctuated equilibrium model of change in Chapter 9 (p. 239). From time to time, though, completely new courses (or products) are developed in response to a need, as illustrated in Vignette 8.2 (p. 203).

The motivation for either product refreshment or NPD will be prompted by:
- demand identified by market research
- declining uptake of an existing course
- launching of new courses by competitors
- demand for new courses from existing clientele
- changes in or additions to examinations or tests
- publication of new textbooks, teaching materials
- availability of new teaching technology, such as interactive whiteboards
- recruitment of staff with new ideas.

TASK

Take a recent new course in your LTO. This assumes that the LTO does have some new courses. It could be that rather than totally new offerings, existing courses have been modified and relaunched as new. For the purposes of this activity, regard such modified offers as 'new'.

1 Identify the motivation for developing the new course.
   - Why was a decision made to develop the new (or modified) course?
   - Who came up with the initial idea?
   - What, if any, external factors (such as competitors) influenced the decision to develop the new course?
2 Make a list of the main stages in course development. All NPD goes through stages, beginning with the initial idea, and proceeding to evaluation, development and launching the new product. Carefully reconstruct the developmental stages for this new product, using the scheme in Figure 8.6 (p. 215) as a reference.
3 List the sections or departments or sections, activities and personnel involved in each stage.
4 List the outcomes of each stage. For instance, at what stage was a course outline or syllabus produced?

How similar was the NPD scheme you followed to the one outlined in Figure 8.6?
   Were there any gaps in your scheme? Were there any additional steps? If so, why? In what ways could you improve your LTO's approach to NPD?

The NPD scheme (Figure 8.6) outlines a widely followed sequence of stages, beginning with initial idea generation. Ideas are evaluated or checked for their feasibility, financial viability and marketability, leading to a decision either to proceed to development, or to go no further. At this stage, questions to find answers to include the following (tutor2U, 2007):

- Is there sufficient demand?
- Will it be profitable?
- What is the likely payback period?
- Does it fit the image of the LTO?
- Does it fit the product portfolio of the LTO?
- What is the likely life cycle of the new product?
- What is the state of the market and the competition?
- Does the LTO possess the capabilities to successfully develop, market and deliver the new product?
- How easy will it be to develop and deliver?

The screening stage is a very important one, since it should draw on a number of criteria relevant to the mission and economic viability of the LTO. Failure adequately to screen a new product proposal, such as occurred with the unsuccessful business course in Vignette 4.2 (Chapter 4, p. 80), can lead to a waste of LTO resources. The post-commercialization review stage is also important as it involves measuring performance against criteria set out in the business and marketing plans. Such criteria are often specified as key performance indicators (KPIs), which are measurements of the improvement in performing an activity that is critical to the business; they are commonly expressed as ratios, e.g. percentages. Thus a KPI for a new product (or course) might be an increase of X% in the level of student recruitment, or achieving an increased level of customer satisfaction or of Net Promoter Score (see Chapter 5, p. 133) among students taking the new course.

At each stage, LTO staff in Marketing and Sales, and Academic and Student services will be involved in a cross-functional team, and once the new product enters the development stage, it should have an 'owner' who is both responsible and accountable for its success. If, having been launched, the new product proves successful, it will then continue as a routine part of the range of products (or courses) provided by the LTO. If, however, the review stage reveals that the new product falls short of meeting success criteria, it will either be substantially modified or withdrawn. It is important to keep in mind that a new product, like any innovation, will tend to follow an adoption curve (see Chapter 9, p. 238), with a slow take-up, followed by more rapid adoption as it reaches the tipping point. Managers need to take this into account when setting targets for a new product. Likewise, they need to remember that, like organizations (see Chapter 2, p. 31) and teachers' careers (below, p. 227), products have a life cycle, and when the adoption curve peaks and a product goes into decline, decisions will have to be made as to its future.

Stage	
1 Idea generation	New ideas from internal and external sources.
2 Idea screening	Evaluating, sorting for pedagogical feasibility, financial viability, marketability. Risk analysis.
3 Concept development & testing	Converting concept into tangible product and testing it with consumers (including agents) to find out if product appeals.
4 Marketing strategy development	Designing a marketing strategy for the new product; doing some formal market research to assess product's potential. See *Marketing plan*, Chapter 4, p. 111.
5 Business analysis	Reviewing sales, cost and profit projections against LTO's goals. Estimate potential sales, income, break-even point, profit and return on investment of new ideas. See *Costed proposal outline*, Chapter 6, p. 153.
6 Product development	Designing and developing the new product, including, for a course, an outline and materials.
7 Test marketing	Small-scale pilot of the new product to assess consumer reactions, and fine-tuning of product.
8 Commercialization	Introducing new product to the market.
9 Review	Evaluating performance of new product against commercial and academic criteria as specified in costed proposal and marketing plan.

FIGURE 8.6: *New product development stages* (adapted from http://www.tutor2u.net/business 2007)

The specification of the new product will typically include the following:
- target customer: demographic, psychographic and academic characteristics
- aims: what customer goals are to be achieved
- content: what the course content will be
- mode: what modes of provision are to be used: face-to-face, blended learning, etc.
- time: how long and in what time units it will be packaged and sold
- when: time of year and day
- cost: how much it will cost to develop and provide
- price: what the market price is.

How many of these were covered in the specification of the new product in your LTO?

Refreshing existing products is relatively low risk, whereas developing and launching a totally original new product is high risk. In either case, an NPD scheme provides a framework and discipline which will help mitigate risk and safeguard the resources and reputation of the LTO.

MANAGING RESOURCES

In Chapter 6 (p. 158), attention was drawn to the importance of having a resource inventory as part of financial planning. This is equally true of academic management, a significant part of which involves obtaining, organizing, replacing and maintaining resources. In an LTO, these resources include people and their skills, materials, hardware, software, and time. The two vignettes below illustrate resource management in two areas: hardware (and associated software), and materials.

Vignette 8.5: Miranda's LTO

The LTO was approached by a third party to do some pilot work on the use of interactive whiteboards (IWB) as part of research and development. Miranda, a teacher with an interest in teaching applications of IT, became involved, developing into a skilled and enthusiastic IWB user and advocate. There was only one IWB in each of the branches of the chain, however, and although Miranda did some in-service training sessions with teachers, there was limited adoption. The fact that there was only one IWB per branch also meant that it was administratively difficult to timetable their use. In turn, this meant that teachers had very restricted opportunity to develop their familiarity and expertise with what was, for them, a new piece of technology. At the end of a prolonged trial phase, it was felt that one branch should be fully equipped so as to encourage adoption, but by the time a decision was reached, the budgets for the forthcoming year had been finalized, and this high-cost item had not been included. The introduction of IWBs across the chain was put on hold for the next annual budget round.

Vignette 8.6: Anne's LTO

Anne was appointed to the post of DOS in a medium-sized LTO. Student recruitment was buoyant and with extra classes there was a need to update and increase the stock of supplementary materials, not only to meet the increased volume of learners, but also to satisfy the teachers' need for up-to-date material. Anne approached the senior management with a request for clarification of her budget for the purchase of materials. She was told that there was not a budget, but that she could purchase 'whatever she wanted'. Cautiously, she placed an order for sets of supplementary materials, only to be told that 'it was too much'. As a result, she had to cut back the order, but still without knowing what the ceiling was on the acquisition of materials. She also had to account for the shortfall in the anticipated provision of new materials to the teachers.

In each of these vignettes, there was a policy gap. In Vignette 8.5, the LTO lacked a technology-enhanced language learning (TELL) policy, so the experimental use of IWB was not part of a pedagogical, let alone a marketing strategy. Furthermore, once a decision had been made to proceed further, no provision was made in the capital expenses budget to resource the purchase and installation of expensive equipment. In Vignette 8.6, the DOS was disempowered by not having a budget she could manage; the renewal of materials did not appear to be planned and costed as part of an annual budget plan. As a result, the teachers, and ultimately the students, were constrained by a lack of attention to effective resource management.

So, the first consideration in resource management concerns the alignment of purchasing policies with the mission and purpose of the LTO, and the maintenance of quality. This means that an academic manager needs to have policy guidelines to budget for the acquisition of:

- renewable resources for the year (part of the annual operating budget)
- additional or new resources (usually part of a capital budget)
- additional or replacement equipment
- training requirements associated with any of the above.

Such acquisition should be in line with projected needs and the state of existing resources. These factors feed into budget planning for the year ahead so that where necessary, resources and equipment are renewed, or significant new purchases are factored in. Purchasing will be phased according to the annual LTO schedule of demand and use, together with the lead times needed to have resources in place and training in their use when needed. As the range of resources used by an LTO is considerable, the purchasing, monitoring and renewal cycles will differ accordingly.

Types of resource

All LTOs have a range of resources which are conventionally categorized under three main headings:

- Consumables: these include items like stationery, which are used up in the process of use.
- Non-consumables: these cover equipment, such as tools, office equipment, computers, teaching equipment with a lifetime of a given number of years.
- Intangibles: these are assets (something the LTO has) and capabilities (something it can do), and include such factors as human capital, knowledge capital, brand, R & D capability, IT and information management capability, and other non-financial resources. Some of these may be part of the intellectual property of the LTO. Such knowledge items include teaching materials and systems (both pedagogical and administrative).

Managing such knowledge is a significant part of resource management in an LTO, whose business depends on providing its clientele with totally intangible services and benefits.

TASK

What are the resources in your LTO? Make lists under the following headings:
- Consumables
- Non-consumables
- Intangibles

Some items have already been given as examples. Your task is to add more.

Consumables	Non-consumables	Intangibles
Stationery	Computers	Course outlines

Briefly state the characteristics of each resource.

Consumables	Non-consumables	Intangibles
Need to be restocked	Need to be maintained	Tend to be processes and outcomes

What is each of these kinds of resources used for?

Consumables	Non-consumables	Intangibles
Administration		Marketing

How are the following resources stored?

Consumables	Non-consumables	Intangibles
Stationery cupboard	Resource centre	

What triggers the acquisition of each of the above type of resource?

Consumables	Non-consumables	Intangibles
	Obsolescence	

REFLECTION

In your LTO, what systems are in place for managing IT equipment and services? In a small LTO, this may be the responsibility of a staff member who is an IT enthusiast; in a larger LTO, this will usually be in the hands of an IT services unit.
- Who was involved in setting up these systems?
- Who 'owns' the systems? Who is responsible for administering them?
- How effective are the present arrangements?
- How could they be improved?

The effective management of intangible resources in an LTO is very important. By their very nature, they are not 'storable' in the same way as physical, tangible resources are. Yet, without a supply of intangible resources, an LTO will be in serious trouble. For the academic manager, the significant intangible resources are those concerned with teaching and learning. Many LTOs have experience of storing, organizing and retrieving resources embodied in a Self-Access Centre (SAC), which exemplifies knowledge management at work. Lessons can be applied from organizing and managing a SAC to the new requirements arising from the widespread and growing use of IT as part of TELL strategy. It has become increasingly common to use electronic databases and virtual learning environments (VLEs) for administering and actually providing courses and materials. Vignette 8.7 illustrates one such use.

Vignette 8.7: Centre for Academic Learning

The Centre for Academic Learning is an IEP in a university. It runs a wide range of courses for aspiring and registered non-native English-speaking students. Over the years, its staff have developed considerable expertise in researching and developing EAP courses and materials, a large body of which has accumulated in filing cabinets and on individuals' computers. In line with university policy, a decision was made to move this material onto a VLE maintained by the university for the systematic administration and use of teaching materials and courses. Two staff took on the role of managing the EAP database. All materials were sent to them for vetting. If considered necessary, editing and rewriting was done by the original writer/instructor. Meanwhile, a classification system was developed and materials were sorted, stored and cross-referenced on the VLE site, to which teachers had password-protected access. Regular bulletins were sent out to notify staff of new postings. The next phase was to develop a student site on the VLE to augment face-to-face instruction.

REFLECTION

In your LTO, what range of teaching and learning material is available?
- How is material used by teachers and students managed, and by whom?
- Is there a SAC? If so, how is it organized and managed? What systems and procedures can be adapted for wider use as TELL requirements become more prominent?
- What new needs are emerging as the range of material diversifies? (e.g. the advent of CD-ROM and DVD materials linked to coursebooks; the development of IWB-based materials)
- How are these new needs to be managed? Who will be responsible? What new systems and equipment may be required?
- What provision for the use of a VLE is envisaged? Or is already in place?
- How are staff being trained in the use of these systems?

Time as a resource

Managing other people's time

A major area of an academic manager's responsibilities – and often a source of problems – is timetabling or scheduling. In a large LTO, this responsibility may be delegated, and it may even be the responsibility of an administrative staff member. Ultimately, however, the academic manager will have responsibility for ensuring that there is a match between classes to be taught, availability of rooms, equipment and teachers. Quite crucially, the academic manager may also be expected to meet a widely used KPI: average class size.

An experienced academic manager, when asked to summarize her approach to timetabling, came up with the following points:

- Know what your teachers can handle (this is the bit that you have to keep in your head).
- Hire flexible teachers (not just in experience of levels, but in dealing with change).
- Stretch the teachers a little bit so they are used to change and can handle crises.
- Get the teachers to change classes every session (10 to 12 weeks).
- Get them to accept that a new student starting in their class each week is a positive for the class.
- Always have two different teachers per class (this is good for both students and teachers).
- Try to have variety of male/female, more mature/young, or strict/easy teachers for each class.

TASK

How applicable are the above points to timetabling in your LTO?

- For example, what would be the problem with aiming for a variety of teacher if your LTO has a policy of one teacher per class throughout the duration of a student's stay? Or if you have a predominance of hourly-paid teaching staff?
- What are the kinds of information about teachers that you have 'to keep in your head'?
- How does this information influence your timetabling decisions?

Phillips (2000) views timetabling, whether paper-based or computer-assisted, as 'the key resource management tool in a language school', as it brings together 'all the key resources that must be managed by the tactical manager: teaching staff, supervisory staff, classes, rooms, time and, in an elegant timetabling solution, physical resources such as videos, OHPs, etc.'

He proposes a spreadsheet-based 'Resource management timetable', a version of which is set out in Figure 8.7 opposite.

Week beginning (date) Week no.

DAYS	TIME	1	2	3	4	5	Reserve	Managers
M		VIDEO	OHP					
	13.30	A13	B13	C13		D13	JD	BR
O	Teacher	AM	KP	RB		CW	JD	
N	15.00	A15	B15	C15	E15	D15	JD	BR
	Teacher	AM	KP	RB	DC	GS	JD	
D	16.30	A16	B16	C16				BR
	Teacher	AM	KP	RB			JD	
A	18.00	A18				B18		VC
Y	Teacher	DC				DC	JD	
	19.30	A19	G19		E19	F19	JD	VC
	Teacher	DC	LR		DC	CW	VC	
		OHP	VIDEO					
	13.30			A132	B132			BR
T	Teacher			AM	KP		JD	
U	15.00			A152		B152		BR
E	Teacher			AM		KP	JD	
S	16.30	A162	STAFF MEETING					BR
D	Teacher	AM					JD	
A	18.00	A18		B182	B183		JD	VC
Y	Teacher	RB		RB	KP			
	19.30			H192		VC	VC	BR

Teachers: AM: Anne Murray, KP: Kathy Probert, RB: Robert Boss, DC: Dominic Chuo, GS: Geronimo Suarez, LR: Lucia Rodrigues, CW: Chuck Williams, FZ: Ferdinand Zapotec

Supervisors available for reserve: JD: Julie Dias, HD: Hugh Dunmore
Managers on duty: BR: Bobby Robinson, VC: Vera Chen

FIGURE 8.7: *Resource management timetable*

To interpret this timetable, we have to understand that the LTO concerned has:

- five rooms, numbered 1 to 5
- five teaching slots of one hour each per day
- eight levels of General English classes, from Level A to Level G
- eight teachers, indicated by their unique initials, e.g. AM for Anne Murray, etc.
- two supervisors (Julie Dias, Hugh Dunmore) and two managers (Bobby Robinson, Vera Chen).

The key points incorporated in this timetable are:

- Information can be accessed in four main ways: by teacher, by class, by room or by time. This means it is possible to see at a glance which teacher is teaching which class in which room at which time on each day.
- It is also possible to see who is on reserve.
- The name of the manager who is on duty at any one time is given. This means that all staff know who to come to in the event of a problem.
- Class names are meaningful: A13 is a class at Level A at 13.30, and so on.
- There is an extra cell for each room for each day. Physical resource information is given there; for example, the video set will be in Room 1 on Monday, but Room 2 on Tuesday.
- Since this timetable is (or should be) on display, distributed or available (as on an intranet) to all members of staff, anyone can guide a student or a new teacher to the correct location.
- Special notices which are time-related can be included on the timetable; for example, D13 in Room 5 is a new class starting on Monday, so the cell is shaded. Likewise, the staff meeting at 16.30 in Room 2.

With a spreadsheet or other form of data management, such a timetable can be set up to consolidate information which will be used for analysis and managing teachers' time and other resources. It can total up the number of hours for each teacher, as well as for all teachers for the day or the week and the month. The utilization of teachers, both full-time and hourly-paid, will usually be aligned to targets for the period concerned, and the scheme can be set up to provide the following:

- number of hours teachers are contracted or have agreed to teach
- number of hours actually taught
- percentage of utilization
- budgeted number of hours
- the difference between budget and the taught amount
- percentage of difference between the budget and the taught amount
- the ratio of contract to hourly-paid teacher utilization.

Such a scheme can also be organized to indicate the running total of hours for each level, providing a useful cross-check with the teacher hours total, while also monitoring performance of different products/courses. Since products will usually be differently priced, yielding different gross margins, it is important to monitor how they are performing. If a high-margin product is down on hours, while low-margin product is exceeding hours taught, the manager will know that in fact profitability has declined, although the number of hours taught has risen. This has implications for the people responsible for sales, who may be devoting too much effort to recruiting students for low-margin products, so that more effort needs to be put into selling the higher-margin courses.

Finally, the spreadsheet can be set up to monitor the KPI mentioned at the beginning of this section: average class size. This is a basic metric, as much else follows from it, including class hour income, the number of teachers' hours and associated cost, and the profitability of each class. The academic manager may be under quite a lot of pressure, for commercial reasons, to maintain a target average class size when, because there is a wide range of student levels, it would be pedagogically desirable to open an extra class to reduce diversity. Reconciling these two pressures is not easy, and much will depend on the nature of the offer made to the consumer, and their expectations formed on that basis.

Teachers are also uneasy about having classes with a wide range of levels, as it makes their work more difficult. If diversifying the range of student intake is part of an LTO marketing strategy (see the Ansoff matrix in Chapter 4, p. 92), instead of dealing with the teaching demands that this gives rise to on an ad hoc basis, the academic manager should consider developing a policy and practices to handle the diversification in a way that reconciles everyone's concerns in a more considered manner. If, for instance, the nature of the market and the offer (such as continuous enrolment) means that mixed-level classes are the norm, attention must be given to developing methods for mixed-level teaching. This, in turn, means devoting some resources to INSET so that teachers are involved in becoming part of the solution to a continuing academic problem.

The scheme which Phillips has proposed may appear to be a long way from where we started: timetabling. What it demonstrates is how timetabling is, above all, concerned with the management of resources within the LTO. Undoubtedly, people's time, skills and commitment are key resources, so they need to be managed wisely and efficiently, while the staff concerned also need to be brought into the picture so that they can see how their work fits into the overall scheme. By being engaged in this way, staff can help contribute to solutions when, as happens, the academic manager is confronted with an unexpected scheduling problem which needs an urgent and effective solution.

Managing your own time

Scheduling is about managing other people's time within the overall requirements of the LTO's activities. What about the manager's own time? How is that to be managed?

One thing is clear: the academic manager often has too much to do, and too little time to do it in. Furthermore, managers' jobs don't stay static; there are plenty of ongoing changes in the environment and the marketplace to ensure that managers are constantly having to adjust and adapt their own jobs and their time.

TASK

To get an idea of what your own job entails, how you approach it, and where the time goes, complete the table in Figure 8.8.

1   Tick according to whether each activity is either operational or tactical.
2   Under 'Time involved', enter a number according to whether the time you devote to the activity concerned is:
   • too much = 3
   • about right = 2
   • not enough = 1

When you have completed the table, consider the following:
   • Which types of activity are 'about right'?
   • Which are 'too much'?
   • Which are 'not enough'?
   • What have you learnt about the time management of your job from this?

As we saw at the start of this chapter, the higher up the management hierarchy you go, the more extensive are your management responsibilities. Thus, someone moving from the post of senior teacher to that of an academic manager, such as DOS, will have to take on responsibility for decisions and systems which affect the work of everyone. If, as an academic manager, you find that you are spending too much time on operational matters, you are probably not making best use of your time.

If you find, for instance, that you are spending too much time on chasing things and people (moving furniture, finding missing equipment/textbooks/materials, tidying classrooms), it looks as if there is a need to review systems, procedures and delegation so that such resources are more effectively managed. If you are spending too much time on administrative tasks (ordering materials and equipment, answering emails), review these areas to reduce their impact on your time. And if you are spending too much time on such professional areas as recruiting and inducting teachers, or planning next term, at the expense of keeping in touch with the day-to-day activities of the LTO by, for example, walking around or being sociable with colleagues, a review is in order to achieve a balance among these various demands on your time and attention.

There are numerous systems and advice for managing time, including electronic time planners. All depend on:
   • clarifying goals for the day, week and month
   • distinguishing between urgent and important activities
   • prioritizing on the basis of urgency/importance
   • allocating time to meetings
   • maintaining time limits and meeting deadlines.

Activity	Management area		Time involved
	Operational	Tactical	
Attending parties and out-of-school meetings			
Being sociable with colleagues			
Channelling information			
Costing courses			
Dealing with agents			
Delegating work to colleagues			
Developing existing or new courses			
Finding missing equipment/textbooks/ materials			
Going to conferences			
Improving systems			
Inducting new teachers			
Keeping an eye on developments in the field			
Meeting with the Principal			
Maintaining staff/student records			
Making coffee			
Meeting parents			
Moving furniture			
Observing classes			
Ordering materials and equipment			
Organizing a professional development programme			
Planning next term			
Recruiting teachers			
Running in-service training			
Running staff meetings			
Teaching			
Timetabling classes and teachers			
Tidying classrooms			
Walking around the school			
Writing emails			

FIGURE 8.8: *Time management*

Although many effective managers like to maintain an 'open door' policy, even they will also close the door when they need to spend uninterrupted, 'quality' time on important activities, such as planning, and they make sure that everyone is aware of the reason for this change of routine. It makes sense to establish such routines because managing your own time also involves restricting other people's ability to disrupt yours.

PROFESSIONAL DEVELOPMENT

Clearly, good teaching is absolutely central to the work of an LTO. However, good teaching does not just happen by accident. Ensuring that it does happen – and continues to do so – is one of the academic manager's major responsibilities. The selection and appointment of good teachers bring together academic and HRM. This will involve drawing up person descriptions of the kind of individual being sought (see Chapter 3, p. 54). Once appointed, the new teacher will require support through orientation, mentoring, provision of materials and resources, observation and feedback, appraisal, and further training (see Chapter 3, *Orientation of new staff*, p. 58 and *Performance management*, p. 65).

Teacher observation

In the Task on p. 212, the requirements for effective teaching in the EAQUALS accreditation scheme were listed. Observation is a way of monitoring the effectiveness of teaching, and most accreditation schemes include observation as part of academic management.

As teachers tend to work independently in their classrooms, being observed is intrusive and potentially threatening, particularly if it is treated as a form of inspection, rather than as part of professional support and development. Teacher observation is not only part of quality assurance; it is also an important aspect of HRM (see Chapter 3, p. 68) .

Teacher observation should:
- involve agreed and clear criteria
- be carried out by trained staff
- include preparation and follow-up
- have provision for mentoring and support for teachers needing help
- involve agreed records which are part of a teacher's personal file and professional portfolio (see below).

This means that the academic manager must ensure that:
- teacher observation is adequately resourced with time and competent staff to do the observations
- it is scheduled in advance as part of an annual programme
- it is part of all teachers' job descriptions
- it is part of new teacher induction.

Ideally, teacher observation will be part of the culture of the LTO, and integrated into institutionally supported professional development.

Continuing professional development (CPD)

In Chapter 3, p. 70, the significance of PD was pointed out, both as part of a 'learning organization', and as part of 'personal mastery'. Indeed, as noted in Chapter 1, p. 10, leading and motivating people is one of the principal management tasks. The concern with long-term staff development is particularly prominent in national education systems in the UK and Australia, under the name of Continuing Professional Development or CPD. CPD differs from in-service training (or INSET) in that it is part of total quality management (TQM) which extends and develops the concept of quality assurance through the creation of a quality culture. In the TQM culture, it is the aim of every member to please, delight and satisfy customers, while the commitment to continuous improvement is achieved through CPD.

The type of CPD which teachers need and want will vary according to their stage in their professional development and their job satisfaction, as described by Huberman (1993), who defined a number of phases in teachers' careers, from early novice through mid to late career, each with its own development needs and aspirations. He found that teachers who sought diversity in classroom teaching or a shift in roles – or what Rosenblatt (2004) defines as skill flexibility – usually attain a higher level of satisfaction. A lack of recurring episodes in which the demands of the situation are slightly beyond one's existing repertoire, be it for children or adults, constrains development (Tsui, 2003). Stretching and extending a teacher's teaching repertoire is at the core of CPD.

State sector education agencies, such as Teachernet in the UK, have raised the profile of CPD in mainstream teaching, emphasizing its relevance to teachers who wish to make progress in their careers. Awareness of the importance of CPD is not confined to public sector teachers, however, as was demonstrated by a group of LTO academic managers and teachers in Australia, who, in a workshop, agreed that PD sessions should have 'impact' by being:

- innovative
- memorable
- practical
- convincing
- hands-on
- entertaining
- useful
- informative
- stimulating
- transferable
- motivating
- team-building.

While CPD is ultimately the responsibility of the individual, nonetheless, making CPD opportunities available is an important responsibility of an academic manager. As Richards & Farrell (2005) show, in PD there is a wide range of activities which can be deployed, from workshops to action research to teaching portfolios. Maintaining a record of CPD activities will add value, for both the individual and the institution. Rather than re-invent the wheel, managers and teachers can, at no cost, download a teacher's portfolio from the University of Cambridge ESOL website.

REFLECTION

What role does CPD have in your own LTO? Answers to this question vary hugely, and some LTOs lack anything that could be considered to be CPD.

What form does CPD take? This can vary from the scrappy, improvised session given by a 'volunteered' staff member, to a carefully planned programme of activities involving both in-house and external trainers.

What differences in PD requirements and motivation appear to characterize teachers at different phases of their life cycle? Academic managers will usually have observed differences in teachers' behaviour, depending on age, length and type of experience. Such differences suggest that a 'one size fits all' PD scheme may be inappropriate.

How is the impact of CPD evaluated for both individuals and the LTO? Curiously, this is an aspect of both CPD and INSET which is often overlooked. Observing teachers is one way of tracking the impact of training opportunities.

As an academic manager, what CPD framework and record scheme would you be interested in establishing in your LTO if no such scheme exists at the moment? Having individual records is part of HRM and is an area where academic management overlaps with other management areas.

MANAGING QUALITY

For the consumers of the teaching and other services of an LTO, it is their actual experience of what the LTO has provided to them that establishes their definition of quality (see Chapter 5, pp. 121 and 129). This experience will have been initiated by the kinds of promise which the LTO made in its promotional material (see Chapter 4, p. 103). Since language teaching and learning is at the heart of what the LTO provides, it makes sense to be as clear and explicit as possible in making this offer. Increasingly, LTOs are representing this part of their offer in terms of competencies organized by level, providing students with a guide to their existing and desired levels.

An example of such a specification is found on the Eurocentres website (Figure 8.9). The Eurocentres scale is aligned to the Common European Framework of Reference for Languages: Learning, Teaching, Assessment (CEFR), Council for Cultural Co-operation, Council of Europe (2001). This divides learners into three broad divisions A, B and C, each of which forms two branches:

Basic User: Breakthrough (A1)
                           Waystage (A2)

Independent User: Threshold (B1)
                           Vantage (B2)

Proficient User: Effective Operational Proficiency (C1)
                           Mastery (C2)

Level 10	– achieve a precise, differentiated expression of thoughts and opinions in a natural style – argue your case and negotiate skilfully – write virtually flawless essays and reports		C2
Level 9	– feel fully comfortable in the language – be creative in the language and develop a personal style – put acrosss complex points of view in meetings, seminars, reports, presentations	This level is important for study at university	C1
Level 8	– intervene in a discussion appropriately – develop ideas systematically – emphasize specific points in meetings, seminars, reports, presentations		
Level 7	– keep up with a lively discussion among native speakers and interaction spontaneously and comfortably – present and defend your own point of view – reliably pass on detailed information	Employers value examination certificates on this level	B2
Level 6	– participate actively in longer discussions – describe problems in detail – react to the comments of others – talk on the phone without difficulty		
Level 5	– join in a conversation unprepared – formulate thoughts – monitor and pass on information – give detailed instructions	From this level you can use the language in the workplace	B1
Level 4	– maintain a conversation and chat with friends – respond flexibly to different situations – express feelings		
Level 3	– make yourself understood in predictable everyday situations – obtain specific information – describe events and personal experiences		A2
Level 2	– obtain simple information – understand answers to questions – discuss what to do – describe activities		
Level 1	– simple communication on holiday – make reservations in hotels – get what you need in restaurants and shops		A1
Level 0	– no knowledge		

FIGURE 8.9: *Eurocentres Scale of Language Proficiency*

The CEFR describes what a learner is supposed to be able to do in reading, listening, speaking and writing at each level, in detail, specified as a series of 'can do' statements, as in this example for level C2:

> Can understand with ease virtually everything heard or read. Can summarize information from different spoken and written sources, reconstructing arguments and accounts in a coherent presentation. Can express him/herself spontaneously, very fluently and precisely, differentiating finer shades of meaning even in more complex situations. (CEFR Global Scale)

As consumers, students (and their sponsors – typically parents or employers) will want to be given an indication on their progress, as Steve found in his survey reported in the case study in Chapter 4, p. 95. The CEFR will be too detailed for such purposes (although it could be adapted to provide a simplified and transparent outcomes specification for such a readership). Simplification can, of course, be taken too far, as is illustrated in the following report on a student's progress from LTO A (Figure 8.10).

LTO A Report			
Reading	3.5	Writing	3.3
Listening	3.5	Speaking	3.5
	Attitude to Study	Attendance and Punctuality	Progress
Excellent	✓	✓	
Very good			✓
Good			
Satisfactory			
Unsatisfactory			

Comments from group tutor:
A well-motivated student who works extremely well with the other members of the group.

FIGURE 8.10: *Sample report, LTO A*

The second example, from LTO B (Figure 8.11) indicates a concern with the interests of the consumer (the learner) and their sponsor (parent or employer). This example also suggests that the management of the LTO really is concerned with quality. As far as academic management is concerned, such a focus on quality involves having:
- a clear and shared view of what is involved in language learning and teaching: vision, mission, philosophy, objectives
- high levels of competence in being able to provide effective learning opportunities: knowledge, skills and motivation of staff

LTO B Report

Grammar	B+	Always asks questions to clarify new grammar points and makes an effort to use them.
Vocabulary	B+	Records and remembers vocabulary well and tries to apply it in spoken and written work.
Speaking & Pronunciation	B	Quite fluent but could stretch himself more.
Listening	A	Listening skills are above average for this level.
Reading	A	Reading comprehension above average for this level and makes good use of techniques learned throughout the course.
Writing	B	Always completes work; his fluency and style are improving.
Homework & Self Study	A	Completes all homework by deadline, good at working independently, attends all exam practice sessions.
Attitude & Effort	B	As he prefers to work by himself, he sometimes finds group work difficult.

Director of Studies' comments:

Harold seems to be afraid of failing, so does not like to go outside what he is comfortable with is therefore reluctant to try something that may be a challenge for him. For this reason, Harold is not confident about doing CPE in December. However, I believe he would be quite ready to attempt it and he has been advised to do so.

FIGURE 8.11: *Sample report, LTO B*

- adequate resources and systems to support such provision: systems for new product development, evaluation and assessment, staff training and development
- ways of measuring the efficiency and the effectiveness of such systems, including placement, progress and achievement tests.

Managing quality should not mean setting up complex processes, systems, checklists and measures as an end in themselves. Many of the measurement systems are likely already to be in place, although the data may not have been used for evaluating quality. For example, the process and outcome of new product development involves the following measures:

- the number of new products under development
- the progress of development (at what stage is each product?)
- the number of new products which have been launched
- their success as measured by student volume, satisfaction and achievement.

Many of these can be expressed as ratios (typically percentages); for example, what is the ratio of new (or improved) products to existing ones? Such ratios also provide ways of making comparisons with sector benchmarks, and they are also indicative of innovativeness, as a very low ratio of new developments in progress or launched will be characteristic of an LTO which is probably stuck in the mud.

Likewise, there are measures for evaluating CPD, beginning with something as obvious as the budget devoted to staff training and development and the allocation for conference attendance. Other measures will include the number of INSET and PD sessions held, the number of staff attending them and the number of staff following external courses. More difficult to evaluate, but important, is the impact of PD on the teaching and learning that takes place in the LTO. Such impact may be best evaluated through action research which, itself, is a form of PD.

CONCLUSION

The job of the academic manager is a particularly comprehensive one. Although assigning staff and scheduling classes will be a significant part of day-to-day, operational work, it is important that the academic manager has the opportunity to look beyond these operational concerns to take account of the broader resource management and product development needs of the LTO, as well as the professional development needs of staff. These aspects must be given due attention if the LTO is to fulfil both its educational and commercial goals. Academic management also involves responding to changes in the market, identifying innovations and successfully implementing them. These are the topics of the following two chapters.

9 Managing change

- CHANGE
- MODELS FOR IMPLEMENTING INNOVATION
- INTERNAL CHANGE
- TECHNOLOGY

INTRODUCTION

Drucker (1973, p. 43) observes that 'management always has to consider both the present and the future; both the short run and the long run'. In the present, the manager must keep the enterprise performing by ensuring that day-to-day operations are successfully carried out. Achieving this will involve the kinds of relatively minor modifications that are made in response to changing circumstances or feedback from customers so as to keep the LTO in a state of productive equilibrium.

A manager also has to redirect resources from areas of low or diminishing returns to areas of high or rising results. In other words, the manager has to be concerned with the future, or, in Drucker's words, the manager 'has to create tomorrow' (Drucker, 1973, p. 45). Implicit in this task is managing change and innovation on a scale which goes beyond maintaining a steady state. Such major change has been termed a 'punctuation' in the 'punctuated equilibrium' model of change (see p. 239).

In fact, change, as such, happens, regardless of managerial intervention. Any difference between a state of affairs at different times can be thought of as change. Innovation, by contrast, has been defined by Audrey Nichols (1983, p. 4) as

> ... an idea or practice perceived as new by an individual or individuals, which is intended to bring about improvement in relation to desired objectives, which is fundamental in nature, and which is planned and deliberate.

The difference between change and innovation is important, although the terms are often used interchangeably, with 'change management' being applied to implementing innovation in the sense defined by Nichols, and 'diffusion of innovation' to the way in which innovations are spread and adopted. In this chapter, 'change' will be used to refer to forces which can impact on an organization, while 'managing innovation' will be concerned with the introduction of new ideas and practices.

CHANGE

External influences: STEP factors

There are numerous forces which continuously affect the environment in which any LTO operates. Figure 9.1 displays such environmental influences.

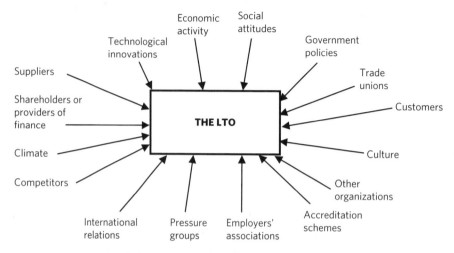

FIGURE 9.1: *Environmental influences on an LTO* (adapted from Mullins, 1985, p.13)

It is abundantly clear that, in the past twenty years, there have been huge changes in the environment of all LTOs, changes over which an LTO has no influence; rather, they are changes which influence the LTO. Such changes are summed up in Figure 9.2, in what are called the STEP (or sometimes PEST) factors:

Social	cultural aspects, demographics (age, gender, race, family size, etc.), lifestyle changes, population shifts, trends, fads, diversity, immigration/emigration, education, health, living standards, housing trends, fashion, attitudes to work, leisure activities, occupations, earning capacity
Technological	inventions, new discoveries, research, energy uses/sources/fuels, communications, rates of obsolescence, advances, information technology, internet, transportation, bio-tech
Economic	economic growth trends, interest, exchange rates and inflation rates, government spending levels, disposable income, unemployment rates, consumer confidence, import/export trends, global warming
Political	tax policy, employment laws, environmental regulations, consumer protection, industry-specific regulations, trade restrictions and tariffs, domestic and international political stability, global warming

FIGURE 9.2: *STEP factors*

A STEP analysis, as will be clear from the list above, involves understanding the external forces – including the competition – affecting the organization. Achieving this involves scanning external events, and assessing the impact on your own sector and, specifically, your own LTO. Sources for such an analysis include:

- newspapers, periodicals, current books and broadcast media
- trade organizations, such as English UK, English Australia
- government agencies, such as departments of education and tourism
- industry analysts, available from governmental and non-governmental organizations
- financial analyses, available from the financial press, and sector analyses.

Taking account of such factors, David Graddol (2006), in *English Next*, a review commissioned and published by the British Council, considers the growth of global English and its implications for the future of ELT. His is the kind analysis which informs strategic, i.e. long-term, planning, although with the speed of change as it is, *English Next* also has implications for medium-term, tactical planning.

TASK

Carry out a current STEP analysis of your sector, focusing on how organizations such as your own may have to change in response to the factors you identify.

You may not be able to fill each STEP category; some events, such as the impact of IT, cover more than one category, while some may not be relevant.

Which are the factors that are critical in influencing or shaping your LTO and its competitors in the future?

How will your LTO respond to the impact of such factors? In other words, what innovations will it have to consider introducing?

Factor	Examples	Time: short, medium, long term	Impact: low, medium, high
Social			
Technological			
Economic			
Political			

External and internal factors: SWOT analysis

SWOT analysis is a valuable tool when reviewing your LTO's activities and laying the ground for strategic planning, not only in planning innovation, but also in strategic financial and marketing planning. Before beginning a SWOT analysis, it is important to decide why you are doing it, and what you hope to get out of it. The identification of internal strengths and weaknesses, and external opportunities and threats, provides the basis for defining strategies by asking these four questions:

1 How can we use each strength?
2 How can we reduce or remove each weakness?
3 How can we exploit each opportunity?
4 How can we defend against or remove each threat?

It is a good idea to have a cross-functional team to do a SWOT analysis, as each member will bring a different perspective to the exercise. Examples of specific SWOT factors are as follows:

Internal factors: strengths and weaknesses

- resources: financial, intellectual, locational/situational
- customer service
- efficiency
- proprietary systems (such as marketing and sales databases and management)
- quality
- human resources
- management
- price
- development time
- cost
- capacity and capability
- relationships with key sector customers
- brand and reputation in the market
- local language and cultural knowledge
- brand reputation

External factors: opportunities and threats

- political/legal
- market trends
- economic condition
- expectations of stakeholders
- technology
- public expectations
- competitors and competitive activities

A good SWOT analysis will indicate areas of the LTO's activities which may require changing; in other words, it provides the basis for identifying innovations. The SWOT worksheet (Figure 9.3) includes a section to identify specifically both the strategies to be pursued in the immediate future and those that are more long-term. From this worksheet, a manager or management team can then map out an implementation plan.

		INTERNAL FACTORS	
		Strengths (S) List 3–5 *internal* strengths here:	**Weaknesses (W)** List 3–5 *internal* weaknesses here:
E X T E R N A L F A C T O R S	**Opportunities (O)** List 3–5 *external* opportunities here:	**SO strategies** List strategies to use strengths and take advantage of opportunities here:	**WO strategies** List strategies to take advantage of opportunities by overcoming weaknesses here:
	Threats (T) List 3–5 *external* threats here:	**ST strategies** List strategies to use strengths and avoid threats here:	**WT strategies** List strategies to minimize weaknesses and avoid threats here:

Immediate strategies to be undertaken:
1
2
3

Long-term strategies to be considered:
1
2
3

FIGURE 9.3: *SWOT matrix*

> **TASK**
>
> Using the worksheet in Figure 9.3, perform your own SWOT analysis on an activity or unit within your LTO. Ideally, work with several colleagues.
> - Begin by agreeing on a reason or reasons for doing the analysis.
> - List at least three items within each category
> - List as many strategies as you can within the matrix for each category.
> - Then prioritize the strategies according to which you would undertake first.

Risk assessment

Refer to Chapter 10, p. 263 for an account of risk assessment, which is important not only in the context of project management, but also in the management of innovation. Risk assessment can be carried out using a risk tolerance matrix (see Figure 10.5, Chapter 10, p. 264).

MODELS FOR IMPLEMENTING INNOVATION

Having considered two useful tools for clarifying a need for change, we will now review some models of innovation so as to provide a framework for and insights into implementing innovation in the LTO context, as exemplified in the case studies to follow. The introduction and adoption of innovations – the process of diffusion – has been much studied, dating back to the work of the French sociologist Gabriel Tarde (1903). Subsequent work by Everett Rogers (1995), studying the adoption of agricultural innovations among farmers, demonstrated how the rate of diffusion, which is essentially a social process, can be plotted on a bell-shaped innovation curve (Figure 9.4), which displays a cumulative percentage of adopters over time. There is a slow start, followed by more rapid adoption, then levelling off until there is only a small percentage of 'laggards' who have not adopted.

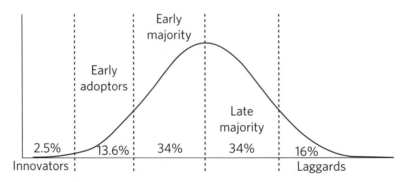

FIGURE 9.4: *Rogers' Adoption/Innovation curve*

Diffusion as epidemic: the tipping point

In recent years, the study of change has drawn on ideas from two unrelated fields: epidemiology and evolutionary theory. The first of these was the subject of a popularization by Malcolm Gladwell (2000) in his book *The Tipping Point*, which refers to the critical point when the spread of a disease becomes an epidemic or a trend becomes common. (In Rogers' curve, this would be the point at which the early majority have adopted an innovation.) Gladwell develops three general themes which he believes influence the development of trends:

- the law of the few: the formation of self-organizing networks which foster the spread of ideas through the work of key individuals
- the 'stickiness' factor of messages
- the power of context.

Social epidemics (such as changes in fashion) are stimulated by the efforts of a few people that he calls Connectors, Mavens and Salesmen. These are people who do not appear as such on an organizational chart, but who will be part of the informal social network through which much information is transmitted and work achieved. Connectors are people who have loose ties to lots of people (rather than close ties to a limited circle). They are good at word-of-mouth transmission of news. Mavens are knowledgeable, trusted information brokers, sharing and trading what they know. Salesmen are charismatic individuals and effective persuaders.

Gladwell shows that the content of information about an innovation is very important; in particular, the quality of what he calls the 'stickiness' of messages is crucial. Is the message memorable? Is it so memorable that it can create change and spur someone to action? In short, is the message like a really good lesson? Does it, in the words of the Australian teachers asked about professional development (see Chapter 8, p. 227), have 'impact'?

His third theme, the power of context, is an environmental argument: behaviour is a function of social context. What really matters is little environmental things which can contribute to the tipping point. The case study on p. 246 describes an 'open door' policy which is an example in an LTO context.

Innovation as punctuated equilibrium

The second example of applying a model from one field to another is found in the 'punctuated equilibrium' model of innovation (Parsons & Fidler, 2005), which has its origins in evolutionary theory. Put simply, in Darwin's theory of evolution, new species emerge through the slow accumulation of random changes over time. The punctuated equilibrium model, by contrast, proposes that change occurs in fits and starts, with prolonged periods of equilibrium during which incremental change occurs slowly, punctuated by periods of rapid, transformational change (Figure 9.5, p. 240).

Organizations typically operate on the basis of equilibrium for long periods, during which evolutionary changes occur, improving organizational efficiency, but without bringing about radical change. In the LTO context, examples of such evolutionary changes would be the updating of existing offers and facilities, or replacing customer-facing staff as part of routine staff turnover. Such changes will tend to be bottom-up, and will be the outcome of 'single-loop' learning (Argyris & Schön, 1978) referred to in Chapter 2, p. 48, which focuses on incremental improvement in organizational efficiency. As they do not challenge or upset the organization's culture, structure and systems – its 'deep structure' – these changes are conservative rather than radical. Indeed, citing Pascale et al, (2000, p. 6), Fullan (2001b, p. 108) points out that 'equilibrium is a precursor to death', as a living system in a state of equilibrium is less responsive to changes around it.

From time to time, however, the life of an organization is disrupted by a major change, such as that which occurs with a change of ownership or the appointment of a new CEO or director. These 'punctuations' will involve 'double-loop' learning, in which quite fundamental questions will be asked about the vision, mission, values, goals and systems of the organization. In other words, the punctuation will involve changes in deep structure.

The relatively brief period of a punctuation may result in stress for organizational members, particularly for those who have to find ways of implementing whatever innovations have been introduced. Their response may be to look for ways of reducing the stress, which can then compromise the innovation. In any case, people find it difficult to sustain prolonged effort, and there is likely to be an 'implementational dip', when motivation, energy and commitment flag. This means that managers responsible for introducing such radical, transformational change have to be prepared to find ways of rewarding and remotivating staff in order to sustain effort and commitment.

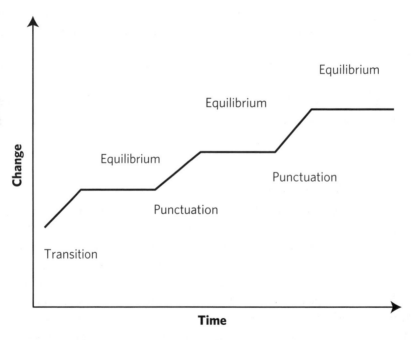

FIGURE 9.5: *Punctuated equilibrium model of change*

Sources of innovation

Models of diffusion provide an insight into the way innovations are spread, with social networks being especially important. What, though, are the sources of innovation?

Finding answers to this question has become especially significant in an era when identifying and implementing appealing innovations help to maintain the competitive advantage of an enterprise. In an international survey of 765 CEOs, IBM (2006) found that the largest single source of innovative ideas was internal: employees, many of whom in an LTO will be the customer-facing staff. The significance of customer contact is further demonstrated in the IBM survey, since customers also make up around one third of sources of innovation, just below another important external source: business partners.

Although collaboration and partnering is 'theoretically easy', it is 'practically hard to do' (IBM, 2006, p. 23). In fact, it may amount to a form of punctuation for both partners, and even internal 'partnering' can be problematic thanks to the silo-ization common in many enterprises. Even so, some very successful LTOs have benefited from the innovations which come from well-managed external partnering and collaboration.

In descending order, after customers, the IBM survey found that the sources of innovative ideas came from consultants, competitors, associations, trade shows and conferences, internal sales and service units, internal research and development, and lastly, academia. The importance of external sources of innovative ideas suggests that an enterprise needs to be constantly scanning its environment and, in an LTO, should encourage staff to be alert to external sources through participating in conferences and monitoring what competitors are doing.

While being open to external sources of innovation is crucial, there are also features of the innovations themselves which influence the tipping point in their diffusion and adoption.

Influences on adopting innovations

Rogers (1995) identifies five important characteristics of innovations as perceived by potential adopters, which influence adoption:

- Compatibility: the degree to which an innovation is perceived as being consistent with the existing values, past experiences and needs of potential adopters.
- Complexity: the degree to which an innovation is perceived as difficult to understand or use.
- Observability: the degree to which the results of an innovation are made available to others. The easier it is for people to see the results of an innovation, the more likely they are to adopt it.
- Relative advantage: the degree to which an innovation is perceived as better than the idea or practice it supersedes.
- Trialability: the degree to which an innovation may be experimented with on a limited basis.

(Rogers, 1995, pp. 15–16)

In the LTO sector, an American researcher, Fredricka Stoller (1997), drawing on this earlier work on innovation diffusion, set out to test the attributes of successful innovation in language teaching by surveying innovations in selected higher education Intensive

English programs in the US. She identified three factors contributing to the acceptance or rejection of innovations.

- Balanced divergence of power: the innovation is viewed as sufficiently divergent but not too divergent from current practices
- Dissatisfaction factor: presence of some degree of dissatisfaction with the current state of affairs
- Viability factor: perception that the innovation is viable.

The balanced divergence factor combines six characteristics, which, when perceived as being sufficiently present, form what she terms a 'zone of innovation', as depicted in Figure 9.6.

	Too little	Sufficient	Too much
Compatibility			
Complexity			
Explicitness			
Flexibility			
Originality			
Visibility			

FIGURE 9.6: *Zone of innovation* (Christison & Stoller (eds), 1997, p. 43)

Stoller concludes that while explicitness and visibility are important in stimulating favourable attitudes towards an innovation, an excess of either can hamper innovative efforts, and she suggests that innovations that are too visible can threaten individuals within the system who are satisfied with things as they are. They in turn may become sources of resistance.

She also finds that difficulty/complexity are similarly perceived. If an innovation is seen as being too simple, the innovation may be regarded as not different enough from current practice to merit the effort of implementing it. Stoller also discovered that difficulty as such was not seen to be a problem as far as her informants were concerned, but she notes that this was in part related to the context in which they worked, since the organizations concerned had a problem-solving orientation and, in Fullan's terms (see next section), had the 'readiness' (i.e. the practical and conceptual capacity) to initiate, develop or adopt a given innovation (Fullan, 2001a, p.63).

Failure and success in managing change

Given the concern with implementing change in virtually all aspects of contemporary society, it is hardly surprising that reasons for failure and success have occupied those concerned with change management. Michael Barber (2007, p. 78) cites a salutary list of the eight most common errors in change programmes identified by Kotter (1996, p. 4).

These are especially relevant when managing the kind of transformational change associated with a punctuation:

- allowing too much complacency
- failing to create a sufficiently powerful guiding coalition
- underestimating the power of vision
- undercommunicating the vision by a factor of 10 (or 100 or even 1000)
- permitting obstacles to block the new vision
- failing to create short-term wins
- declaring victory too soon
- neglecting to anchor changes firmly in the corporate culture.

Reasons for failure and success in educational change have been extensively studied by Michael Fullan (2001a & b) in mainstream education. Among the reasons for failure he has identified are:

- believing that complex problems can be solved quickly
- adopting innovations which have only symbolic benefit
- responding too quickly to fads
- misunderstanding resistance as an attempt to block, rather than as indicating a need for help and support
- allowing pockets of success to fail through lack of support.

Successful change management is supported by keeping in mind that:

- Change is a learning process (and therefore needs to be regarded as such).
- Change is a journey, not a blueprint: it involves not just one-off solutions, but continuous planning and adjusting.
- Problems arise from the change process; these are natural and expected and must be identified and solved.
- Change is resource-hungry, so adequate resourcing is essential.
- Change requires local power to manage it; it cannot be managed by remote control from a central power source.
- Change is systemic: it involves linkages and interconnections among many systems and issues in the organization.

The relevance of Fullan's conclusions is seen in the 'change' examples reported in this and the previous chapter. Complex problems, such as setting up a new course or introducing or changing coursebooks, cannot be dealt with quickly, as demonstrated in Vignette 8.5 (p. 216) and the case studies in this chapter (pp. 246, 249, 250–1).

Change and collegiality

Turning to the numerous examples of advice concerning change management, Fullan concludes that much of it is 'non-actionable' (Fullan, 2001b, p. 33). This is why many people have concluded that change cannot actually be managed. Nevertheless, change can be led, and effective leaders are skilled at establishing and sustaining a professional community which is high on sociability and solidarity, two key factors in the Goffee & Jones model discussed in Chapter 2 (Figure 2.5, p. 38). Drawing on research by

McLaughlin & Talbert (2001), Fullan (2001b, p. 68) contrasts two departments in the same school (summarized in Figure 9.7): one department was a professional community, with high collegiality, the other was not. One functioned well, the other functioned poorly, resembling a fragmented organization.

English department	Social Studies department
Share lessons, materials	Don't share lessons, materials
Collegial support and interaction	Lack collegial support
Treat colleagues as resources	Don't treat colleagues as resources
Positive view of students	Negative view of students

FIGURE 9.7: *Comparison of departments*

Creating collegiality in an institution where it is lacking may be an innovation in itself. There is, however, a note of caution to keep in mind on the benefits of collegiality: Parsons & Fidler (2005, p. 461) conclude that 'unfulfilled punctuations are more likely at collegial institutions', and Fullan (2001b, p. 67) observes that unless collaborative cultures 'are focusing on the right things they may end up being powerfully wrong'. Ultimately, though, successful innovation which results in improvements in relationships and the ways of doing things in an organization are outcomes whose benefits Fullan believes should not be underestimated.

INTERNAL CHANGE

In this section, we will look at some innovations which may be prompted by a combination of internal and external factors. A common source of change with profound internal consequences involves the appointment of new personnel, particularly at middle and senior management level, and this is the first example of internal change to be considered.

Personnel: new staff

In general, the appointment of new staff, especially at senior management level, is motivated not only by the need to manage succession planning, but also by the desire for change. It is rare for a new CEO to be appointed in order simply to continue running things as they were before. This means, then, that the new appointee will usually have a mandate from the ownership or from the board to introduce changes, and, indeed, it is very likely that in the job interview, the new CEO or senior manager will have been asked to suggest what initiatives he or she would envisage implementing. In short, new personnel, by importing new ideas and practices, are significant change agents and they can prompt the kind of revolutionary change associated with a punctuation in the equilibrium of the LTO.

The attitudes towards the newcomer will depend on the history of the organization, particularly its recent history. If the LTO has been going through difficult times, surrendering market share to the competition, losing volume, profitability and confidence, the new appointee will be expected to 'turn things round'. If, however, the LTO has been very successful, a different kind of challenge may face the newcomer: complacency. Whatever the case, the wise newcomer will spend some time learning about and analysing the LTO. This will involve listening to what people have to say and observing what they actually do, as well as analysing sales and marketing and financial data. On the basis of this analysis, the newcomer will be in a position to identify and prioritize areas for innovation, and initiate making the changes.

In the meantime, the newcomer will also be wise to carry out some symbolic acts which indicate that things are going to be different. The case study on p. 246 illustrates what happened when a new manager in a large, international chain took over from one who had been distant and isolated. It also illustrates the effect of Gladwell's 'power of context'.

Personnel: organizational changes

In Chapter 2, we considered lines of authority and responsibility, or line management, which is depicted in the form of an organizational chart. Also discussed there was a feature of LTO organizational structure which is virtually universal: one part which is concerned with administration, and another which deals with teaching. These two parts occupy different silos, and a dysfunctional feature of some LTOs is a lack of cross-silo communication and co-operation. In the NPD scheme outlined in Chapter 8, we suggested that collaboration across silos is important for effectively developing new products. Initiating such cross-functional collaboration may, in some LTOs, be an innovation in itself, calling for careful management and support from senior management.

Within an LTO, it is not uncommon to observe very different spans of control within silos. For example, the administration silo may be relatively small, with one manager being responsible for a handful of staff. By contrast, the teaching or academic silo may have a large number of staff, with a mixture of full- and part-time teachers. This results in one manager, usually the DOS or equivalent, having an excessively wide span of control, with lots of direct reports, resulting in overload. Reducing the load and increasing efficiency will require a structural innovation by delegating some of the management responsibilities to intermediate staff, such as an ADOS or equivalent. This is what Rick did in the case study on p. 246, by setting up co-ordinator posts, while also enriching the jobs of the staff concerned. Likewise, establishing assistant or deputy posts will push down responsibility and reduce the span of control.

Implementing such an organizational innovation will require consultation, analysis of work, grouping of jobs which most appropriately go together, communicating the changes to all affected staff, monitoring the effect of the staff changes and making adjustments if necessary. It may also involve training for staff taking on new responsibilities. This kind of organizational innovation, which is obviously intended to bring about an improvement, will only be successful if it is clearly communicated, and continuing efforts are made to support implementation, since members of the organization will be learning new ways of doing things and building new kinds of work relations.

Case study: Rick

When Rick took over from his predecessor, morale among teaching staff was low, so he had a difficult job. He began by taking advantage of the brief honeymoon from which any new manager will benefit. Firstly, he linked the staffroom computers to the intranet, and teachers each had their own email address. This meant that staff could contact Rick without having to knock on his door, although, in fact, he operated an open-door policy right from the start, the only time of the year when he discouraged staff from coming to him being the period when he was involved in the annual budgeting. For the rest of the time, he encouraged staff to go to him with grievances rather than bottling them up. Such meetings were also opportunities to come up with new ideas, and as teachers felt that they were being given a fair hearing, an atmosphere of trust was established.

He introduced fortnightly staff meetings, and he would publish in advance a list of items which he wished to discuss. Staff could also add items which they wanted to discuss to the list. The meetings themselves were managed by rotating the chairperson and secretary roles, which meant that over a year, everyone had a turn at managing the staff meeting.

Rick was prepared to delegate to staff by, for instance, setting up a system of co-ordinator posts, e.g. Business English Co-ordinator, Examinations Co-ordinator. Although this meant that the post holders had extra work (albeit with a slightly reduced teaching load), they did have an opportunity to develop new skills and promote their own professional growth. At the same time, Rick obtained more time for himself, enabling him to deal with planning and development. Furthermore, an increase in the headcount of teaching staff for whom he was responsible enhanced Rick's status and reputation, so that both he and his colleagues gained.

He also implemented a job-plan scheme. Individual staff agreed specific goals at the start of the year, and these were reviewed as part of an appraisal at the end of year. Rick maintained a record of appraisal meetings and staff realized that their achievements would be documented for future promotion or employment. In fact, staff turnover declined during the period of Rick's tenure.

TASK

Referring back to the work you have already done in previous chapters, particularly regarding the organization of your LTO and the analysis of your own job, list some changes in the personnel in the LTO. Concentrate on such aspects as span of control, scope of jobs, and benefits to be gained from reorganization of existing staff or setting up of a new post or posts.

Place

The location of an LTO tends to be taken for granted, yet there is no doubt that being in the wrong place can have serious effects on its viability. An LTO whose core clientele are young learners needs to be in a residential district where such students live, whereas one concerned with executive and corporate training will be best located in the Central Business District. Proximity to homestay accommodation (in the case of an LTO serving a mainly offshore market), public transport links and secure parking are also key considerations.

In Vignette 8.1 (Chapter 8, p. 202), we learned how, on accepting the offer of the post of branch manager, Loraine was informed of the forthcoming change of premises, a change which she would have to manage. This change of premises had been triggered by several STEP and SWOT factors, some linked to the ending of the current lease, the prospect of a considerably higher rent if a new lease were entered into, as well as the need to find premises which more closely matched the capacity requirements of the branch and the convenience of its clientele. After a protracted search, new premises, at an affordable rent, were found and a new lease signed. The choice of both the location and the design of the new premises were determined by the strategic plan for the branch, and Loraine's responsibility as project manager was to liaise with the architect, builders and suppliers on the one hand, and with the central senior management of the chain on the other, to ensure that the new branch would be open and functioning with a minimum of downtime. She also had to maintain business as usual and involve staff in preparing for and taking part in the move to the new premises.

Taking account of the limitations of the existing premises, Loraine and her colleagues set about ensuring that its inefficiencies would not be replicated at their new location. High among these was ensuring that all of the key staff would be located on the same floor so that they could actually see and speak to each other on a daily basis and sustain the collegiality which Loraine had already encouraged among her colleagues. Working within the constraints of the new premises, Loraine drew on the experience and suggestions of her colleagues, while also taking into account the predicted expectations and requirements of the clientele.

Clearly, the solution to limitations imposed by place cannot always involve a major relocation. Even so, changing dysfunctional features of an existing location, such as the fragmentation and inefficiencies that occur when staff are scattered around the premises, can significantly improve working practices, staff motivation and customer satisfaction. Identifying and rectifying such servicescape problems are part of managing place-related innovation.

Product

Changing premises happens only occasionally, if at all, in the life of an LTO, whereas in comparison, introducing new products occurs on a relatively frequent basis. From the viewpoint of the LTO manager as professional, introducing new products involves curriculum development, including planning a new course and selecting new coursebooks. In Chapter 8, we outlined a system for new product development. Now we will consider two examples of curriculum and new product development in the form of introducing a new course and selecting new coursebooks. The LTOs involved operated on quite different scales: the first (opposite) was small, and relatively new, whereas the second (pp. 250–1) was part of a long-established, very large college of further education. Despite their disparity, these examples illustrate aspects of managing innovation which can be extrapolated and applied to LTOs of any size.

The two case studies illustrate how external and internal factors stimulated innovations. In *Introducing a new course and coursebook*, the LTO was entering an unfamiliar sector, which required developing entirely new courses for a lower age level. Although experienced in course development, with transferable skills, what was lacking was actual experience of teaching juniors.

By seeking advice, recruiting new staff, and selecting a new coursebook aimed at juniors, the academic manager was filling gaps in institutional knowledge and competence. Time pressures meant that she was unable to carry out one vital step: trialling the materials with the intended students by the teachers who would be using them. It is clear from what happened that the new teachers, who had not been involved in the coursebook selection, found themselves in a situation that no teacher is comfortable with: using inappropriate materials. This is a threatening experience for most teachers, and the teachers' reaction is only to be expected. Fortunately, the academic manager paid attention to what the teachers were saying, rather than treating it as unhelpful resistance, and took remedial action. Failure to do so would undoubtedly have led to further problems.

Selecting new coursebooks reads like a textbook example of how to manage innovation effectively in an LTO staffed entirely by casually employed teachers. To begin with, Astrid, the HOD, took her time. In fact, the whole exercise occupied around 18 months, doubtless a luxury in many other contexts, but one which was considered vital given the scope and significance of this important innovation. With such a timescale, Astrid was able to plan the innovation carefully, and to involve key stakeholders right from the start. Indeed, it was feedback, collected as part of routine course evaluation, which had alerted her to the need to review the coursebooks. This means that the initiative to change coursebooks was prompted by a recognized need. In short, it fell within the 'zone of innovation'.

Case study: Introducing a new course and coursebook

The LTO, which had been in existence for about five years, was already teaching teenagers when a demand for teaching much younger children was identified, and so the director decided to start some courses for 'juniors'. The decision to do this was made towards the end of the academic year and advice from affiliated centres in the LTO's network was sought. Of particular concern was the selection of a coursebook and supplementary materials for this level, as copies had to be ordered in advance so as to be in stock for the forthcoming academic year, when the new course would begin.

As none of the existing teachers had any experience of working with children of this age group (7–10 years), some new teachers, who had relevant experience of teaching juniors, were recruited. The new teachers were provided with some training, the teaching programmes for juniors were devised, and other start-up activities were completed before teaching was due to begin.

Initially, everything went quite smoothly until the point at which teachers actually started teaching the juniors and using the coursebook that had been purchased. It turned out that most of the teachers did not want to use it. Even though the coursebook had been recommended by two other schools in the network, the new teachers did not find it to be appropriate for the juniors they were teaching. In their opinion, there was a mismatch in content and level with the background and level of the junior learners. So the teachers decided to spurn the coursebook.

This meant the LTO was faced with quite a problem: potentially, money spent on the teaching materials had been wasted, yet the teaching programmes had been based on that same coursebook, and the students had already been recruited. Having core teaching materials which were deemed not to be usable was a disaster. The bright side of this situation was that at that time there were fewer than half a dozen groups of juniors, and only four dozen coursebooks had been purchased. Even so, a solution had to be found, and quickly.

Fortunately, Daiva, the director, when faced with the problem, listened to what the teachers had to say, and then set about repairing the problem by assigning one of the teachers to do some curriculum development, identifying those parts of the books which could be omitted, and devising supplementary materials so that, rather than ditching the books, they could continue to be used in ways which matched local needs. The repair worked: teachers were happy with the changes, and the LTO avoided scrapping an expensive set of materials and, by doing so, upsetting a very significant customer – the parents of their young learners.

Case study: Selecting new coursebooks

This large adult education institution has a programme consisting of three types of courses: intensive courses working through one level of the CEFR (see Chapter 8, p. 228) within a period of five to six weeks, twice-weekly courses working through one level per semester, and once-weekly courses needing three to four semesters to complete a level. One coursebook series is used so that participants can change between course types, and can continue with the same approach.

Having been in use for a decade, the coursebook series had started to become dated and the subject of criticism among teachers and students, the former regarding it as too academic and grammar-focused as well as difficult to use in the kind of mixed-ability classrooms that were the norm. Teachers perceived a new textbook as both a challenge and as a way of avoiding boredom caused by teaching the same texts they had been using for ten years. Meanwhile, publishers' representatives kept enquiring about an opportunity for changing the coursebook, as such an institutional adoption represents substantial sales.

Information gathering and preparation

A need for change having been determined, Astrid, the HOD, together with the DOS, evaluated a number of coursebook series using assessment criteria adapted from a published source. The availability of a starter level, as well as the price, were important considerations for the LTO's clientele, and were also incorporated among the criteria. The DOS and HOD then reduced the list to three series: A (the latest version of a series already in use), B and C.

The DOS approached a number of qualified teachers with experience across a range of levels and asked them to participate in the piloting process. It was agreed to pilot levels A1 and A2 of each of the three coursebook series since the majority of the LTO's participants attended courses at these levels. In addition to this, piloting was to cover a range of classes per level.

Having selected the series and planned the piloting phase, the HOD contacted publishers to negotiate the terms of piloting their courses. The terms included:
- free student books, teacher's books and audio material for the English department
- free student books, teacher's books and audio material for teachers of pilot courses
- free student books for participants of pilot courses
- complimentary workshops for all teachers, introducing them to the series and offering them a free copy of a student book.

In order to collect meaningful data, the LTO attempted to ensure that there was the same mixture of participants on pilot courses as in ordinary classes. No mention was made of free books for those registering at the beginning of the semester, so that those who found themselves in the pilot classes discovered that they had a small bonus in the form of a free textbook.

The HOD and DOS developed individual questionnaires for each series, and they organized the piloting so that some teachers taught the same level of one series in different types of courses, others used two elementary coursebooks in different classes, while another teacher tried out the transition from one level to the next by teaching sequential levels of the same coursebook.

Communication

Throughout the process, teachers not engaged in piloting were provided with relevant information in the department's letters to staff as well as in teachers' meetings. This kept everyone 'in the loop', even though none of the teachers was on a permanent, full-time contract. Workshops on the piloted coursebooks introduced them to the series and their methodology.

Evaluation

After two semesters, feedback from both teachers and participants was very positive for all series. A final decision then had to be made. In the end, it was decided not to adopt coursebook A, the latest version of the series that they had already used, since it was felt that by doing so they would have passed over the opportunity of introducing new material and a different approach to teaching. An exception was made for level A1 (false beginners), for whom the new version of coursebook A proved to be the most effective.

Deciding between coursebooks B and C was difficult since both were up-to-date publications using task-based learning and including all the supplementary material that was needed. In the end, coursebook C was chosen.

Implementation

Shortly before the start of the new year, the publisher organised a second workshop to familiarize teachers with the series and its underlying approach. The autumn then saw the introduction of C for all courses starting at the beginning of a level and the new version of A for refresher courses at A1 level. The implementation went very smoothly, and minor problems were quickly solved.

Continuation

After two semesters of working with the series, a workshop gave teachers the opportunity to reflect on the implementation process and provide feedback to the academic managers. Overall, the feedback was very positive.

Changing coursebooks, particularly in such a high-profile public sector institution, involves risk. So, Astrid took some risk-mitigating measures. Firstly, she drew up a set of criteria for evaluating candidate replacement coursebooks. The criteria included pedagogical as well as practical considerations. Secondly, she involved teachers by recruiting some who would be prepared to trial or pilot candidate coursebooks across a representative sample of classes. Thirdly, she involved another key stakeholding group: the publishers. Knowing that they would compete with each other to secure an adoption, she was able to resource the piloting at minimal cost to her LTO.

Fourthly, she kept all teachers in the picture so that they knew what was happening. This was important because the teachers are the one group of stakeholders who will be most affected by a change of coursebook; they are also the group who can ensure its success or failure, as we saw in *Introducing a new course and coursebook*. If teachers are unhappy with a coursebook, they will often use alternative teaching material, which undermines the confidence and satisfaction of students, particularly if they have acquired a book which is little used. It also means that in an LTO which has a large clientele who expect continuity and smooth articulation from one level or course to another, the absence of a core coursebook series can lead to confusion and dissatisfaction, ultimately resulting in a decline in student recruitment.

As a result of the piloting, Astrid and the DOS were able to obtain a rich fund of information on which to make a final selection. The teachers who had trialled the materials were able to make their voices heard, while their colleagues knew that the piloting had been carried out by people like themselves, with students like the ones they taught. This lent credibility to the exercise, so that when the final selection was made, teachers had confidence in the choice. They also knew that the publishers concerned would be running in-service courses to help familiarize them with the new materials so that, rather than feeling deskilled when using the new textbooks, they would have some confidence in being able to use them effectively. This would also benefit the students, all of them fee-paying, who would not be made to feel that they were being used as guinea pigs.

This example illustrates a number of features of managing innovation discussed earlier. In particular, it demonstrates how to manage an innovation 'which is intended to bring about improvement in relation to desired objectives, which is fundamental in nature, and which is planned and deliberate' (Nichols, 1983, p. 4). Teachers were encouraged to develop and deploy their skill flexibility (Rosenblatt, 2004) because they wanted the teaching and learning benefits which adopting new coursebooks would provide. Indeed, a significant stimulus for changing the coursebooks had come from the teachers themselves, and they were ultimately rewarded for their efforts by the adoption of new materials which met their requirements and those of their students.

TECHNOLOGY

Vignette 8.5 (Chapter 8, p. 216) deals with the introduction of IWBs, a new piece of technology, in an LTO chain. There is a growing literature on the introduction and diffusion of communications technology, such as the IWB, in mainstream education (e.g. Moss, Jewitt, & Levaãiç et al, 2007) which provides some useful pointers for ELT. It is clear that simply installing hardware and associated infrastructure, while obviously necessary, is not sufficient to ensure that the investment will be fully integrated and used effectively. Without training, few teachers will have the knowledge, understanding and confidence to incorporate the new technology into their teaching effectively. As it happens, IWBs are relatively easy to accommodate into existing teaching practices, though without in any significant way transforming them. With training, familiarity and practice, teachers will be in a position to extend and finally transform their teaching using the new technology.

It is also clear that with the introduction of communications technology, such as the IWB, teachers will initially be required to do extra work to develop both their expertise and materials. Quite quickly, teachers will accumulate teaching material of varying quality and transferability. From an academic manager's point of view, it makes sense to share such material by building up a bank of IWB resources. For this to be effective, teachers will need training in developing materials which can actually be used by others, since teachers typically devise materials for their own lessons, to be taught by themselves. Again, the academic manager will need to work with teachers to develop a system for devising materials so that they can be effectively incorporated and shared in a resource bank (see Vignette 8.7, p. 219). An LTO with experience in managing a Self-Access Centre will be well placed to develop such a bank of teachers' resources.

Finally, there is a duty of care dimension to the installation of communications technology. In the enthusiasm to adopt exciting new equipment, potential dangers to users (in this case, both staff and students) may result in overlooking side effects, such as the danger to eyesight in the case of IWBs. A health and safety audit, and the provision of training and protection, should therefore be part of the evaluation and implementation of such innovation.

CONCLUSION

For much of their life, LTOs operate in a state of equilibrium, managing incremental changes as they adapt to the environment and the market. From time to time, though, either external factors or internal influences disturb the steady state, ushering in a period of radical, transformational change. Managing the changes brought about by such a punctuation will involve time, resources and a range of skills which are brought together in project management, the subject of the next chapter.

TASK

Take one of the situations discussed in the case studies in this chapter, and complete the checklist in Figure 9.8 (p. 254). Then use the same checklist to review an example of innovation implementation in your own LTO.
- What insights into the innovation process have been revealed?
- What changes would you make in managing implementation in the future?

Factor	Present?	Comment
The situation		
Dissatisfaction with current state		
The innovation:		
Acceptability		
Feasibility		
Relevance		
Viability		
Relative advantage of innovation:		
Compatibility		
Complexity		
Explicitness		
Flexibility		
Originality		
Visibility		
Emphasis on teaching and social issues		
Influence of:		
Connectors		
Mavens		
Salesmen		
Senior management		
Stickiness of messages		
Resistance		
Provision of:		
Resources		
Time		
Outcome		
Improvement in state of affairs		
Satisfaction among adopters/users		

FIGURE 9.8: *Task checklist*

10 Project management

- PROJECT MANAGEMENT: AN OVERVIEW
- PROJECT PLANNING
- EXTERNALLY FUNDED PROJECTS
- MONITORING AND EVALUATION
- PROJECT COMPLETION

GOALS
OBJECTIVES

INTRODUCTION

In discussing change and the management of innovation, we have considered factors which influence dissemination and adoption. Managing change can be very complex, involving decisions at many levels, and the efforts of many people. While there is no totally foolproof way of managing change, we believe that project management provides an effective methodology and set of tools for change management. Although conceived and developed for large-scale projects, up to and including those on a national level (as described by Barber, 2007, in the context of public service reform in the UK), project management can be usefully adapted to the smaller scale of the LTO, and in this section we will outline an approach to project management which can be applied or adapted to implementing innovation at local level.

Increasingly, project management is seen as an essential element of management on a wider scale. Indeed, project management can teach us many valuable lessons regarding management writ large. But what is a project? The three examples below illustrate the range of activities covered by projects.

1   The academic director of an IEP associated with a undergraduate programme in a US university is tasked with designing a new course to assist students with the demands of academic writing. She forms a team to develop the course, and together they develop a plan for creating the course and materials.
2   A not-for-profit LTO in Poland decides to develop e-learning materials for potential students who are unable to attend English classes onsite. They build a partnership of like-minded institutions in other European Union countries, all of whom are interested in similar work, and apply for funds through the European Commission. The Polish co-ordinating LTO is charged with managing the international project, and submitting a report and the final product to the Commission.
3   The co-ordinator of the writing programme at a Middle Eastern university decides that he would like to reorganize the computer lab in order to make it a more conducive place for learning. He writes a proposal and submits it to the Dean of the department, and subsequently is responsible for monitoring and evaluating the changes as they go ahead.

PROJECT MANAGEMENT: AN OVERVIEW

From these examples, we see that a project is an undertaking which is designed to achieve specific objectives within a given budget and within a specified period of time. Often a project is structured towards the production of some kind of tangible product, such as a new curriculum, a set of teaching materials in some area, or a new look for the school cafeteria.

Unlike the ongoing operations of an LTO, a project eventually comes to an end. For many activities in an LTO, of which new course design and provision, or new product development (see Chapter 8, p. 213), are typical, a project approach is appropriate because there will be a specific outcome (or 'deliverable'), such as a course, to be developed by given deadlines and provided over a period of time (such as a term or a semester), with a development team assigned to the project for a fixed period, and using resources allocated to them. The development and provision process will typically be broken down into specific tasks, often with team members assigned separate tasks and responsibilities. Throughout, information flows within the team and from them to other stakeholders will be maintained, and feedback systems will ensure that all parties are able to keep on target and make adjustments as necessary. Finally, projects are typically one component in a larger whole; for instance, in an LTO a course is simply one component among the offerings of the organization. A project should be developed with clear reference to the broader goals for the organization. Indeed, in many cases a project may represent one of the steps along the way towards realizing the organizational vision.

Usually a project involves forming a team of people, making a plan of action, and then carrying out that plan while constantly monitoring and evaluating progress. In short, it is a fairly similar process to management writ large, and as set out in Chapter 1, Figure 1.2, p. 11.

Projects can be, and are, undertaken at all levels of an LTO, and can involve any number of people, although they normally involve a team, often drawn from different parts of the organization, such as marketing and sales, student services and academic (as outlined in the NPD scheme in Chapter 8, p. 215). Projects have become a conventional part of organizational management, particularly for carrying out organizational strategies, such as opening a new branch as reported in Vignette 8.1 in Chapter 8, p. 202, or implementing innovation, such as developing a new product or introducing an institution-wide change of coursebooks as reported in the case studies in Chapter 9, pp. 249 and 250–1.

Generically, projects have the following characteristics:
- a life cycle, with phases and stages
- a beginning and end
- specific objectives which are to be achieved, e.g. increasing student volume, raising levels of customer satisfaction, increasing repeat business
- time and cost constraints, such as those incorporated in the costed proposal outline in Chapter 6, p. 153
- definable tasks
- 'deliverables': specific end product(s), such as a new course, test or service
- unique sets of activities.

Internal and external projects

Projects can be divided into two distinct types: internal and external. An internal project is one in which a goal of the organization is addressed using funding and resources only from internal sources.

An external project, on the other hand, is one in which the funding (or at least a significant part of it) comes from an external source. This could be locally, such as a local government source; nationally, from a national foundation or ministry; or internationally, from an international foundation or an international funder such as the EU or USAID.

While the sources of funding in these two types of projects are radically different, the work that should go into the project is much the same. Externally funded projects tend to have quite rigorous proposal stages and subsequent reporting requirements to ensure that the money is being spent as intended and with tangible outcomes. While such strict requirements are not usual in internal projects, it is important to take the same steps in monitoring and evaluation so as to ensure that the organization's money is being well spent as part of good financial practice. It is also often necessary to submit a full proposal even for an internal project.

PROJECT PLANNING

As with any other aspect of management, there is a need to define where we want to go, what route we will take, and how exactly we will get there. Broadly speaking, the following questions should be addressed in order to define the project:

- What are the general areas of concern that the project will focus on?
- What is the project aiming to achieve?
- Who are the major stakeholders? How will they be involved?
- Who is working on the issue already? What are they doing?
- Who will implement the project?
- What is the intended duration of the project?
- What is the intended level of funding?
- Who will fund the project?

As the project is much more specific than general programme management, it is best to start with a specific situation, e.g. a need for a new coursebook, or the creation of a café for the LTO.

REFLECTION

Reflect on your own work situation.

- Think of an area where you are dissatisfied with a situation, or you can identify a need.
- Define the problem (e.g. the LTO's premises are not wheelchair-accessible).

This is the situation that we will discuss throughout this section of the text.

Having identified the situation that you want to address, it is time to define your goals and objectives for the project. These have multiple uses. Firstly, and most importantly, they provide direction. They serve to show what you want to do or accomplish, and they provide the basis for choosing strategies and judging them. They will also help to answer the crucial question 'Are we best suited to do it?' (This question is probably more relevant for external projects, though may also apply to internal projects.) And lastly, they serve to provide the basis for knowing and judging success, i.e. what the situation will look like and feel like when resolved.

Goal/aim

To start with, we define the goal. This is a broad general statement of proposed accomplishments. Since we are working to provide a solution to a problem, the goal is that solution. It is, in short, the end point of the process. The goal is sometimes also referred to as the 'aim'. The goal should fit into the organizational needs as shown in Figure 10.1.

> **REFLECTION**
>
> Taking the problem you defined above, develop a goal statement that 'solves' the problem you identified, e.g. to enable wheelchair users to access the classrooms and secretary's office.

FIGURE 10.1: *Organizational goal*

Objectives

As this goal is very broad and general, it needs to become more concrete. This is done by developing objectives. An objective may be defined as a desired state of affairs which makes the goal concrete and specific in terms of precisely what is to be accomplished, where and by when. Objectives are specific accomplishments necessary to attain the goal.

An objective statement contains the following elements:
- When (future state)
- Who
- Where

- Scope (how much, how many)
- What (will be achieved).

As mentioned in Chapter 6 (p. 161), objectives should always be 'SMART':
- Specific: objectives should state clearly what they are setting out to achieve (What, Who, Where)
- Measurable: the criteria for meeting the objectives should be quantified (Scope)
- Agreed: the objectives should be agreed among those responsible for meeting them, and their managers
- Realistic: objectives should be achievable given the resources available, and not merely aspirational
- Time-bound: a schedule and deadline for meeting the objectives should be stated (When).

Sometimes alternative expanded forms are used, e.g. 'A' (attainable, achievable), 'R' (relevant).

TASK

Examine these objectives and say what is wrong with them. Then try and rewrite them to be SMART:

1 to improve reading skills in young adults and to enable 50% of applicants to pass the FCE and to increase enrolment by 15% by September 2010
2 to improve the English skills of children aged between 7 and 11
3 to enable 95% of applicants to English universities to attain the language qualifications needed to enter.

See Appendix, p. 276, for a possible response to this Task.

TASK

Taking the goal statement you developed previously, create two or three objective statements that will make your goal concrete. Ensure that they are SMART, e.g. 'to build a concrete ramp from the pavement level up to the entrance of the building by the beginning of the next academic year'.

The objectives lead towards the overall project goal like this:

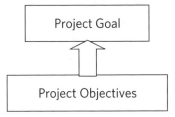

FIGURE 10.2: *Project objectives*

Strategy

Having developed your objectives, the next step is to design a strategy to achieve them. This is done by breaking the objectives down into tasks and activities. Tasks are identifiable steps that can be scheduled on a timeline or a calendar and which can be assigned to specific people. All the tasks taken together should result in the achievement of the objective.

> **TASK**
>
> Take one (or all) of your objectives, and break them down into specific tasks which could be undertaken to achieve your objective, e.g.:
>
> 1 Check on planning permission needs.
> 2 Approach other occupants of the building.
> 3 Get quotes from five local builders.

Slotting the tasks and activities (strategy) into the hierarchical representation of all of the above steps creates the following outline of how the various aspects of the project plan fit into the goal and the organizational needs:

FIGURE 10.3: *Project planning hierarchy*

Action plans and Gantt charts

An action plan is a schedule setting out the activities in sequence, and who does what by when. This kind of plan can also be used for ongoing monitoring and as actions are completed, they are ticked off in the plan.

The initial action plan can also be used for working out the critical path, which is the shortest route to completion of the project. All projects involve a series of activities, some of which can be carried out simultaneously, some of which can only be initiated once other activities have been completed. A critical path analysis enables the manager to:
- identify relationships and dependency sequences in the activities
- determine where parallel activity can be performed
- assess the shortest time in which a project can be completed
- identify resources needed to execute a project
- prioritize tasks
- ascertain the most efficient way of shortening time on urgent projects.

Often tasks and activities leading towards an objective are outlined on a Gantt chart. A Gantt chart is a graphical way of showing tasks on a timeline. It is particularly useful when a project needs a large number of tasks to be carried out, some of which are dependent on other tasks being completed first and some of which can be done in parallel with other tasks.

A brief example of a Gantt chart is shown in Figure 10.4:

						July											
#	Task	Start	Days	Finish	Owner	M-02	T-03	W-04	Th-05	F-06	Sa-07	Su-08	M-09	T-10	W-11	Th-12	F-13
1	Perform needs analysis	2-Jul	3	4-Jul	Paula	▓	▓	▓									
2	Design workshop	5-Jul	4	8-Jul	Paula				▓	▓	▓	▓					
3	Prepare worksheets etc.	7-Jul	2	10-Jul	Ben						▓	▓	▓	▓			
4	Deliver workshop (pilot)	11-Jul	1	11-Jul	Paula										▓		
5	Revise workshop design	12-Jul	2	13-Jul	Paula											▓	▓
6	Document process	2-Jul	12	13-Jul	Erika	▓	▓	▓	▓	▓	▓	▓	▓	▓	▓	▓	▓

FIGURE 10.4: *Sample Gantt chart*

You will note that in the Gantt chart above, each activity is given a time frame of how long it is anticipated to take, and crucially an 'owner', i.e. the person responsible for that particular activity (who is not necessarily the person who will actually carry it out but is responsible for making sure it gets done). Some activities can overlap in time, i.e. one particular activity does not necessarily need to be completed before another begins. Finally, it is worth noting that here there is an activity referred to as 'document process'. In order that valuable information and learning is not lost, it is worth writing the ongoing activity of documentation into the project so that records are kept and consequently lessons can be learned.

> **TASK**
>
> Take the tasks that you identified above and create an activity plan and a Gantt chart with them, outlining the critical path.

Milestones

A 'milestone' is an event that signifies the completion of a major deliverable or set of deliverables, meaning that there should not be too many of them. These deliverables will be the product outcomes of a stage or phase. Milestones are used as project checkpoints to monitor progress against trajectories (or 'stocktaking'), and they indicate a point at which significant decisions will be made. Milestones can be flagged on a Gantt chart.

Additional development tools

As part of the planning and development phase of the project, there are a number of other factors that are considered. These include a stakeholder analysis and a risk assessment.

Key stakeholders

Any project involves a number of parties who perform different but complementary roles.

> **TASK**
>
> Make a list of stakeholders in your LTO project.
> - Consider which of these stakeholders will be most affected by the outcomes or results of the project.
> - List the stakeholders with most power or influence over project outcomes.
> - Complete the table below with your list of stakeholders and your assessment of the project's impact on them, and of their influence on the project.
>
> | Stakeholder group | Impact of result | Power/influence |
> |---|---|---|
> | | | |
> | | | |
> | | | |

What are the implications of such a stakeholder analysis? Briefly, there are two:

• Involve those on whom the project will impact.
• Communicate with those with influence.

In other words, those affected by the project should be involved from an early stage in planning and decision-making. This is illustrated in the two case studies concerned with new coursebooks (Chapter 9, pp. 246 and 250–1).

In the first, the teachers, who would be highly impacted by the choice of books, and who had considerable influence of their use, could not be consulted in the choice. Subsequently, their teaching (and the performance of their young learners) was affected by the mismatch experienced between the books and learners. The teachers had sufficient influence to give rise to a major problem as far as management were concerned.

In the second, teachers were involved right from the start. In feedback to the academic manager, they identified shortcomings of existing materials and established a need for change. They were then involved in piloting and all teachers were kept informed throughout the year-long piloting phase as to what was happening.

Obviously, there are differences in the extent of involvement which is practicable, and in some cases it may be difficult to involve everyone, as it was in the first of the two cases mentioned above. However, the difficulty of doing so may be a warning, because parties who are most affected by outcomes can be those who will usually want to have some input to decisions concerning these outcomes.

Similarly, those parties who have high power or influence over a project need to be in the communication loop so that they are not omitted, with potentially dire effects when, eventually, they learn what is going on.

REFLECTION

Referring back to your completed table, consider how stakeholders were involved, or could be involved, as appropriate.

It will help when doing this to look at each phase of the project and identify those who will be affected by each of these phases.

Risk assessment

'Risk' refers to a situation which may occur in the future and which, if it were to occur, could affect the ability of a project or programme to achieve one or more of its goals or objectives. It is important to assess risks when planning a project and to plan what to do to mitigate or reduce the risk.

Assessing a risk involves firstly considering the likelihood of the risk happening:

High (H):   more likely to occur than not (>60%)
Medium (M):   fairly likely to occur (20–60%)
Low (L):   unlikely to occur but not impossible (<20%).

Next, the assessment considers the impact of the risk on the LTO's strategic aims or objectives, or those or a project:

High (H):   major impact on the achievement of one or more of the aims or objectives

Medium (M): significant impact on the achievement of one or more of the aims or objectives

Low (L):   not expected to have a significant impact on the overall achievement of the aims or objectives.

Risks can be plotted on to a risk tolerance matrix (Figure 10.5). Each asterisk in Figure 10.5 represents a risk, which would have a reference number and be linked to a numbered list with details of the risk. Those which have high probability and high impact will call for counter-measures, while those with low probability and low impact can be safely ignored. Risks should be reviewed in the light of such counter-measures and the assessment of residual risk recorded. Such a matrix for assessing project risks will be useful for the project team.

The assessment and management of risk is recorded and monitored using a risk register. This register will include a description of the risk, who is responsible for dealing with it, its probability and impact, counter-measures and the residual probability of its occurring once counter-measures have been taken, its revised impact and the current status of the risk.

Probability

	Very Low	Low	Medium	High	Very High
Very High					★
High	★★		★		
Medium	★		Risk tolerance line		
Low		★★	★★		
Very Low			★		
	Very Low	Low	Medium	High	Very High

Impact

★ = Risk

FIGURE 10.5: *Risk tolerance matrix* (Office of Government Commerce)

TASK

Using the risk matrix, analyse the risks to your project. In the case of a completed project, consider what risks and counter-measures occurred and what the impact was of any residual risks.

EXTERNALLY FUNDED PROJECTS

Proposal writing

It is an increasingly important skill for educational organizations to be able to submit project proposals to external funding agencies. These agencies may be governmental or, more likely, foundations, but they can be a very important source of income for the LTO.

Having thought about the problem, its solution (the goal), the objectives, and the strategy, you have in fact already done much of the work necessary to complete a project proposal.

A proposal is usually submitted in response to a Call or Request for Proposals (often called an RFP) from the funding agency. These agencies usually have a set of priorities which they hope that applicants will address, and the RFP will reflect those priorities. It is worth keeping an eye on the websites of such donor organizations to see if their priorities are in line with your organizational mission and capabilities.

Having discovered an RFP that seems to be in line with your organizational goals, the next step is to work with some of your key staff to brainstorm and conceptualize some form of suggested approach that would fit the needs identified. Having agreed on an approach, the next stage is to write up the project proposal. Normally the funder has a desired format for such a proposal, with various elements required, including a specific budget format.

In the event that the funder does not provide their own checklist, the following is a list of the categories that might be on a proposal. It is unlikely that every single one of these would be necessary, but this list contains all the likely categories that you may need to complete when submitting such an application.

1   Preliminary information
    • cover letter
    • title page
    • table of contents
    • executive summary (a one-page summary of the proposed project)
    • list of abbreviations
2   Project overview
    • introduction and background
    • problem statement
    • needs assessment
    • proposing organization (who you are and why you are qualified to do this work)
3   Project description
    • goals and objectives
    • strategy and rationale
    • activities
    • resources (which of your resources you will 'donate' to the project as part of something often called 'cost-share')
    • participation
    • sustainability

- constraints and assumptions
- personnel structure
- schedule of activities
- project schematic (for example, a Gantt chart)

4 Monitoring, evaluation and reporting
- baseline measure
- monitoring system
- evaluation system
- reporting schedule

5 Budget
- budget spreadsheet
- budget narrative

When writing a project proposal it is important to keep in mind that the purpose of your writing is:
- to present the idea
- to promise something
- to outline a plan
- to request support
- to persuade.

To do this you need to keep the following in mind at all times: the proposer (yourself), the audience (the funder) and the idea itself. Above all, keeping in mind the '5 Cs' will enable you to write a good proposal that is liable to be well received.

A good proposal is:
- clear
- coherent
- complete
- communicative
- convincing.

Advantages and disadvantages

Externally funded projects can be an extremely valuable source of revenue for a privately funded (for-profit or not-for-profit) LTO. They can provide a much needed source of income and make the LTO less vulnerable to downturns in the market (as having a diversified set of revenue sources tends to do).

Project work is naturally different from the core business of the school, and so it often provides some very useful professional development opportunities for your staff. In addition, developing and participating in projects can be an extremely valuable networking tool, while often giving your organization much greater visibility. Project work in general is also a very helpful organizational tool, allowing staff from different departments to work together in the achievement of a common goal, and preventing the kind of silo-ization noted in Chapter 2.

On the downside, developing projects and writing proposals is extremely time-consuming work. Putting together a proposal in response to an RFP can often take up a vast number of person-hours. And at the end of the process there is, of course, no guarantee that the funding will be forthcoming. Indeed, estimates suggest that an organization which develops good, well-written proposals can expect to receive approval and funding for around 10% of those proposals.

Even if a proposal is funded, the amount of income that an organization receives from the grant is limited. Moneys cannot be redirected to other needs at the school (unlike tuition income, for example), and often institutional overhead cannot be included in the budget. All expenditure must be accounted for in the reports. Usually, the income benefit to the school comes in the form of staff costs (salary) which would otherwise be met out of other incomes. Finally, reporting requirements can be quite strict and involve significant work on behalf of the project manager and accountant.

Project work, in short, is by no means an easy or a safe source of income. But it can be rewarding and have lots of less tangible benefits for the organization. The decision to enter into the project work market, as an example of significant innovation, is one that cannot be taken lightly.

MONITORING AND EVALUATION

Monitoring and evaluation should be aspects of any management system, not just for the management of a project. They answer the questions of whether the project is doing what you hoped and whether it could be doing so any more efficiently or effectively. They are also tools used for assessing the effectiveness of the project after it is finished in the hope that lessons will be learned for future work.

As teachers, we may see monitoring as observing students' performance during the lesson as it goes on to see if we need to make any changes to that particular lesson (or maybe subsequent lessons). Evaluation, on the other hand, is a judgment of students' progress – either formally or informally – to inform the curriculum or for an external audience. Evaluation should also inform our teaching – what we are doing that seems to be working, what needs to change, etc. Similarly in management, monitoring is the ongoing process of, in a sense, keeping an eye on things, and making sure that things are on track. Evaluation is broader, and while there is a component of evaluation which should happen at the end of a project, and periodically throughout, there is also a component of ongoing evaluation that should take place.

Monitoring and evaluation systems are absolutely crucial parts of any project proposal, underpinning regular stocktakes. A good evaluation system should in the proposal stage not only list the desired effects of the project and how these will be observed and confirmed, but also describe the actions that will be taken to adjust the project if necessary (and ideally, what indicators will let the project manager know that it is time to adjust things).

One way of designing an evaluation system is to ask the following questions:
- What will we evaluate?

- Who will evaluate it?
- When will it be evaluated?
- How will we evaluate it?
- What will be done with the results of the evaluation?

Returning to the project proposal, we can look at all of the tasks and activities and ask these questions of all of them. This provides a very comprehensive set of evaluation tools. In many cases the evaluation of an activity will be the clear evidence that it has been done, or that the desired outputs have actually been produced.

A project entails change, so a good monitoring and evaluation system will:

- show whether change is occurring
- indicate the results of the activity, including eventual impacts, whether these changes are intended or not intended, direct or indirect, positive or negative, primary or secondary
- suggest how to improve the efficiency of implementation, the extent of the desired results achieved and their sustainability.

The monitoring and evaluation system will also tell you what actions can be taken at different levels of concern:

- Modify the project design and/or continue.
- Expand the scope of the project: is the project going very well? Would it be worth expanding it? Or contracting it?
- Terminate the project: if the project is not achieving what was hoped, there must be an option to end it. The longer an ineffectual project goes on, the more costs are accrued.
- Replicate the project elsewhere.
- Replan the programme to which the project contributes: this would be the 'double-loop learning' or systems thinking level of analysis (see Chapter 2, p. 48).

One starting point for measuring the effectiveness of the change is a baseline study.

Baseline studies

Once it has been determined what the project is setting out to accomplish and how it will be evaluated, it is often important to carry out a baseline study to determine what the current situation is in relation to the project objectives and goals – and therefore whether the project actually acts to facilitate change.

The baseline study might typically include the following pieces of data:

- contextual information (STEP factors: see Chapter 9, p. 234)
- exploration of stakeholder interests
- historical information
- description of current situation
- sources of other information.

The baseline study is just one element in the monitoring and evaluation plan and is structured to assess systematically the circumstances in which the project takes place. It provides the basis for subsequent assessment of how efficiently the project is being implemented and the eventual results achieved. Mid-term reviews, project completion reports and other evaluations will judge progress largely based on comparisons with the information from the baseline study.

Reporting

Most external funders require fairly stringent reports, in terms of both narrative description and details of expenditure. Those responsible for disbursing the money need to ensure that no embezzlement or fraud is taking place, or even to ensure that things are on track and proceeding as planned. These reports are usually submitted to a predetermined schedule and are written in a formalized way. It is wise to keep records of all expenditures associated with a project; even if they are not required by the funder, there is always the possibility of an unexpected audit.

Even if the project is internally funded it is worth following the rigorous format of project management required by external donors. The reasons that various requirements exist are almost always good ones, and have almost always come out of many years' experience with administering funds. That is not to say that the LTO needs to become bogged down in paperwork as even the smallest project can generate file after file of reports and shoe boxes full of receipts. Obviously there are limits to how much is practical or desirable, but keeping track of how a project is progressing is always worthwhile. It also ensures that those involved with the project are able to account to senior management or to the board of directors on the use of the LTO's resources.

PROJECT COMPLETION

On completion of the project, it is important to review project outcomes and lessons learned. Outcomes can be summarized on a form such as that shown in Figure 10.6.

Deliverable/ milestone from Project plan	Budgeted cost from Project plan	Final cost	Scheduled date from Project plan	Final date
Totals				

FIGURE 10.6: *Project outcomes form*

For each project milestone or phase, identify what worked, what didn't work and ways to improve the process the next time. These can be summarized as in Figure 10.7.

Milestone/phase	What worked	What didn't work	Ways to improve

FIGURE 10.7: *Project milestones form*

As a project should have its own file, in which all project documentation is systematically stored, project completion reports should be filed there for future reference. If an LTO is to be a learning organization (see Chapter 2, p. 42), it is vital to manage such institutional knowledge and to make use of it for developmental purposes. Even maintaining a simple log of actions, decisions and outcomes when implementing change can be of great value when reviewing what happened and what can be learned from it. A reconstructed narrative and analysis after the event will generally suffer from information gaps and potentially precious information may be lost.

CONCLUSION

Project management provides a methodology for implementing innovation. In the LTO context, innovations can be, and often are, incremental in nature, being modifications to existing practice in order to bring about improvement, though without transforming the enterprise. Using a full-scale project methodology when implementing such innovations would not necessarily be appropriate, although some of the tools, such the action plan and Gantt chart, are useful aids. Where, however, the innovation involves a 'punctuation' (see Chapter 9, p. 239) or transformation, project methodology comes into its own, and in such circumstances it is difficult to envisage achieving implementation without applying a project management methodology which will help ensure that the parties involved are focused, co-ordinated, accountable and, above all, successful.

Appendix

The Appendix contains possible answers to the final Tasks from Chapters 2, 3 and 10, along with the job and person descriptions from Chapter 3.

CHAPTER 2 TASK (P. 50)

Organigram for The International Centre

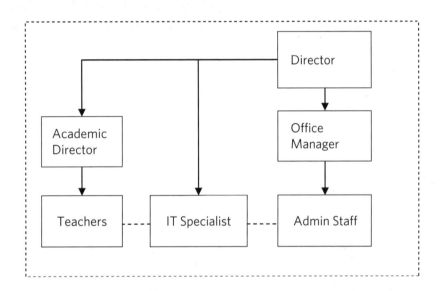

Organizational analysis of the school

Chain of command
- Fairly flat on academic side, a little bit deeper and more hierarchical on admin side.
- Fairly typical for LTOs.
- Problems with clarity of chain of command on admin side: people sidestepping line management and going to the top (previous line manager).

Departmentalization
- Few departments – essentially two: admin and academic.
- Advantages: little silo-ization; easy to communicate within departments.
- Disadvantages: may lead to a lack of skill in certain areas; the LTO could be carving out a niche, but at present is not doing so.

Formalization
- Mixed: some positions very formalized, others not at all.
- Problems:
  - Mixed levels can lead to resentment (those with very formalized roles may resent those who have much more freedom, while those with less clarity of purpose may resent those who have much more structure).
  - They can also lead to a lack of clarity from customer's point of view – not sure who to go to for what problem/question (and staff may be similarly unsure).

Span of control
- Quite high. The academic director has a very large span of control – thirty teachers with no middle management. On the admin side, the span is lower, but still relatively high – approximately fifteen people theoretically reporting to the office manager, though many may actually be reporting to the director. Recent changes designed to reduce the director's span of control have only been partially successful.
- Problems:
  - The academic director has too great a span of control: she cannot possibly do the job successfully and act in a successful performance management role at the same time (coaching/mentoring/supporting staff)
  - Likewise office manager.
  - The Director's span of control has been brought down to more manageable levels, but needs to be more clearly formalized.

Centralization
- Very centralized, with an attempt to reduce centralization.
- Likely to be too great an amount of centralization – clearly staff still feel they should check things with the director – culture of centralization difficult to break. Large span of control means that there is still likely to be a very high degree of centralization even after the changes.
- Disadvantage is that the LTO is inflexible – no one is able to take decisions without reporting to the director, which is limiting.

Work specialization
- Not clear from the information given. No analysis possible in this area.

Action to improve the school's structure
Possible steps include:
- Formalize those positions which are currently non-formalized.
- Make the chain of command clearer and ensure that everyone knows what it is.
- Create three or four senior teacher positions and promote people into them. Senior teachers are each responsible for level co-ordination responsibilities and performance management of between seven and ten teachers.
- Departmentalize the admin side slightly: create two middle management positions below office manager, and have staff report to one of the two depending on their focus

(actual division of admin positions in this way would depend on context – could be 'customer-facing staff' and 'other support staff', or 'maintenance' and 'office', or some other division logical to the LTO). Bring the IT specialist into one of these departments.

- Ensure links between staff are not lost in restructuring; teachers can still talk directly to the IT specialist for example, and do not need to go through a complex chain to have access.
- Changes should be made in consultative participatory manner: increasing buy-in, understanding of new systems, and bringing staff from both sides of the LTO together.

CHAPTER 3 JOB AND PERSON DESCRIPTION (P. 54)

Sample job description

International Language Centre
Job Description

Job title: EFL Teacher
Department: Academic
Reports to: Director of Studies
Prepared by: John Smith, Director of Studies
Prepared date: May 23, 2007
Approved by: Jane Doe, Director
Approved date: May 29, 2007

SUMMARY
Teaches up to 25 class hours of General English per week. Plans classes, teaches levels as assigned, marks student homework and completes ILC paperwork as required.

ESSENTIAL DUTIES AND RESPONSIBILITIES include the following. Other duties may be assigned.

- Plan classes according to syllabus guidelines.
- Teach up to 25 hours per week (as assigned). Levels may include Adult General English from Beginner to Advanced level, Young Learners levels 1–8, Business English classes as required.
- Mark all student homework within one week of receiving it.
- Set and grade end of term tests. Submit all grades to receptionist.
- Complete register for every class, including listing the areas/topics/materials covered in each lesson in the form provided.
- Inform receptionist when any student misses two classes consecutively, or four classes over the course of a term.
- Attend weekly teacher meetings, and monthly level co-ordination meetings for levels taught.
- Prepare for and attend parent–teacher meetings once per term.
- Participate fully in annual performance review process.

- Observe two colleagues per term and be observed by two colleagues per term in peer observation system.
- Assist in placement testing and registration at the beginning of each term.
- Teach up to one hour per week as a substitute for an indisposed colleague.

Sample person description

International Language Centre
Person Description

QUALIFICATIONS

To perform this job successfully, an individual must be able to perform each essential duty satisfactorily. The requirements listed below are representative of the knowledge, skill, and/or ability required. Reasonable accommodations may be made to enable individuals with disabilities to perform the essential functions.

EDUCATION and/or EXPERIENCE

CELTA or equivalent teaching certificate, plus 2 years' teaching experience in offshore English language teaching school, or CELTA grade B or higher and 1 year's experience.

LANGUAGE SKILLS

Native speaker proficiency in English is a must. Ability to speak Spanish an advantage, but not essential.

LEVELS

Ability and willingness to teach different class levels: Beginners, Advanced, Exam classes, Children (from age 7 upwards), Young Learners, and Business English.

PERSONAL QUALITIES

Ability to work as part of a team. Willingness to work evenings and Saturday mornings. Enthusiastic and highly motivated. Ability to work well with people from different cultural backgrounds.

ORGANIZATIONAL SKILLS

Good time management. Ability to keep up-to-date and legible records.

OTHER

EU passport or Spanish work permit. Driving licence an advantage.

CHAPTER 3 TASK (P. 78)

Dealing with the issues

Using the idea of the learning organization as a guide, the important thing here is not just to come up with a quick fix to the problem. Think systems and think strategically. Are there are any double-loop learnings here?

It would seem that one of the main problems is a split between the two staffroom groups. Can a plan be devised which brings these two groups together, increases the sense of organizational belonging and shared vision, motivates the staff, and in so doing ensures that some of the expatriate staff stay on longer, which benefits the LTO all round? This should be the starting point for planning a strategy to deal with the current issues.

One starting point might be to use the opportunity to ask all staff to work together to produce an internal vision statement (see Chapter 2, p. 41). This could be done via a facilitated meeting and discussion, in which all staff (teachers and admin staff) come together to thrash out what kind of work environment they want the LTO to be. This statement could then be used as a guide for internal strategy and discussion on HR-related matters.

Motivating both groups

Expatriate staff

We can see that there is a problem with the 'maintenance factor' of salary (see Chapter 3, p. 61). Assuming for now that increasing salaries across the board is not an option, what other motivators could be put into place that would counter this demotivation? Is there a way to increase teachers' sense of recognition and achievement? Some teachers might, for example, enjoy doing some outreach teacher training at local schools. Others might feel motivated by being involved in teamwork on projects of some description. Think about the section on job enrichment (see Chapter 3, p. 61) and let that guide your thinking.

Local staff

For this group, it seems clear that the issue is a lack of recognition for their work. Salary doesn't seem to be a demotivator, but possibly feeling less important than those who may be less qualified could be causing some sense of alienation. One option, for example, could be to set up mentoring relationships in which local teachers are paired with incoming foreign teachers. Their brief would be to help the new teachers adjust to the culture and city, to help them understand the students' perspectives – their learning backgrounds and their cultural perspectives, and possibly to pass on some tips for addressing these questions. In this way not only are they likely to feel more valued and appreciated, but also the foreign teachers will hopefully be assisted with life in the new city and with dealing with culture shock/bureaucratic issues they may be facing. Importantly, these 'buddy' systems could also help to bridge the staffroom divide.

It might also be possible to set up a system of professional development workshops. These could be offered to all teaching staff by individual teachers – local teachers would get the chance to share their knowledge and experience, and foreign teachers would get valuable (and motivating) professional development. This would not be limited to the local/foreigner direction – foreign teachers might also elect to give workshops on some methodological innovation that might be new to the local teachers.

Other strategies

One other issue that may need to be fixed is the orientation/induction system – the buddy/mentor system mentioned above would be a start, but if foreign teachers really are feeling that living in the city is difficult, then it seems that a simple solution would be to offer more support and to revamp the orientation programme somewhat. This also would be a good time to bring people in to the 'shared vision' that has been created to enhance the feeling of involvement in the LTO.

Ultimately, what's important is that teachers enjoy working for the LTO, and therefore feel that the average salary is more than compensated for by the fact that they work for the best LTO in which to be a teacher in the city. It is also important to remember that different people are motivated by different things; while some might be inspired by working towards improving the LTO as part of a project team, others might be more enthused by feeling that the job is secure and that all is relatively stable.

Use the ideas on motivation and job enrichment on p. 61 to guide your brainstorming of possible strategies.

CHAPTER 10 SMART OBJECTIVES (P. 259)

The following are possible responses to the Task:

1   Too many objectives are combined together. Some are not measurable, e.g. 'to improve reading skills'. Divide into two objectives:
    - to increase reading and other skills in young adult students, such that 50% of those who start the course are able to take and pass the exam by September 2010
    - to increase enrolment by 15% over current levels by September 2010.
2   This is not specific (who, how many, all?), measurable (improve by how much, what assessment?), or time-bound (by when?). A possible rewrite might be: Offer courses to 100 children between ages 7 and 11 of A1 level (using the Common European Framework as a guide), and over the course of one year, bring them all to level A2, by July next year.
3   This is not realistic (95% pass rate?) or time-bound (every year? just this year?). A possible rewrite might be: Offer university entrance exam preparation courses for up to 50 students who already have a 5.5 level in IELTS, such that over the course of the academic year, 75% of them take IELTS and attain a level 6.0.

References & further reading

12Manage. Available at: www.12manage.com/management_dictionary.html

Accreditation UK. Available at: www.britishcouncil.org/accreditation.htm

Accurate English. Available at: www.accurateenglish.com/

Advisory Council for English Language Schools. Available at: www.acels.ie/schoolsregulations.htm

American Marketing Association. Available at: www.marketingpower.com/content4620.php.

AOI College of Languages. Available at: www.aoicollege.com

Argyris, C. & Schön, D. 1978. *Organizational learning: A Theory of Action Perspective*. Reading, Mass, Addison Wesley.

Argyris, C. & Schön, D. 1996. *Organizational Learning II: Theory, Method and Practice*. Reading, Mass, Addison Wesley.

Australian Government: Australian Education International. Available at: aei.dest.gov.au/AEI/MIP/Statistics/StudentEnrolmentAndVisaStatistics/Recent.htm#Final

Barber, M. 2007. *Instructions to Deliver*. London, Politicos.

Block, S. B. & Hirt, G.A. 1994. *Foundations of Financial Management*. Toronto, Irwin.

Bolman, L. & Deal, T. 1991. *Reframing Organizations: Artistry, Choice, and Leadership*. San Francisco, Jossey-Bass.

Brookson, S. 2000. *Managing Budgets*. London, Dorling Kindersley.

Brown, A. 1995. *Organisational Culture*. London, Pitman Publishing.

Brown, P. & Levinson, S. C. 1987. *Politeness: Some universals in language usage*. Cambridge, Cambridge University Press.

business.gov.au. Available at: www.business.gov.au

Business Link. Available at: www.businesslinkwm.co.uk

BusinessDictionary.com. Available at: www.businessdictionary.com/

Butler, P. (ed.) 1991. *Numbers Guide: The Essentials of Business Numeracy*. London, The Economist Books.

Carlzon, J. 1989. *Moments of Truth*. London, HarperCollins.

Charles, D. 1993. 'The Fronted Organigram: Questions of Management in English Language Teaching'. In Boswood, T., Hoffman, R., & Tung, P. (eds). *Perspectives on English for Professional Communication*. Hong Kong, City Polytechnic of Hong Kong. pp. 217–224.

Christison, M. A. & Stoller, F. L. (eds) 1997. *A Handbook for Language Program Administrators*. Burlingame, CA, Alta Book Centre.

Collins, J. 2005. *Good To Great and the Social Sectors*. New York, HarperCollins.

Common European Framework of Reference for Languages: Learning, teaching, assessment. 2001. Council for Cultural Co-operation, Council of Europe. Cambridge,

Cambridge University Press. Available at: www.coe.int/t/dg4/linguistic/CADRE_EN.asp

Commission on English Language Program Accreditation. Available at: www.cea-accredit.org/standards.php#services

Cooper, C. L. & Argyris, C. (eds) 1998. *The Concise Blackwell Encyclopaedia of Management.* Oxford, Blackwell.

Couros, A. 2003. *Innovation, Change Theory and the Acceptance of New Technologies: A Literature Review.* Available at: educationaltechnology.ca/couros/publications/unpublishedpapers/change_theory.pdf

Cristobal, E. & Llurda, E. 2006. 'Learners' preferences regarding types of language school: An exploratory market research'. *System.* 34, pp. 135–148.

Daft, R. L. 1992. *Organizational Theory and Design.* West Publishing, St. Paul, Minnesota.

Davidson, J. O. & Tesh, J. S. 1997. 'Theory and practice in language program organization design'. In: Christison & Stoller (eds) 1997. *A Handbook for Language Program Administrators.* Burlingame, CA, Alta Book Centre. pp. 177–198.

Dawson, S. 1986. *Analysing Organisations.* London, Macmillan.

De Lano, L., Riley, L. & Crookes, G. 1994. 'The meaning of innovation for ESL teachers'. *System.* 22/4. pp. 487–496.

Department for Children, Schools and Families. Available at: www.dfes.gov.uk/

Division of Instructional Innovation and Assessment, The University of Texas at Austin, 2007. Focus Groups. *Instructional Assessment Resources.* Available at: www.utexas.edu/academic/diia/assessment/iar/tech/plan/method/focus.php

Drucker, P. 1973. *Management: Tasks, Responsibilities, Practices.* New York, Harper Business.

Drucker, P. 2001. *The Essential Drucker.* New York, HarperCollins.

Dudeney, G. 2000. *The Internet and the Language Classroom.* Cambridge, Cambridge University Press.

EF Language Schools. Available at: www.ef.com/master/ils/teaching/why/

Eurocentres Scale of Language Proficiency. Available at: www.eurocentres.com/en/eurocentres/Scale_of_Language_Proficiency,43.html

European Association for Quality Language Services. 2007. Available at: www.eaquals.org/about/thecode.asp

Financial Accounting Standards Board (FASB). 1985. *Statement of Financial Accounting Concepts, No. 6: 'Elements of Financial Statements'.*

Fitzsimons, P. 1999. *Managerialism and Education.* Available at: www.ffst.hr/ENCYCLOPAEDIA/managerialism.htm

Freeman, D. 1989. 'Teacher Training, Development, and Decision-Making'. *TESOL Quarterly* 231, pp. 27–45.

Free Management Library. Available at: www.managementhelp.org

Fullan, M. 2001a. *The New Meaning of Educational Change* 3rd ed., New York, Teachers College Press.

Fullan, M. 2001b. *Leading in a Culture of Change.* San Francisco, CA, Jossey-Bass.

Fullan, M. Available at: www.michaelfullan.ca

Galton, M. (ed.) 1980. *Curriculum Change: The Lessons of a Decade*. Leicester, Leicester University Press.

Garratt, B. 2000. *The Twelve Organizational Capabilities*. London, HarperCollins Business.

Gladwell, M. 2000. *The Tipping Point: How Little Things Can Make a Big Difference*. Boston, Little, Brown.

Goffee, R. & Jones, G. 1996. 'What Holds the Modern Company Together?' *Harvard Business Review on Managing People*. Boston, MA, Harvard Business School Press.

Graddol, D. 2006. *English Next*. London, The British Council. Available at: www.britishcouncil.org/learning-research-englishnext.htm

Graves, K. 2000. *Designing Language Courses: A Guide for Teachers*. Boston, MA, Heinle & Heinle.

Handy, C. 1985. *Understanding Organizations*. 3rd ed. Harmondsworth, Middlesex, Penguin.

Herzberg, F. 1987. 'One More Time: How do you motivate employees?' *Harvard Business Review*. Sept–Oct 1987.

Heyworth, F. A. 2002. *Guide to Project Management*. Graz, Austria, Council of Europe Publishing.

Hockley, A. 2006. 'What Makes Teachers Tick?' *ELT Management*. March 2006.

Hofstede, G. 1991. *Cultures and Organisations: Software of the Mind*. London, McGraw Hill.

Hofstede, G. 1987–2003. *Cultural Dimensions*. Available at: www.geert-hofstede.com/

Huberman, M. A. 1989. 'The Professional Life Cycle of Teachers'. *Teachers College Record*. 911. pp. 31–58.

Huberman, M. A. 1993 *The Lives of Teachers*. New York, Teachers College Press.

IBM. 2006. *Expanding the Innovation Horizon: the Global CEO Study 2006*. Somers, NY, IBM Global Services.

Internet World Stats. Available at: www.internetworldstats.com/stats.htm

Intrax International Institute. Available at: www.intraxinstitute.edu

Jobber, D. 2001 *Principles and Practices of Marketing*. 3rd ed. London, McGraw-Hill.

Johnson, R. K. 1989. *The Second Language Curriculum*. Cambridge, Cambridge University Press.

Kelly, P. 1980. 'From innovation to adaptability: the changing perspective of curriculum development'. In: Galton, M. (ed.) 1980. *Curriculum Change*. Leicester, Leicester University Press.

Kohn, A. 1995. *Punished by Rewards: The Trouble With Gold Stars, Incentive Plans, A'S, Praise, and Other Bribes*. Boston, MA, Houghton Mifflin.

Kolb, D. A. 1984. *Experiential Learning*. Englewood Cliffs, NJ, Prentice Hall.

Kotler, P. 1997. *Marketing Management, Analysis, Planning, Implementation and Control*. 9th ed. Upper Saddle River, NJ, Prentice Hall.

Kotter, J. 1996. *Leading Change*. Boston, Harvard Business School Press.

Lake, N. & Hickey, K. 2002. *The Customer Service Workbook*. (*The Sunday Times Business Enterprise Guide* series). London, Kogan Page.

Language Systems International. Available at: www.languagesystems.com/home.asp

Law, S. & Glover, D. 2000. *Educational Leadership and Learning*. Buckingham, Open University Press.

Lovemarks.com. Available at: www.lovemarks.com/index.php?pageID=20040

McLaughlin, M. & Talbert. J. 2001. *Professional Communities and the Work of High School Teaching*. Chicago, Chicago University Press.

McNamara, C. 1997–2007. *Basic Overview of Organizational Life Cycles*. Available at: www.managementhelp.org/org_thry/org_cycl.htm

Mintzberg, H. 1983. *Structure in Fives: Designing Effective Organizations*. Upper Saddle River, New Jersey, Prentice Hall.

Moran, P. 2001 *Teaching Culture: Perspectives in Practice*. Boston, Heinle & Heinle.

Moss, G., Jewitt, C., Levaãiç, R., Armstrong, V., Cardini, A., Castle, F. 2007. 'The Interactive Whiteboards, Pedagogy and Pupil Performance Evaluation: An Evaluation of the Schools Whiteboard Expansion (SWE Project)'. *London Challenge. Research Report 816*. London, Institute of Education.

Mullins, L. J. 1985. *Management and Organizational Behaviour*. London, Pitman.

Mullins, L. J. 2002. *Management and Organisational Behaviour*. 6th ed. Harlow: Pearson Education.

National ELT Accreditation Scheme Limited. Available at: www.neasaustralia.com/fst.html

Net Promoter Score. Available at: www.netpromoter.com/

New Zealand Ministry of Education Code of Practice for the Pastoral Care of International Students. Available at: www.minedu.govt.nz/index.cfm?layout=index&indexid=6666&indexparentid=6663

New Zealand Qualifications Authority. Available at: www.nzqa.govt.nz/for-providers/aaa/index.html

Nichols, A. 1983. *Managing Educational Innovations*. London, Allen & Unwin

Nominal group technique. Available at:
www.joe.org/joe/1984march/iw2.html
www.mycoted.com/Nominal_Group_Technique
www.uwex.edu/ces/pdande/resources/pdf/Tipsheet3.pdf

Parasuraman, A., Zeithaml, V. A. & Berry, L. L. 1988. 'Communication and Control Processes in the Delivery of Service Quality'. In *Journal of Marketing*. 52, April 1988, pp. 35–48.

Parasuraman, A., Berry, L. & Zeithaml, V.A. 1991 'Understanding Customer Expectations of Service'. *Sloan Management Review*. Spring, pp. 39–48.

Parsons, C., & Fidler, B. 2005. 'A new theory of educational change – punctuated equilibrium: the case of the internationalization of higher education institutions'. *British Journal of Educational Studies*. 53/4. pp. 447–65.

Pascale, R., Millemann, M. & Gioja, L. 2000. *Surfing the Edge of Chaos*. New York, Crown Business Publishing.

Payne, A. C. M., Clark, M. & Peck, H. 1997. *Relationship Marketing for Competitive Advantage*. Oxford, Butterworth Heinemann.

Phillips, T. 2000. 'Resource management timetabling'. *EL Gazette*.

Pickering. G. 1999a. 'Roads to quality street: perspectives on quality in ELT'. *ELT Management*. 28 December, pp. 5–9.

Pickering, G. 1999b. 'The learning organization: an idea whose time has come?' *ELT Management*. March.

Podolny, J.M., Khurana, R. & Hill-Popper, M. 2005. *How to Put Meaning Back into Leading*. Available at: www.hbsworkingknowledge.hbs.edu/item.jhtml?id=4563&t=leadership

Porter, L. 1982. 'Giving and Receiving Feedback: It Will Never Be Easy, But It Can Be Better'. *NTL Reading Book for Human Relations Training*. Bethel, ME, NTL Institute.

Reicheld, F. 2006. *The Ultimate Question: For Driving Good Profits and True Growth*. Boston, MA, Harvard Business School.

Richards, J. C. 2001. *Curriculum Development in Language Teaching*. Cambridge, Cambridge University Press.

Richards, J. C. & Farrell, T. S. C. 2005. *Professional Development for Language Teachers: Strategies for Teacher Learning*. Cambridge, Cambridge University Press.

Robbins, S. P. 2001. *Organizational Behavior*. 9th ed. Upper Saddle River, NJ, Prentice Hall.

Roberts-Phelps, G. 2001. *Customer Relationship Management*. London, Thorogood.

Rogers, E. M. 1995. *Diffusion of Innovations*. 4th ed. New York, Free Press.

Rosenblatt, S. 2004. 'Skill flexibility and school change: a multi-national study'. *Journal of Educational Change*. 5. pp. 1–30.

Schein, E. H. 1985. *Organizational Culture and Leadership*. San Francisco, CA, Jossey Bass.

Senge, P. 1990. *The Fifth Discipline: The Art and Practice of the Learning Organization*. London, Century Books.

Shenkar, O. 1994. *Global Perspectives of Human Resource Management: Collected Readings*. Upper Saddle River, New Jersey, Prentice Hall.

Shim, J. K. & Siegel, J. G. 2000. *Financial Management*. New York, Barron's Educational Series.

Shostack, G. L. 1984. 'Designing Services That Deliver'. *Harvard Business Review*. 62/1, pp. 133–9.

Smith, M. K. 2001 'David A. Kolb on experiential learning'. *the encyclopedia of informal education*. Available at: www.infed.org/biblio/b-explrn.htm#jarvis

Stoller, F. L. 1997. 'The catalyst for change and innovation'. In: Christison & Stoller (eds) 1997. *A Handbook for Language Program Administrators*. Burlingame, CA, Alta Book Centre. pp. 33–48.

Sydänmaanlakka, P. 2002. *An Intelligent Organization*. Oxford, Capstone.

Tarde, G. (trans E.W. Parsons) 1903. *The Laws of Imitation*. New York, Holt & Co.

Teachernet. Available at: www.teachernet.gov.uk/professionaldevelopment/

Tomlinson, B. (ed.) 1998. *Materials Development in Language Teaching*. Cambridge, Cambridge University Press.

Tsui, A. B. 2003. *Understanding Expertise in Teaching*. Cambridge, Cambridge University Press.

tutor2U. 2007. *New Product Development*. Available at: www.tutor2u.net/business/presentations/marketing/newproductdevelopment/

Underhill, A. 2004. 'The Learning School'. *Humanising Language Teaching*. Available at: www.hltmag.co.uk/jan04/mart1.htm.

University of Cambridge ESOL Teacher Portfolio. Available at: www.teacherportfolio.cambridgeesol.org/

University of Connecticut. Available at: admissions.uconn.edu/virtualtour/

Walker, J. 1997. 'Blueprinting the EFL Service Provision'. *ELT Management*. 24 July 1997. pp. 18–22.

Walker, J. 2001. 'Client views of TESOL: expectations and perceptions'. *International Journal of Educational Management*. 15/4, pp.187–196.

Walker, J. 2003. 'Client satisfaction with English language centre service: insights from a New Zealand national survey'. *International Journal of Educational Management*. 17/7. pp. 294–302.

Ward, B. *Creating Customer Loyalty: The Customer Loyalty Grid*. Available at: www.excellence2.com/customer-service/Creating_Customer_Loyalty_The_Customer_Loyalty_Grid.shtml

Weihrich, H. 1982. *The TOWS Matrix: A Tool for Situational Analysis*. Kidlington, Oxon, Elsevier Science Limited.

Wheelen, T. L. & Hunger, J. D. 2000. *Strategic Management & Business Policy*. 7th ed. London, Prentice Hall.

White, R., Martin, M., Stimson, M. & Hodge, R. 1991. *Management in English Language Teaching*. Cambridge, Cambridge University Press.

Wikipedia. Available at: wikipedia.org/wiki/Main_Page

Zeithaml, V., Berry, L. L., & Parasuraman, A. 1988. 'Communication and control processes in the delivery of service quality'. *Journal of Marketing*, 52 April, pp. 35–48.

Index

360° feedback 66–7

academic management
  curriculum management 207–15
  LTO managers 16
  professional development 226–8, 231
  quality management 228–31
  resource management 216–26
  roles and responsibilities of the
    academic manager 201–6
  scales of language proficiency 228–30
  time as a resource 220–6
academic side of the LTO, comparison
  with administrative side 29, 33–4
'accommodating' style of conflict
  management 74, 75
accountability of management,
  corporate governance 13–15
accounting standards compliance 175–6
accreditation schemes 4, 121–2, 136–8
Accreditation UK 4
action plans, project planning 261
active listening 75–6
administrative responsibilities
  LTO managers 16
  principal/head teacher 19
  subject leader/DOS 18
  teachers 17
administrative side of the LTO,
  comparison with the academic side
  29, 33–4
advertising 103–4
alignment of values, and LTO
  effectiveness 2
analytical tools, financial management
  160–6
annual operating budget 178–83
Ansoff matrix 92–3
atmospheric features of the LTO
  location 107–8
attitudes of others, LTO managers'
  understanding of 21–3
autonomy, and organizational structure
  30
'avoiding' style of conflict management
  74, 75
awareness, self-awareness in LTO
  managers 22–3

balance sheet 171
Barber, Michael 242–3
baseline (incremental) budgeting
  178–80
baseline studies 268–9
behavioural variables, segmentation of
  customers 96–7
benchmarking 168–9

benefits see compensation systems
blueprinting 145–50
Boston Consulting Group Matrix
  99–100
brainstorming 43
break-even analysis 101, 162–4
budget adjustments 190–3
budget components 183–8
  budget notes 187
  costs/expenses 184–7
  direct costs 185–6
  indirect (overhead) costs 186–7
  revenue 184, 185
  start-up costs 187
budget reporting 193–5
budgets 177–83
  aims of budgeting 177–8
  analytical tool 162
  annual operating budget 178–83
  baseline (incremental) budgeting
    178–80
  capital budget 178, 183
  for marketing and sales 110
  inflation rates 178–80
  Life of Project budget 178, 183
  monitoring and control 188–90
  time scale 178
  types of 178–83
  zero-based budgeting 180–3
business functions and departments
  12–13
business management, LTO managers
  16 see also management
business partnering, source of
  innovation 241
business plan models 153

capital budget 178, 183
Carlzon, Jan 123
cash flow 196–8
cash flow statement 171–3, 196–8
centralized organizational structure 30
chain of command 26–7
change
  definition 233
  distinction from innovation 233
change management
  appointment of new staff 244–5, 246
  changing the location of an LTO 247,
    248
  collegiality and change 243–4
  definition 233
  environmental influences on an LTO
    234–5
  forces which influence change 234–8
  influences on adoption of innovations
    241–2

internal change 244–52
  introducing new products in an LTO
    247–52
  introducing new technology 252–3
  models for implementing innovation
    238–44
  organizational changes 245
  reasons for failure and success 242–3
  risk assessment 237–8
  sources of innovation 240–1
  STEP analysis 234–5, 238
  SWOT analysis 236–7, 238
  see also project management
client satisfaction rating scales 130–1
clients of LTOs 82–3 see also customers
codes of practice 136–41
'collaborating' style of conflict
  management 74
collegiality and change 243–4
Common European Framework of
  Reference for Languages: Learning,
  Teaching, Assessment (CEFR)
  228–30
communal organization 38, 39
communication
  lines of communication 27–8
  problems within organizations 27–8,
    29
compensation systems 61, 63–4
competitive bidding 101
'competing' style of conflict
  management 73–4
competitor-orientated pricing 101
complaints handling, policy and
  guidelines 138–40
'compromising' style of conflict
  management 73–4
conferences, LTO participation 103,
  105–6
conflict management 72–7
  accommodation 74, 75
  active listening 75–6
  advantages and disadvantages of
    conflict 72–3
  avoidance 74, 75
  collaboration 74
  competition 73–4
  compromise 73–4
  dealing with grievances 76–7
  manager as arbitrator in conflict 75–6
  manager as participant in conflict 76
  styles of conflict management 73–5
conflict management styles 73–5
consumers of LTO services 81–3 see also
  customers
continuing professional development
  (CPD) 24, 227–8, 232

continuous improvement in effective LTOs 3
contracts
    fixed type 60
    hourly-paid staff 60
    new employees 58
    terms and conditions of service (TACOS) 58
contractual compliance issues 175–6
controlling function of management 10
corporate governance 13–15
corporate leadership role, LTO managers 16
corrective action, management control 10–11
costed proposal outline 153–8
critical path analysis, project planning 261
cross-departmental teams 46
cross-selling 103
cultural influences within LTOs 33–4
curriculum management 207–15
    course and product development 213–15
    frameworks and guidelines (level 2) 208–10
    specific products or services (level 3) 210–12
    statement of principles 208
    vision, mission and values (level 1) 207–8
customer expectations 82–3, 113–16 see also customer satisfaction
customer feedback systems 129–36
customer journey 122–9
    building customer loyalty 142–5
    customer buying cycle 122–4
    customer retention strategies 145
    customer satisfaction feedback 127–9
    effective touchpoints 123–4
    gaps in service provision 127–9
    'moments of truth' 123
    post-purchase phase 123, 127–9, 142–5
    pre-purchase phase 123, 124–7
    purchase phase 123, 124–7
    relationship marketing 142–3
customer loyalty, building 142–5
customer preferences, by group 114–16
customer recommendation predictors 113–15
customer relations role, LTO managers 16
customer retention strategies 145
customer satisfaction
    feedback surveys 127–9
    gap between expectations and experience 127–9
    predictors 114–15
    questionnaires 129–30
    zone of tolerance 127–8
customer service
    blueprinting 145–50
    codes of practice 136–41
    customer buying cycle 122–4
    customer journey 122–9, 142–5

documentation sent to or received from customers 124–7
    duty of care 140–1
    effective touchpoints 123–4
    gaps in service provision 127–9
    handling complaints 138–40
    health and safety issues 140–1
    identifying customers and consumers 116–18
    managing risk 141
    measuring performance 129–36
    'moments of truth' 123
    service provided by LTOs 118–22
customer service research 113–16
    customer expectations of the language school 113–16
    customer preferences by group 114–16
    customer recommendation predictors 113–15
    customer satisfaction predictors 113–14
    offshore market (New Zealand) 113–14, 116
    onshore market (Spain) 114–16
customers of LTOs 81–3
    finding out what they value 94–7
    identifying customers 116–18
    internal customers in an LTO 117–18
    segmentation of customer groups 96–7

decentralized organizational structure 30
decision-making
    and organizational structure 30
    in a learning organization 46
delegating 70–2
demographic segmentation 81, 96–7
departmentalization (silo-ization) 27–8, 29, 145
departments
    business functions 12–13
    lack of communication between 27–8, 29
    silo-ization 27–8, 29, 145
diplomatic role, LTO managers 16
direct selling 103
disciplinary procedures 69
diversification strategy 92, 93
documentation sent to or received from customers 124–7
domestic markets see onshore markets
DOS (director of studies)
    job focus 18
    job responsibilities 18–19
duty of care, to stakeholders 140–1, 174–5
duty of care (financial management) 173–6
    accounting standards compliance 175–6
    financial risk management 173–4
    legal and contractual compliance 175–6
    responsibility to stakeholders 174–5

EAQUALS accreditation scheme 4
EAQUALS code of practice 136–8
educational events and conferences, LTO participation 103, 105–6
EFL (English as a Foreign Language) 85
ELT salesperson, characteristics required 108–9
English Australia 4, 106
English UK 4, 106
entrepreneurial role, LTO managers 16
environment, influence on organizational design 33
ESL (English as a Second Language) 85
ESOL (English for Speakers of Other Languages), diversity of contexts 5–8, 9 see also TESOL
ethical behaviour
    corporate governance 13–15
    human resource management 77
Eurocentres Scale of Language Proficiency 228–9
European Foundation for Quality Management (EFQM) 122
excellence, commitment in effective LTOs 2–3
experiential learning cycle 47
EYL (English for Young Learners) 85

feedback
    360° feedback 66–7
    and performance management 65–7
    customer satisfaction 127–9
    formative 127
    giving effective feedback 65–6
    instilling a culture of 65–7
    making use of 135–6
    summative 127
financial management see operational financial management; strategic financial management
financial statements 170–3
    balance sheet 171
    cash flow statement 171–3
    profit and loss statement (income statement) 170–1
focus groups 134–5
formalization, and organizational structure 30
formative feedback 127
fragmented organization 38, 39
full-cost pricing 101
Fullan, Michael 243
functions and departments 12–13

Gantt charts, project planning 261–2
'Gaps' model for service provision 128–9
geographic segmentation 96–7
geographical location of the market 81
Gladwell, Malcolm 239
Global English 85
goals, and LTO effectiveness 2
going-rate pricing 101
grievance procedures 76–7
gross margins and profitability 94

growth, impact on organizational design
34–5
growth strategies 92–3

Handy, Charles, organizational cultural
framework 35–7
head teacher/principal
job focus 19
job responsibilities 19–20
headroom for growth 90
health and safety issues 140–1
Herzberg, Frederick 61
human resource management
conflict management 72–7
delegating 70–2
ethical behaviour 77
legislation 77
motivation 61–4
negotiation 72–7
performance management 65–70
staffing 51–60

IATEFL (International Association of
Teachers of English as a Foreign
Language) 4
IBEU (Instituto Brasil Estados Unidos),
learning organization case study 45
identity and character of effective LTOs
3
IDLTM (International Diploma in
Language Teaching Management) 1
income streams and profitability 94
inflation rates, use in budgets 178–80
information technology, influence on
organizational design 33
innovation
definition 233
diffusion of 233
distinction from change 233
influences on adoption 241–2
models for implementation 238–44
sources of 240–1
zone of 242
see also change management
innovation and adaptability, effective
LTOs 3
innovation diffusion models
diffusion as epidemic (tipping point)
238–9
influences on adopting innovations
241–2
punctuated equilibrium model
239–40
Rogers' adoption/innovation curve
238
Internet resources for LTOs and
managers 4
interviewing job applicants 57
investment decisions 167–8
IWBs (interactive whiteboards),
introduction of 216–17, 252–3

job description 54
job enrichment, and staff motivation
61–3
job model 54

KASA (Knowledge, Skills, Attitudes
and Awareness) framework 20–3
key performance indicators (KPIs) 169
knowledge requirement for LTO
managers 20–1, 23
Kohn, A. 61

language proficiency scales 228–30
leadership responsibilities
principal/head teacher 19–20
subject leader/DOS 18–19
teachers 17
leading/motivating function of
management 10
learning by doing model 47–8
learning models 47–8
learning organization 42–50
application to an LTO 44–50
awareness of mental models 43
communication and feedback 44–6
cross-departmental teams 46
decision-making process 46
definition 42–3
effective LTOs 3
experiential learning cycle 47
IBEU (Instituto Brasil Estados
Unidos) case study 45
model of learning by doing 47–8
participatory decision-making 46
personal mastery (constant learning)
43
professional development 48–9
punctuated equilibrium model of
change 48, 239
reflection 46–8
role of performance management 70
shared vision 43, 44
single-loop and double-loop learning
48, 239
systems thinking 44
team building 44, 46
team learning 43
transparency 44, 46
legal compliance issues 175–6
legislation, human resource
management 77
Life of Project budget 178, 183
listening and learning, in effective LTOs
2
lovemarks concept 144–5
lower management level 13
LTO (language teaching organization)
design
influence of environment 33
influence of national culture 33–4
influence of purpose and strategy 33
influence of size 33
influence of technology 33
LTO location 98, 107–8
atmospheric features 107–8
moving to new premises 247, 248
servicescape 107–8
LTO manager
as arbitrator in conflict 75–6
as participant in conflict 76

balancing professional and
managerial concerns 20
changing job perspectives 17–20
job perspectives at different
management levels 17–20
job responsibilities 15–17
KASA framework for self analysis
20–3
making the transition from teacher
20–3
meeting educational and commercial
demands 20
LTO staff, job enrichment 61–3
LTO teachers, motivators 61
LTOs (language teaching organizations)
academic and administrative sides
compared 29, 33–4
balance between managerial and
professional priorities 5
becoming a learning organization
44–50
characteristics of effective LTOs 2–3
cultural influences within 33–4
diversity of ESOL contexts 5–8, 9
local variations in corporate
governance 14–15
organizational culture 37, 39–40
portfolio of courses and market
segmentation 96–7
responsibilities of principal/head
teacher 19–20
responsibilities of subject leader/DOS
18–19
responsibilities of teachers 17–18
variety of forms of organization 25–6

management, definition 8, 10
management accountability, corporate
governance 13–15
management by walking around
(MBWA) 67
management control system 10–12
management functions 10
management hierarchy 13
job perspectives at different levels
17–20
responsibilities of principal/head
teacher 19–20
responsibilities of subject leader/DOS
18–19
responsibilities of teachers 17–18
management levels, and job focus 17–20
management personality 22–3
management responsibilities
principal/head teacher 19–20
subject leader/DOS 18–19
teachers 17–18
managerialism, contrast with
professionalism 5
marginal-cost pricing 101
market development strategy 92
market-orientated pricing 101
market penetration strategy 92
market position 90–1
market segmentation 81
market trend data analysis 92–3

marketing
  budgeting for marketing and sales 110
  clients of LTOs 82–3
  consumers of LTO services 81–3
  customer expectations 82–3
  customers of LTOs 81–3
  defining the customer 81–3
  defining marketing 81
  demographic segmentation 81
  finding out what customers want
    94–7
  geographical location of the market 81
  monitoring performance 110–11
  onshore and offshore markets 81
  product-driven approach 80
  psychographic segmentation 81
  relationship marketing 81
  retail LTO markets 82
  sales targets as drivers 79
  segmentation of customer groups
    96–7
  segmentation of the market 81
  sponsors of LTO services 82–3
  strategic marketing process 83–94
  transaction marketing 81
  wholesale LTO markets 82
marketing mix 98–111
  packaging of LTO services 98
  people with whom the customer has
    contact 98, 108–9
  physical evidence of LTO services 98
  place where the service is provided
    98, 107–8
  pricing approaches 98–102
  process(es) involved in service
    provision 98, 109
  product specification 98, 99–100
  promotion 98, 103–7
marketing plan 111–12
meaningful work, in effective LTOs 2
mechanistic organizational structure 34
mental models 43
mercenary organization 38, 39
middle management, responsibilities 13,
  18–19
milestones, project planning 262
mission, use in the recruitment process
  52–3
mission statements 40–1
modelling, financial management tool
  164–6
models of ELT 84–5
  EFL (English as a Foreign Language)
    85
  ESL (English as a Second Language)
    85
  EYL (English for Young Learners) 85
  Global English 85
models of learning processes 47–8
monitoring performance 10–11
  marketing 110–11
moral purpose, in effective LTOs 2
motivation of others, LTO managers'
  understanding of 21–2, 23
motivation of staff 61–4
  compensation systems 61, 63–4

job enrichment 61–3
prioritization 64
salary 61, 63–4
satisfiers and dissatisfiers 61
service to students 61

national culture, influence on
  organizational design 33–4
NEAS accreditation scheme 4
negotiation see conflict management
net promoter score (NPS) 114, 133–4
networked organization 38–9
New Public Management 5

offshore (overseas) markets 81, 85–9
  customer service research (New
    Zealand) 113–16
onshore (domestic) markets 81, 85–6,
  88, 90–2
  customer service research (Spain)
    114–16
operational financial management
  aims of budgeting 177–8
  budget adjustments 190–3
  budget components 183–8
  budget monitoring and control
    188–90
  budget reporting 193–5
  cash flow 196–8
  operational use of a budget 188–95
  systems within the LTO 198–200
  types of budgets 178–83
organic organizational structure 31, 33,
  34
organigrams 26–9
  academic and administrative sides of
    the LTO 29
  chain of command 26–7
  formal reporting relationships 26–7
  fronted organigram 29
  inverted hierarchy type 28–9
  lack of communication within
    organizations 27–8, 29
  lines of communication 27–8, 29
  sideways-on model 29
  span of control 26
organizational change management 245
organizational charts see organigrams
organizational culture 35–40
  communal organization 38, 39
  definition 35
  factors influencing development
    37–40
  fragmented organization 38, 39
  functions 35
  Handy's cultural framework 35–7
  LTOs 37, 39–40
  mercenary organization 38, 39
  networked organization 38–9
  person culture 36–7
  power culture 36
  role culture 36
  sociability vs solidarity model 38–40
  task culture 36
organizational design 31–5
  impact of growth 34

impact of organizational history and
  context 31, 33
influence of environment 33
influence of national culture 33–4
influence of purpose and strategy 33
influence of size 33
influence of technology 33
influence on capacity and capability
  34–5
mechanistic structure 34
organic structure 31, 33, 34
organizational life cycles 31, 32
transition from organic to
  mechanistic 34
organizational life cycles 31, 32
organizational objectives
  mission statements 40–1
  strategic planning 41–2
  vision statements 41
organizational structure 26–40
  and staff autonomy 30
  centralization 30
  chain of command 26–7
  departmentalization 29
  formalization (rules and regulations)
    30
  influence of organizational culture
    35–40
  lines of communication 27–8, 29
  organigrams 26–9
  organizational design 31–5
  span of control 26, 30
  work specialization 30–1
organizations
  definition 25
  variety of forms of LTOs 25–6
organizing function of management 10
orientation of new staff 58–9
overseas markets see offshore markets

packaging of LTO services 98
participatory decision-making in an
  organization 46
pay scales 63–4
people management roles, LTO
  managers 16
people with whom the customer has
  contact 98, 108–9
performance appraisal system 67–9
performance/importance (PI) surveys
  131–3
performance management 65–70
  and the learning organization 70
  case study 71
  disciplinary procedures 69
  importance of feedback 65–7
  performance appraisal system 67–9
  professional development 69, 70
  teacher observations 68–9
performance measurement
  client satisfaction rating scales 130–1
  customer feedback systems 129–36
  customer satisfaction questionnaires
    129–30
  focus groups 134–5
  making use of feedback 135–6

net promoter score (NPS) 133–4
performance/importance (PI) surveys 131–3
performance monitoring, marketing 110–11
performance-related pay systems 63–4
person culture 36–7
person description (recruitment) 54, 55
personal mastery, in learning organizations 43
personal selling 103
physical evidence of LTO services 98
Pickering, George 121–2
place where the service is provided 98, 107–8 *see also* LTO location
planning and analytical tools, financial management 160–6
planning function of management 10–11
portfolio of courses, planning 99–100
power culture 36
pricing approaches 98–102
  break-even analysis 101
  competitive bidding 101
  competitor-orientated pricing 101
  full-cost pricing 101
  going-rate pricing 101
  marginal-cost pricing 101
  market-orientated pricing 101
  USP (Unique Sales/Selling Proposition/Point) 101–2
principal/head teacher
  job focus 19
  job responsibilities 19–20
prioritization, and motivation 64
process(es) involved in service provision 98, 109
product, introducing in an LTO 247–52
product development strategy 92–3
product-driven approach to marketing 80
product life cycle stage, marketing decisions 93
product portfolio planning 99–100
product specification 98, 99–100
professional development 69, 70, 226–8, 232
  continuing professional development (CPD) 24, 227–8, 231
  in a learning organization 48–9
  teaching observation 226
professional leadership role, LTO managers 16
professionalism, contrast with managerialism 5
profit and loss statement (income statement) 170–1
profitability measurement 94
project management
  baseline studies 268–9
  documentation 262, 269, 270
  external projects 257
  externally funded projects 265–7
  features of projects 256–7
  internal projects 257
  monitoring and evaluation 267–9

overview 256–7
project completion and review 269–70
project planning 257–64
proposal writing 265–6, 267
reporting 269
types of activities covered by projects 255
project planning 257–64
  action plans 261
  critical path analysis 261
  defining goals/aims 258
  deliverables 262
  developing objectives 258–9
  Gantt charts 261–2
  identifying tasks and activities 260–2
  milestones 262
  questions to address 257
  risk assessment 263–4
  risk tolerance matrix 264
  SMART objectives 259
  stakeholder analysis 262–3
  strategy to achieve objectives 260–2
project proposal writing 265–6, 267
promotional mix 98, 103–7
  advertising 103–4
  cross-selling 103
  direct selling 103
  personal selling 103
  public relations 103, 105–7
  publicity 103, 105–7
  sales promotions 103, 104–5
  trade and educational events and conferences 103, 105–6
proposal writing 265–6, 267
psychographic segmentation 81, 96–7
public relations 103, 105–7
public schools
  responsibilities of principal/head teacher 19–20
  responsibilities of subject leader/DOS 18–19
  responsibilities of teachers 17–18
publicity 103, 105–7
punctuated equilibrium model of change 48, 239–40

quality management, academic managers 228–31 *see also* blueprinting; Total Quality Management
quality standards 121–2

recruitment process 52–8
  advertising the position 54–5
  checking qualifications 57
  contracts 58
  creation of a shortlist 56
  criminal record check 57
  defining the organization's needs 52–3
  hiring committee 53
  interviewing 57
  job description 54
  job model 54

legal requirements 55
offering the job 57–8
person description 54, 55
reference to vision and mission 52–3
references 57
response to unsuccessful applicants 55–6
salary and benefits 58
scoring and ranking of applicants 56
sources of potential applicants 54–5
terms and conditions of service (TACOS) 58
time-sensitive nature 58
reflection, importance in a learning organization 46–8
relationship marketing 81, 142–3
representational role, LTO managers 16
reputation, effective LTOs 3
resource inventory 158–9
resource management
  academic managers 216–26
  LTO managers 16
retail LTO markets 82
risk assessment
  management of innovation 237–8
  project planning 263–4
risk management 141
  financial 173–4
risk tolerance matrix 237–8, 264
Rogers, Everett 238, 239, 241
Rogers' adoption/innovation curve 238
role culture 36
rules and regulations, and organizational structure 30

safety issues 140–1
salary, as motivation 61, 63–4
salary bands 63–4
sales
  advertising 103–4
  cross-selling 103
  direct selling 103
  personal selling 103
  see also marketing
sales promotions 103, 104–5
sales staff, characteristics required 108–9
sales targets, as marketing drivers 79
scheduling (timetabling) 220–3
segmentation of customer groups 96–7
segmentation of the market 81
self-awareness in LTO managers 22–3
Senge, Peter 42
senior management, responsibilities 13, 19–20
service provided by LTOs 118–22
  accreditation schemes 121–2
  characteristics of a service 119–20
  customer's viewpoint 122
  customising to customer needs 119–20
  definition of service 119
  differentiation on quality standards 121–2
  ESOL as a service 118–19
  fluctuating demand 120

service provided by LTOs (cont.)
  inseparability of production and consumption 119
  intangibility of evidence of service provision 119
  perishability 120
  providing evidence for potential customers 119
  quality standards 121–2
  quality variability 119–20
  range of LTO services 120–1
  student services manager 118
  Total Quality Management (TQM) 121–2
  variability/heterogeneity of service quality 119–20
  see also customer service
servicescape of the LTO location 107–8
silo-ization of departments 27–8, 29, 145
single-loop and double-loop learning 48
size, influence on organizational design 33
skills requirement for LTO managers 21, 23
SMART objectives 111, 259
sociability vs solidarity model of organizational culture 38–40
span of control, and organizational structure 26, 30
sponsors of LTO services 82–3
staff, commitment and loyalty in effective LTOs 2
staff appointments, change management 244–5, 246
staffing 51–60
  contract types 59–60
  hourly-paid and fixed-contract staff 52, 60
  organizational fit 51–2
  orientation of new staff 58–9
  recruitment process 52–8
stakeholder analysis, project planning 262–3
standards of performance, management control 10–11
STEP analysis 160–1, 234–5, 238
Stoller, Fredricka 241–2
Strategic Business Units (SBUs) analysis 99–100
strategic financial management
  benchmarking 168–9
  break-even analysis 162–4
  budget as analytical tool 162
  business plan models 153
  costed proposal outline 153–8
  decision-making and communication 151–2
  defining success, improvement and failure 159–60
  definition 151–2
  distinction from accounting 151

duty of care 173–6
financial outcomes of strategic planning 153–60
financial statements 170–3
investment decisions 167–8
long-term goals/plan outcomes 159
management level and responsibilities 151
modelling 164–6
planning and analytical tools 160–6
resource inventory 158–9
STEP analysis 160–1
strategic goal implementation 161–2
strategic plan implementation 166–7
strategic planning 153–60
SWOT analysis 160–1
strategic goal implementation 161–2
strategic management, in effective LTOs 2
strategic marketing 83–94
  analysis of market trend data 92–3
  Ansoff matrix 92–3
  comparison with other suppliers 90–1
  data required for decision-making 94
  diversification strategy 92, 93
  external information 84–8, 89
  finding out what customers want 94–7
  growth strategies 92–3
  headroom for growth 90
  income streams and profitability 94
  internal information 88, 90–4
  market development strategy 92
  market penetration strategy 92
  market position 90–1
  models of ELT 84–5, 86
  offshore (overseas) markets 85–9
  onshore (domestic) markets 85–6, 88, 90–2
  potential market size 88, 90
  product development strategy 92–3
  product life cycle stage 93
  profitability measurement 94
strategic plan implementation 166–7
strategic planning 41–2
  defining the current reality 41
  definition 41
  determining strategy 42
  monitoring and evaluation 42
  setting goals and objectives 42
  SWOT analysis 41
strategy, influence on organizational design 33
subject leader/DOS
  job focus 18
  job responsibilities 18–19
summative feedback 127
SWOT analysis 111, 160–1, 236–7, 238
systems thinking, in learning organizations 44

Tarde, Gabriel 238
task culture 36
teacher observations 226
  performance appraisal 68–9
  professional development 226
teachers
  job focus 17
  job responsibilities 17–18
  KASA framework for self analysis 20–3
  managerial responsibilities 17–18
  potentially conflicting roles 18
  transition to manager 20–3
teaching personality 22–3
team building 46
team learning, in learning organizations 43
teams, cross-departmental 46
technological change management 252–3
technology, influence on organizational design 33
terms and conditions of service (TACOS) 58
TESOL (Teachers of English to Speakers of Other Languages) 4
time management 220–6
timetabling 220–3
tipping point for diffusion of innovation 238–9
Total Quality Management (TQM) 121–2
  see also blueprinting
trade and educational events and conferences, participation 103, 105–6
trade associations 4
transaction marketing 81
transparency, in a learning organization 46

USP (Unique Sales/Selling Proposition/ Point) 101–2

values alignment, and LTO effectiveness 2
vertical expansion of jobs 61
vision
  and LTO effectiveness 2
  shared 43, 44
  use in the recruitment process 52–3
vision statements 41

Walker, John 113–15
wholesale LTO markets 82
work specialization, and organizational structure 30–1
World Wide Web, resources for LTOs and managers 4

zero-based budgeting 180–3
zone of tolerance 127–8